Crispin Swinhoe ... Dorset, was brou... boarding school i... years as a doctor in the Ro... 2015.

He has enjoyed a varied, interesting ... unorthodox life. Well-travelled and well-read he has developed a cosmopolitan view of life based on his many experiences.

Crispin has lived in Yorkshire for 25 years, the past 11 of these in Barnsley with his wife Julie.

Crispin has four children: Fiona, Alec, Heidi and Harry - and a step-daughter; Bethany.

Published 2016

©2016 Crispin Swinhoe

Cover illustration
Jim Finnerty

The Reluctant Doctor

&

More Important Stuff

My Life & Times

Crispin Swinhoe

Chapters

1

Introduction

WRITING A STORY ABOUT ONE'S LIFE IS ARROGANT I suppose.

Why?

Because one assumes people will want to read it, and that it is worth reading!

Or perhaps one doesn't assume that, yet feels there are messages to impart that others will find useful to receive and understand earlier in their life's journey than oneself.

I have messages in this book that I believe to be useful, which if no-one reads will be lost forever, but if they're thus lost then I suppose it doesn't really matter - and maybe they aren't that good anyway - however, I can't help thinking that had I known and understood earlier what I do now, then my life might have been a whole lot easier.

The title of this book recognises the fact that I am not important, as neither is anyone who might write an autobiography, even if they are a politician, sportsperson, or actor for example. I am simply a collection of carbon, hydrogen and oxygen formed into a 'being' that happens to have a clever brain; the 'being' in general not specifically me. However, we all have a brain that conjures the thought that we humans are more important than other animals, or even plants come to that, which of course is simply not true. This is just our 'ego', created as a result of our life's experiences making us believe that we have some over-inflated significance. More and more - particularly in western society - this arrogance is daily reinforced by what is said to us, not least in the news, on television and elsewhere.

Our family Dalmatian, Charlie, and other animals live in the moment. They react by reflex and instinct. They do not continually look ahead, or back into the past - they cannot do that. Consequently they are not calculating, manipulative nor evil, unlike some of us humans, with whom they are obliged to share the world. When animals kill they do so instinctively, in order to survive, not to oppress others. If animals procreate with a beautiful, powerful partner they do so to ensure the creation and survival of the best possible individuals in their species, not to strut around with their mate boosting their 'ego'. And if they strut, they do so by instinct and not from any misguided sense of self-importance. They have no 'ego', which probably makes them a whole lot better than us. They are what they are. We don't find animals trying to be something they are not.

More than once in this book I shall be mentioning the problems that the ego and self-importance create for us humans. In fact, 'ego' and self-importance are essentially one and the same. In one way or another it is usually the ego that causes all the strife in the world. Think about the saying: 'No self, no problem'; how true this is, and expresses so aptly in one short phrase what it is I am trying to explain.

So I am not writing this book because I think I'm important, but because I would like to put my life and thoughts into words. So if someone or even a few out there wish to read it all well and good. I will be delighted, will hope that you enjoy it and trust that perhaps it might give you food for thought. What I have to write is neither right nor wrong, but just the thoughts my brain has generated as a result of my life's experience.

Where should I start?

At the beginning, I guess.

However, I feel that a chronological account of my life would be less than interesting or exciting, so I will skip things around a bit interlinking everything with much comment about the world as I see it. I hope some of my thoughts will be found to be amusing, interesting and at times provocative. Remember though - they are just *my* thoughts and not necessarily the truth or otherwise, and as they are read I am sure they will develop responsive thoughts in the mind of their reader. They will be different to mine, but we won't argue about that because my thoughts and my readers' thoughts will be no more important, less important, right, or wrong than those of anyone else.

However, before we start let me share my favourite poem with you the reader, to the sentiments of which, it is pretty much universally agreed it is worth aspiring.

If

If you can keep your head when all about you
Are losing theirs and blaming it on you;
If you can trust yourself when all men doubt you,
But make allowance for their doubting too:
If you can wait and not be tired by waiting,
Or, being lied about, don't deal in lies,
Or being hated don't give way to hating,
And yet don't look too good, nor talk too wise;

If you can dream - and not make dreams your master;
If you can think - and not make thoughts your aim,
If you can meet with Triumph and Disaster
And treat those two impostors just the same:
If you can bear to hear the truth you've spoken
Twisted by knaves to make a trap for fools,
Or watch the things you gave your life to, broken,
And stoop and build'em up with worn-out tools;

If you can make one heap of all your winnings
And risk it on one turn of pitch-and-toss,
And lose, and start again at your beginnings,

And never breathe a word about your loss:
If you can force your heart and nerve and sinew
To serve your turn long after they are gone,
And so hold on when there is nothing in you
Except the Will which says to them: "Hold on!"

If you can talk with crowds and keep your virtue,
Or walk with Kings - nor lose the common touch,
If neither foes nor loving friends can hurt you,
If all men count with you, but none too much:
If you can fill the unforgiving minute
With sixty seconds' worth of distance run,
Yours is the Earth and everything that's in it,
And - which is more - you'll be a Man, my son!

Rudyard Kipling

2

The Early Years

I WAS BORN IN WEYMOUTH, DORSET, ON SUNDAY 29th July 1956.

The event occurred early that morning at my maternal grandparents' house. They had retired to the south coast from London, where my granpy had worked on the Great Western Railway most of his life and on the trains in France during the First World War. My granny had been a housewife, looking after my mum, Anne, and my uncle - mum's brother Paul.

My dad came from the north-east, where his mum had a coal-delivery business. His dad had died of septicaemia when my dad was young, so my northern 'grandpa' was in fact a step relation, but he was still a favourite of mine.

So it was Granny and Granpy on the south coast and Grandma and Grandpa up north. Each pair resided by the sea, so as a kid I always associated grandparents with the beach!

My mum was born in Hammersmith in London, where she lived for much of her childhood. Granny and she were evacuated to the country during the Blitz. However, when aged 16 my mum joined the WRNS (Women's Royal Naval Service) and went to work at *HMS Owl* in the north of Scotland where the Fleet Air Arm pilots practised dropping torpedoes. She became engaged to an Australian member of Bomber Command who was then lost in action in 1944 - a lucky break for my future existence, if not for him!

Mum was demobbed (left the WRNS) in 1945 and returned to London to do nurses' training at St. Mary's Hospital, Paddington. She finished her training and worked for a while, before deciding to visit Australia to meet her late fiancé's family. She travelled all the way on her own by ship, which was the only option in the early 1950s and no mean feat for a young lady. She planned to stay in Australia and work there for a while, but because the Korean War started she decided to come home, there being a real fear at the time that this might be heralding the start of World War Three.

Back in London she returned to nursing at St. Mary's, and that's where she met my father.

My dad was brought up in the northeast, near Sunderland. At the start of the war he was sent to school in Staffordshire to escape the bombing; first to Smallwood Manor Preparatory School and then on to Denstone College, more of which later, because in due course I was to go to the same school and medical school as him.

When he was 16 he volunteered to join the Royal Navy, but was turned down because of colour blindness; another lucky escape for my future existence, perhaps. I am sure a young man on a Naval warship in the Second World War did not have too great a life-expectancy!

His having volunteered during the war was to cause problems later. When Dad left school to go on to medical school it meant that he was called up to do his National Service, which was normally deferred until one's medical training was complete. However my grandma, who was a formidable woman, sorted it all out. She knew someone in the appropriate office, and somehow Dad's 'papers' became 'lost', so off he went to Cambridge and later to St. Mary's Hospital Medical School, London, where I would follow some 25 years later.

The scene was thus set for my parents to meet each other at St. Mary's, Praed Street, Paddington, on Lewis Carrol Ward, the children's ward, and Peter Swinhoe and Anne Borrough then duly became married on Saturday 27th March 1954.

National Service unavoidably then claimed Dad, and he and Mum went to live in Chester, where my sister, Kate, was born on 2nd January 1955, barely nine months after their marriage; a 'honeymoon baby', my mum always maintained!

Everything was now in place for *my* arrival in July of the following year.

His National Service now finished, Dad had become a general practitioner in Thornton Heath, South London, but my parents did not have an established home yet; thus my arrival on this planet was to be in Weymouth.

We soon moved though, and found ourselves living in Brigstock Road in a ground floor flat conveniently located in the self-same building as Dad's general practice.

My memories of this period are scant, but consist of playing in the garden with my sister Kate on her tricycle, climbing trees, my dad building a sailing dinghy out in the garage, and generally being happy with life.

My parents, my dad in particular, believed that children should entertain themselves a significant amount of the time. I thought my dad was great, but I was also scared of him. He worked long hours every weekday, alternate nights, and every other weekend. Even on his weekends off he had a Saturday surgery to run. It was only during his time off that he was able to build the dinghy, and we children 'fitted in'.

In those days, and definitely in our family, children usually did what their parents wanted to do; not like today's opposite extreme, when life revolves around the children. I am sure there should be a happy balance between the two, but I do not seem to see it. Of course, this balance is further disturbed these days by both parents wanting to work, as well as each having their own individual personal time. I see my friends who still have young families trading weekends and evenings with their spouses, allowing each of them to have some 'kid-free' time! This can't be the best way either, although perhaps it feels so for the wives, who somehow usually seem to do better out of the deal.

I have a theory about marriage, of which you will later discover I have *significant* experience.

The theory is this.

When they are out seeking a lad, girls tend to prefer the 'man's man' type; the guy who likes a beer with his mates, plays or watches sport on a Saturday and looks rugged and masculine. So, one would assume, the girl surmises that this is what this (unsuspecting) bloke is like, and wants to be.

She strikes.

They fall in love, marry and have children, at which point the wife is apparently surprised to discover that her Mr Man has not turned out to be quite so good at doing the housework, changing nappies, or cooking as she thought he would. She exerts control, and her new husband changes his ways. His wife is happy again, but the poor guy now feels downtrodden. He doesn't want to complain to his wife, because he loves her, or perhaps because he fears the retribution!

When I was at school there were plenty of boys who hated sport and were not at all 'in' with the lads.

Where are they today?

Presumably settled down in happy marriages!

I know there can be a balance and I hope everyone has or will find it, but beware the following saying holds much truth. 'Men marry expecting their wives never to change and women marry expecting to change their husbands and each is potentially sorely disappointed!'

Back to my early days.

Mum was a good old-fashioned housewife, so there were no issues on the 'who would do what' front. Dad went to work and in his limited spare time we did whatever *he* wanted. Mum looked after us children and all the domestic stuff. Everything ran smoothly and there were no major issues, and yet for some reason, somewhere along the line, I became a desperately shy child. I was also a thumb-sucker and a bed-wetter, long beyond the period when I should have been. None of this really mattered at home all day, with Mum, but the situation was soon to rear its troublesome head with school looming.

Mum had a state education, but Dad went to private school, which is where my sister Kate and I were scheduled to go as well. For as long as I remember, I was always going to go to boarding school when I was older. However, for now, at the age of four, I was off to Rosedean, a little prep school just down the road.

In those days few children went to any kind of pre-school, so I do not think I was well socialised that first day when I had to say goodbye to my mother at the school's front door.

The school was very small with several year-groups sitting at different tables all in one room, so my sister Kate was fairly close by, but this did not help at all. I made no friends and most of the time I just sat there feeling homesick.

The toilets made things worse!

They were outside, and stank.

The urinal had a window above it and the sport of the older boys was to see if they could wee out of it onto anyone foolish enough to be standing below. I would not go into them unless I really had to, and so sat in class becoming more and more desperate. This was compounded by being too shy and scared to ask to be excused in class. So many an accident occurred, further denting my limited confidence. What an unhappy kid I was.

How this kid went on to become a doctor, join the Royal Navy, do his Commando Course and work with the Royal Marines and Special Forces, go to two wars, do Ironman Triathlons and the rest you are going to hear about I have no idea. I suspect it was in spite of the shyness and not because of it, as well as a few other things along the way.

To clarify that, I have often done things that I know I will find very difficult, to prove I can to myself and others!

Anyway, back to Rosedean, or as it happened, moving on to greater things.

Two events occurred around this time. Dad finished the dinghy, which was good because he was able to emerge from the garage at last, and I took a test to go to Dulwich College Preparatory School, supposedly the best prep school in the land at the time! The test I had to take was not that hard. I needed to know my address and a few other simple things about myself and home, but somehow? . . . I suspect because of my shyness at the interview, I managed to fluff even this, so was deferred for a year, which meant me continuing to be deprived of useable school toilets until the age of six.

With the dinghy now complete, it needed to be sailed.

There followed a tense first launch at Wisley Pond in Surrey, and a naming.

Dilemma.

I have no idea specifically why we called her that, but I can think of a few suggestions as to what the 'dilemmas' might have been. One of them was that Dad wanted to race. This meant an accompanying crew of one: Mum. My parents joined a sailing club at Frensham Ponds in Surrey, so . . . what was then to become of their five- and six-year-old children?

Racing took place in the morning, so we left home early at weekends for our 'day at the races'. This involved Mum and Dad heading out onto the water in *Dilemma,* leaving Kate and me wandering around the pond on our own.

Now, a small digression.

I do not hold with the modern view that any child under 14 in a public area on his or her own is more than likely to be assaulted, kidnapped, mugged, raped or worse. This belief, as we all know, leads to many children being driven to school in unnecessarily big cars, even when they live only a mile or so away. This results in added pollution, a traffic jam at the school gates, and - worse than that - a good chance of one's child being totalled as they step off the curb by someone else's 4x4 'Chelsea Tractor'. I don't believe there are any more weirdos around today than when I was a youngster. I can remember there being men in dirty macs by the play park when I was a child. If there were enough of us kids around to do so, we simply used to taunt them, or if on our own - run away. Both of which were the sensible and obvious options to take.

However, apart from the fact that Kate and I might somehow or other have injured ourselves, fallen in and drowned, or met the Frensham Pond paedophile, our parents' activity was hardly conducive to a 'happy family' kind of weekend. We did have a picnic lunch together after the racing, and a family sail in the afternoon, but these activities seemed like a bit of an afterthought. Kate ripped her hand open once, on some barbed wire. Fortunately it was at lunchtime so help was nearby. Her hand was wrapped in a bandage, and we then went off to visit Mum's brother and family *en route*, and so brave Kate's wound was eventually stitched up by Dad when we arrived back in London; no rush! It was only a hand!

And the Frensham Pond toilets were even worse than those at Rosedean, so for me that meant more 'holding on', or accidents.

Back at home, change was afoot.

I went to school one day from Brigstock Road and returned to Dunheved Road North.

We had moved.

My parents had bought a large Victorian house, which had previously been a nursing home. As might be imagined, a lot of work needed to be done, from which emerges an amusing story comparing how we lived then, with living today.

Dad had fitted central heating to the house.

Bear in mind he was a doctor, who understood human physiology. However, when he fitted the radiators none were put in the bedrooms, because in the early 1960s this was considered unhealthy. So in the mornings we leapt out of bed and dressed in front of the gas fire in my parents' room. The good thing about this was it hardened me up for my days at boarding school, where each winter's morn we awoke to ice on the *inside* of the dormitory windows. Perhaps this also contributed to my being able to 'toughen up' a bit in later life. I am sure most people in those days did not have any central heating at all, but that seems a lot less odd to me than going to all the trouble and expense of installing it, but then not extending it to include the bedrooms!

Ours was a nice house, with plenty of space. We were happy there and went into a phase of pretty good normal family living. Dad had a third partner at work, who he did not like, but at least it meant Dad was at home a bit more.

The house had seven bedrooms, so one of them was made into a playroom and I was to get my first scooter.

This state-of-the-art machine had big wheels and a brake. I loved it and went tearing round and round the block on it on the pavement, which included the main London to Brighton Road, but being far less congested and manic in those days, this was considered to be fine.

I was still being more than a mite tardy on the making friends front though, and so one day Mum decided that enough was enough. She had noticed that another young boy of my age lived at the top of the road, so she walked me up to his house, knocked on the door and asked his mother if he could come out and play with me. His mother happily agreed, and that's how I became firm friends with Peter Edwards, who was a year older than me and later also went to Dulwich Prep. We continued to play at home together until our paths went their separate ways, but never at school, with him being a year older; such was the way in the young male breeding ground.

The time then came for me to start at Dulwich Prep.

I was in Miss Bacon's class.

Miss Bacon was old and had a funny smell about her, but she liked me, which was fortunate considering my continued shyness and school phobia.

The reason for her favouritism was two-fold. First I was good at maths and learnt all my times-tables in good time. Second, and more importantly, I loved running.

Miss Bacon had two favourite punishments.

For individual offences she rapped our knuckles hard with the edge of a ruler, but for group misdemeanours she sent us all running round the playground; a punishment that was perfect for me because I loved running.

Playtime saw us all back in the playground.

One of the boys - Hugh Dehn - was a bit of a little thug.

There was a climbing frame in the middle of the playground, but none of today's sissy modern health-and-safety protective accident-proof soft stuff underneath it. Falls from *our* climbing frame meant we went straight onto the tarmac.

Hugh Dehn and his gang thought they owned this climbing frame, which they didn't of course, so frequent battles took place to usurp him and his gang; battles that all ended with the combatants receiving various injuries. I kept out of this, eventually becoming friends with Hugh and his mates. We went to a variety of birthday parties together, and to see films like *Battle of the Bulge, Tobruk* and *A Man Called Flint*. For one of my parties my dad took us to see the motor-racing at Crystal Palace. I am not sure if James Hunt and Nicki Lauda were there on that occasion, as portrayed in the British Academy Award Winning biopic about them - *Rush*.

Some of the less popular boys who were not in 'the crowd' would also invite us to their parties. One of these was a lad whose Christian name I don't recall, but whose surname was Leone. He seemed to be, (and in fact was), quite a personality, perhaps seeming so, because we were not a very cosmopolitan lot in those days. As might be guessed, Leone was Italian. He lived in a posh house in Dulwich with lots of marble and *very* Italian parents. We played various games out in their garden and on his skateboards, the likes of which we had never set eyes on before . . . then it was time for tea. Well . . .

. . . we went to the table, to be confronted by all this strange Italian food, including some weird stuff his mum had made called *pizza*; a new one on us. She implored us in a very Italian voice at least to try some, so out of politeness Hugh took one mouthful, immediately turned green and hughied all over the party food.

After that there were no more trips for us to Leone's house.

Pizza Hut was a long time off hitting the shores of Britain. The only burger one could get was at *Wimpy* and my parents did not approve of such places anyway. Bottles of ketchup and Sarsen's on the table? How common! My friend Peter Edwards's parents took me out with them all once, which I thought was great. My parents were somewhat snobbish and had already mentioned that Sylvia Edwards put the milk bottle on the table. God forbid; so they were not surprised when they heard we had been taken to a *Wimpy* Bar.

Talking of burgers and *pizza* there were hardly any fat kids around in those days - for which there were two reasons.

First and most obvious; we ate less.

There was no snacking at all during the day.

Sweets and pop were far from being the near daily indulgences they are today.

I was given six old pence pocket money a week.

This amount bought six 'penny chews', twenty-four 'black jacks', or twelve 'flying saucers'. These were bought and eaten all in day one, and that was it for the rest of the week.

There was the Corona van, a 'modern invention', which delivered pop to your house, but that was a rare treat.

The only drink allowed at meal times was water.

Sometimes on a Sunday evening we would get to share a few sweets with Mum and Dad in front of the television - a quarter of Everton mints or some such joy, and we had crisps at a picnic occasionally; those crisps with the salt twisted into their accompanying little blue packets. In those days, the cheese and onion option, and all the others that followed, were some way off arriving in the shops.

The other reason for not being a fat kid was that it would result in being teased remorselessly at school over it; so obesity as we see it today was generally pretty much non-existent.

In the politically correct times in which we live today the teasing aspect may seem awful to many, but that is what happened. I can only remember one fat boy in my year at school, and I am sorry to say that he did not have a very happy time of it. I remember his name and nickname, (the likes of which one can imagine), but my lips are sealed.

Back to the playground.

Before I joined the school the fastest runner in the year was one Martin Dorman.

There were regular races organised by the boys and once I had overcome my reluctance to show myself up I raced and easily beat Martin. This established me as being 'one of the lads', which helped my self-esteem enormously, but unfortunately this was soon to be destroyed by an evil teacher.

Two of my other friends at this time were James Weatherup and Andrew Hirst, the latter being one of the three sons of one of Dad's practice partners'. When I was a little older I came to fancy Andrew's sister Juliette, but she was several years senior to me and I would not have dared talk to her anyway, because girls - particularly those I liked - reduced me to a quaking, silent wreck; an affliction that I kept well into my late teens and to some degree beyond!

I lost touch with James Weatherup when he left the Prep at the age of eleven, and only recently heard of him again in connection with the *News of the World* phone-hacking scandal.

Another friend of mine was Tim Dowdall.

Tim left the school early on, when his father was posted to a job in Germany. Tim attended an international school there, later returning to us again as a boarder in the sixth form, in the meantime having become much more worldly-wise than me. He knew all about girls, pop music *and* had long hair, each a benefit of an American-style education in a co-ed school. Tim later went to a progressive school in England and I met up with him again, by which time he had become even more worldly-wise. At that time I was acutely conscious of not benefitting from what some might describe as a 'rounded education', since I boarded at an all-boys' public school.

That year's Sports Day was approaching, and I was confident of winning the 100-yards race for under sevens.

Why do people become teachers?

A love of children maybe?

Or in the case of an all-boys' school - little boys?

That last statement doesn't sound too appropriate, does it - so let me explain.

Through all my years at school there were a lot of single male teachers, some of whom perhaps liked their charges a little too much, but at no time at all did I ever hear of, or experience any impropriety occurring whatsoever. In the England rugby hooker Brian Moore's autobiography, however, he relates a different story, and so I must believe that certain 'indecencies' did take place in some schools.

I liked a number of my teachers and they were good to me, but there were some - both men and women, married and single - who from their behaviour seemed to harbour a genuine dislike of children!

One such of these was Miss X.

I do remember her name, but must remain silent in case she still exists, or someone of her family does and gets to read this book, not that she is likely to have had any younger close family because she gave every indication of being a confirmed spinster.

I have always thought the word 'spinster' sounds so evil. It must have been made up by a jilted man - or maybe a boy at an English prep school!

Sports day came and we all sat cross-legged in the field awaiting our races, both heats and finals. I'd managed to saunter through successfully to the final of the under sevens' 100-yards.

The finalists lined up, the starter's pistol fired and off we all shot . . . with me crossing the finishing line yards ahead of Martin Dorman.

I was thrilled . . .

. . . until Miss X walked over.

"You're disqualified," she sniffed aloofly at me, "you didn't run straight and then you cut in front".

I stood there speechless with disbelief, aghast at this harridan's effrontery. How *dare* she challenge my moment of triumph?

Now - the facts.

The race had been held on a grassy playing field.

There were no white lanes marked to follow, and I had been ahead all the way.

Why did this witch dislike me so much?

I had never even met her before this occasion. She taught class 2B, and I was two years below, in the Annexe, as it was called.

These days one can appeal to have one's GCSE's re-marked, but back then in my young days one could not even challenge the disputed result of the under sevens' 100-yards! Today there would be video footage of the alleged misconduct on a parent's smartphone. Actually, there might not be, because as we all know in today's climate one has to sign some sort of affidavit before a parent can video small children - even their own!

So - the result stood, and Martin Dorman officially became the fastest under-seven runner.

It was the unfairness and injustice of that moment that were to define certain aspects of my future personality.

Thus soured, I would tend to be wary of those around me, until they proved themselves worthy of my trust.

Also, I was to become a driven and fiercely competitive person, always pushing myself to the limits of my ability.

In due course I was to graduate to Miss X's class, when it became even more apparent that she really didn't care for me at all.

That year, the year I joined 2B, the 100-yards heats were held before sports day.

We all sat cross-legged on the grass awaiting our turn to run, but mine never came.

Miss X was running the show, so quashing my nervous anxiety I went to ask her when I would be called to run.

"You've already been called", she said, "but failed to show, so you've missed your heat. You were probably mucking around and not listening, or something".

The miserable old bat must have just whispered out my name, or more likely not called it out at all.

The school records will show that in years three, four, five and six, Crispin Swinhoe rightfully won the 100-yards, beating Martin Dorman. (By the way, Martin was a nice lad and none of what I have related was his fault in any way at all).

If these early 'school years' of mine seem confusing, they were based on working up to year six at prep school, by which time one was aged 12 going on 13 and ready to leave for public school, where the years then started at 'year three'. I suppose then in the state system one would have gone to grammar school at age 11, which would have been two years behind, and called 'year one'. No need to get too bogged down.

In the early 1960s, because the then Labour government had decided to introduce the comprehensive system, thereby ensuring that all children were equally stupid rather than some showing promise and becoming more accomplished than others, Grammar schools were on their way out anyway, to be replaced by a system whereby no one fails, they just don't do so well!

Things at home were progressing well, and I now had a bicycle, having learnt to ride on a friend's by getting on and falling off until I got it right.

No one would have been seen dead with stabilisers in those days, since it would have led to severe teasing, when the word 'sissy' would no doubt have been used. (Interestingly, the modern trend is to realise that stabilisers are not such a good thing anyway).

No helmets were worn either back then, yet I am still alive to tell the tale.

Peter Edwards, my friend, got a racing bike with derailleur gears, something which I then craved having for years, but to no avail.

Meanwhile, my mother had passed her driving test.

Our cars had progressed from an Austin A35 to a Sunbeam Rapier Mark 1, then a Mini Traveller, followed by a Bond

Equipe. I am prepared to wager that not many people today will have heard of a Bond Equipe. It was a snazzy little sports coupé made by a company called Bond. It had a fibreglass body powered by a 1500cc, or perhaps it was 1300cc, Triumph Spitfire engine. Its top speed was about 97mph and it was my dad's pride and joy. I liked the idea of Dad having a sports car, but would have preferred him to have had a MKII Jaguar like the father of one of my friends; he was a builder and a bit of a 'wide-boy', so the car that at the time was the desired getaway car of crooks, suited him quite well I think.

An issue with the Bond was that it was tiny in the back, so my sister Kate and I were squashed in. We also had to suffer Dad's incessant pipe-smoking. Today he would be considered a villain for such behaviour. At least, because he smoked until he died at age 85, and not then from lung, or throat cancer, I like to think that I am safe from the spin-off ravages of passive smoking. Our family must have good anti-cancer genes, but more of that later.

Despite Mum having passed her test, we were only a one-car family, so when Dad was at work we used public transport. Two-car families were rare, and many had no car at all. Nowadays I see three and four cars drawn up outside houses. Just down the road from where I live, a 17 or 18-year-old girl has just passed her test. Outside their abode there now stands a gleaming 65-plated car, presumably bought for her by her parents. This is in Barnsley, not Cheltenham, and they live in a three-bedroom semi, so are not wealthy. I must assume that now it is expected for an 18-year-old to be bought a brand new car by his or her parents.

And we wonder why our roads are so crowded?

When I was a kid the comics I read displayed pictures of futuristic cities with fantastic overhead monorails and other integrated public transport systems. Now that we've arrived here in future-land, what have we done instead? We have made ourselves more reliant on the car by moving shops and other amenities out of the towns and cities, while at the same time doing little to improve other modes of transport. For those of us who like cycling, we daily run the risk of death at the hands of car drivers who consider us an obstruction with no right to be on the roads at all. Even pavements get narrower and are being half-parked upon. When crossing the road on foot we encounter drivers who have clearly not read the Highway Code, which would tell them that once a pedestrian has started a perilous journey across, it is he or she who has 'right of way'.

The motor car was invented in the 19th century.

We now believe that progress on the transport front is to equip our vehicles with an electric motor instead of the internal combustion engine. At a very early age in my science classes I learnt that when it comes to energy one cannot get something for nothing. So although an electric car may possibly be more efficient in terms of energy-use per mile, it still has to be charged. Plug it into the socket and it ultimately creates CO2 or nuclear waste, unless one lives near a wind farm! It is ridiculous that even with only one person in a car it would cost much less in fuel to travel 200 miles from A to B than it would cost to take the train. Yes, there is the added expense of the car, insurance and tax to consider, but with the way society is these days most of us need a car for our daily lives, so those items have to be paid anyway, rendering them irrelevant to this debate! I must admit that my wife and I both have a car each, and I have a motorbike. To me the latter is what a personal vehicle should be; a hobby for sunny days and holidays. Other journeys should be made on a cheap, efficient public transport system. If only one was available.

Earlier I mentioned the current habit of taking children down the road to school in a gas-guzzling, unnecessarily big, potential child-killing 4x4.

Let me tell you about *my* school journeys.

When I first started to attend Dulwich Prep a group of parents would take us to school on a rota basis. When it was my father's turn we always arrived there early and would sit listening to the radio in the car. I can remember back to hearing the news of the Great Train Robbery being announced, in 1963.

Then, at the age of eight it was decided that I should travel to school alone. The journey there was five miles by car, which according to Google even today should take about 28 minutes.

However, I now had to walk to the end of our road, cross the main London to Brighton Road and wait at the bus stop. The bus took me to West Croydon Station, where I caught the train to Gypsy Hill. I then had to walk to school, a distance that Google tells us is only a mile, but seemed a lot further than that to me as an eight-year-old. An additional issue was that there were trains only every half-hour, on the hour, and at half-past. School finished at 3.40pm, so on the way home I often missed the 4pm train and had sit on the station for nearly 30-minutes! The whole journey home would then take me more than two hours.

Added to this were two other factors.

The trains' carriages were those compartments which once 'in' you were unable to get 'out' of, (except by defenestration onto the flashing rails), until arriving at the next station. So if anyone 'dodgy' happened to entrain into the same compartment, one was stuck with them. Worse was when the train then went through a tunnel, and the carriage lights failed.

I hasten to add that I was never attacked.

Well, not on the train I wasn't, but the walk from Gypsy Hill carried further perils. The final leg of the trek necessitated passing an example of an undesirable invention - a Secondary Modern School!

There I was in grey shorts, long grey socks, shirt, blazer and a cap, regularly being confronted by older boys from the rougher end of town.

My school cap was the main target.

I would have it whipped from my head and nicked, either tossed out into the road - in which case it had to be retrieved - or stolen, which would result in a bollocking and detention for not having it with me when I arrived at school.

Most of the boys at school did not have to walk from Gypsy Hill, but came from the other direction, so they didn't have to endure the rigours of going via the Secondary Modern.

Enough about public transport.

Another episode that I must describe because it further dented my self-confidence as well as my public-speaking skills for years after - is the *cuccumber* incident.

Yes, I have deliberately spelt it incorrectly, so that the English scholars out there will read it with a short 'u'.

There was a reading competition held each year, with the best readers being selected from each class in each year to perform up on stage in front of the assembled school.

My form teacher at the time had told us to prepare a passage overnight to read out to our class next day, so that he could select the best.

This process was flawed.

33

I was not a fluent reader, but I could learn a passage by heart, which I did. As a result I was selected to represent our class. On the day of the competition proper however, I only had a short time to prepare the previously unseen piece, and no parents on hand to tell me how to pronounce any awkward words.

I could not work out what the hell a cucumber (*cuccumber*) was.

The word appeared several times, and on stage was read out as *cuccumber* every time by me, with a lot of hesitation. Clearly I did not win the competition, and my seeming stupidity was the source of much teasing for a while to come.

Big change was afoot in the Swinhoe household.

Some time in 1965 Kate and I were playing outside in the garden - or perhaps we had been deliberately sent there to play.

Why?

Because our parents were having a long conversation in the dining room.

In due course we were summoned back into the house and told that Dad did not want to be a general practitioner anymore, so had decided that he was going to re-join the Royal Army Medical Corps (RAMC). The consequence of this was that his first posting would be an 18-month 'unaccompanied' (bachelor) tour in the rank of major, as senior medical officer out in Sharjah on the Persian Gulf, home of the Middle East's romantic-sounding Trucial Oman Scouts - and after that somewhere else abroad, with Mum. So we were to be off to boarding school earlier than expected. I think we were asked our opinion regarding this unforeseen upheaval, but at that age children assume that parents know best!

The family home stayed in Dunheved Road. Now wearing khaki again Dad went away sometime in 1966, and I continued my daily journey to school. He came home once on leave in the middle of his tour and I remember him coming to school to watch me play rugby a lot in those six weeks; some form of guilt, perhaps?

During his Middle East tour our mother made one trip out to see him, when Kate and I were looked after by Grandma.

3

Boarding

AS ALREADY MENTIONED, I WAS ALWAYS GOING
to go to boarding school, following in father's footsteps by
attending Denstone College, but because of our family's
changed circumstances boarding was now going to have to
start earlier. This meant me going to Brightlands - a definite
misnomer as far as I was concerned - the boarding house for
Dulwich Prep.

My friend Peter Edwards had started there a year earlier,
and did little to ease my apprehension when he told me how
homesick he was. My sister Kate, who was already boarding,
had also been very homesick.

I was due to start my new regime in the summer term of
1968. We still lived in Dunheved Road, but Dad was back
from the Middle East and he and Mum were going off to
Malaysia in September, meaning I had a term in which to
prepare myself for our more permanent separation.

My day of departure duly arrived and Dad took one very
apprehensive young Crispin the five miles to the boarding
house. I liked to think the exclusively male venture was

because Mum couldn't have borne the thought of separation from her precious son, but more likely it was because they both knew I would be less likely to 'kick off' in front of Dad.

I knew boys from my year in the boarding house, but none of them were my friends yet. I was shown to my dormitory, shared between eight or ten others. Apart from the vivid recollection of my desperate homesickness, my memories of that first term are poor. However, there was one particularly worrying aspect of being there which might or might not be going to happen to me.

It was common knowledge in the school that there was a boarders' initiation ceremony to be endured. Rumour was that it involved being taken to the woods in the grounds and beaten with stinging nettles and sticks. In the event it never happened to me, but I know that some of the less popular boys had to go through the ordeal. Maybe the fact that I was only a term short of my final year at the school played a part in my being spared.

The year before I joined, Mr Maclean had been Head of the Boarding House. He was a Latin teacher; very grumpy and a hard man to please. However, he was fair and decent if one worked hard, and he liked me because he was also the rugby coach and I was his star winger. It was a shame he was no longer at Brightlands, because the new Head and I did not get on at all. I am not sure he really liked any of us. He lived in a house in the grounds with his wife, who was also a teacher.

The daily routine went something like this.

We were woken by one of the masters walking round the dormitories, ringing a bell. We had to leap out of bed and queue with our towel around our waist to take a cold shower. This was not a wash, but I assume simply to wake us up. We were only in the shower for ten seconds each, but it felt like some sort of punishment despite having done nothing wrong. We all had baskets under our beds for our clothes, so then we dressed, made our bed and went to breakfast. I cannot remember much about the food. It was not gruel as such, but I do remember that lunches at the main school during the day were disgusting, so I doubt it was too good. Lunch was the typical salt meat, clear gravy, boiled cabbage and mashed potato with black bits in it served with an ice-cream scoop. This whole culinary delight was complemented with the odd hair or two, and, if lucky, a dirty finger nail from the dinner ladies. Pudding was of course cold semolina or rice pudding, only made edible by the traditional dollop of jam. Ironically, our Christmas treat for the boarders the term after I started at Brightlands was a trip to see the musical *Oliver!*

After breakfast we walked to school, which was a mile or so away. Our school day was the same as for the day boys, after which we walked back, had our tea, did our homework, played either outside in the grounds or indoors, and then it was time for bed and lights out.

Weekends we had Saturday morning school, and then the rest of our time was spent at Brightlands.

On Sundays we walked in line to church, and then most of the rest of the day was ours to do with as we wished, although late Sunday afternoon was always set aside for letter writing.

There were no mobile phones in those days, nor did we have access to pay phones, so writing letters to and receiving them from our parents was our only form of communication.

Letter writing was a pain. What does an eleven-year-old boy at boarding school ever have to say? *I got up, had a cold shower, went to school, came back to Brightlands, had tea, did homework and went to bed. I got . . .* an exaggeration perhaps, but in my first term my parents only lived five miles away, yet there I was being made to struggle to write letters to them! With hindsight of course it can be seen that this exercise was good training and instilled self discipline. How many children, or even young adults today know *how* to lay out or write a proper letter?

Some Sunday evenings we went to Dulwich College, the big boys' school, to watch a film with their boarders. One evening it was *Bridge Over The River Kwai*. This was in 1968, when the Second World War had finished only 23 years before, so the whole of WWII's events were fairly recent history then, and the effects and consequences of a world war much more familiar to us than they are today. In fact, I suspect most modern children know very little at all about that global confrontation, when the parents of my generation, either served in the Forces, lived through the Blitz or endured other horrors. Even the First World War of 50 years before was still very real to us. My granpy had served in France throughout that war, and my great uncle Horace died in the trenches.

As a child, because of their ingrained enmity against their former foes I knew many adults who on principle would never buy anything of German or Japanese origin.

I served in the Falklands War and the First Gulf War; 33 and 24 years ago respectively. Both are now longer ago than the end of the Second World War was in 1968!

I fear that the lessons of these huge previous conflicts are being lost. Since the fall of the Iron Curtain we find ourselves living in a more and more unstable world. The rise of Hitler was due to the poverty and depression in Germany in the 1920s and early 1930s, as a result of the measures put in place after the Great War (WWI).

Now we see similar problems in the Middle East. Desperate people have nothing to lose by fighting. There is enough food in the world to feed everyone. In the West we unheedingly waste appalling amounts of the stuff, whilst elsewhere others are starving and living in poverty.

Since 2008 the word 'austerity' has increasingly crept into news reports when referring to the west's standard of living, yet in the past 50 years we have enjoyed unprecedented improvement in our degree of prosperity. Maybe this has slowed in the past seven years, but not sufficiently, by a very long way, to be described as austerity. Even the less well-off are prepared to pay, perhaps up to four times the price for an item, because it displays a *designer-label*, even though this doesn't make it any more useful or functional.

People living on welfare benefits are walking around using permanently topped-up mobile phone life-support systems!

If one had owned a house in London, or any other city or town, in 1940 one might well have watched it destroyed by a bomb, losing one's roof, walls and all one's worldly goods and possessions without hope of receiving compensation for any of it – *that's* austerity.

That first term as a school boarder I was miserable and homesick, which became even worse after my first short visit home at half-term. However, it was not all bad. Despite my shyness, slowly I began to make new friends. I remember Mum coming to pick me up at the end of term and taking me to Godalming, in Surrey, where we had now moved, and even though I had never been car sick before I was on that occasion, caused - I am sure - by my utter relief that the summer holidays had arrived at last.

In September Dad left for his new posting to 16 Commonwealth Field Ambulance at Terendak Camp, on the Malacca coast of Malaysia, with Mum due to follow him there shortly afterwards. I returned to school, and I think it was at that point in life I subconsciously realised that from then on I had to look after and fend for myself.

A Mr Decker had now joined the staff at Brightlands, along with Messrs Smith and Tanner (inevitably called sixpence). The latter I believe was undergoing some form of teacher-training, because he seemed to come and go at regular intervals.

Mr Smith was a nice, much-liked man, despite the fact that his favourite classroom punishment was to pull us up by our ears! Mr Tanner was good too, and keen on sport like me. The pair of them helped me to come to terms with boarding school.

Life went on.

I was now in Form 6A, during which time my friend Tim Dowdall returned from Germany and taught me some of what he had learnt about life there in the meantime. At the tender age of 12 I went with him to the Rolling Stones free concert in Hyde Park. We were supposed to be with his grandma for the day, but instead we went alone.

Another escapade was when I went with another boy to watch cricket at the Oval; cricket wasn't my cup of tea really, but it was a good day away.

One other weekend I stayed at a friend's house in Kent; his family had some land there and an old Lambretta scooter, which we hacked around on. This was when I first started my life-long affair with motorised bikes; a love which I continue to this day, and still, never being able to bring myself to call a scooter a motorbike!

Let me now tell you about a funny episode we had with one of our teachers.

Mr Decker's first name - Desmond - was the same as in one of the Beatles' songs, and after lights out one night we started singing this song, making reference in it to one of our female teacher's names. Desmond heard us and came storming up the stairs with a leather slipper in his hand. On hearing him approach we had obviously stopped our ribald singing, but there was such an evil glint in his eye that we knew in order to vent his ire he fully intended to use the slipper if he could. "Come on sing it, *sing* it I <u>dare</u> you," he shouted, slapping his slipper across into his other hand. When we dumbly desisted to oblige, he withdrew downstairs, whereupon we'd resume belting it out again, when he'd come dashing back up once more, getting hotter and hotter under the collar each time. Eventually we gave in and packed up the torment. He coached us at rugby and was a nice bloke with whom I got on well. On this occasion we had definitely been provoking him to make him act so mean!

Another episode which took place at this time was with Brightlands' Head; a truly outrageous and unfair event that was perpetrated specifically against me. Even to this day I don't understand what he thought he was doing, treating a young boy the way he did. This is what happened . . .

. . . it was nearly the end of term and my sister Kate and I were off to Malaysia to spend Christmas out there with Mum and Dad. My parents had sent me £5 for the journey. More correctly I suppose they should have sent it to the housemaster to give to me, but they didn't. I took it to school that day and proudly showed it off to a few boys, because £5 then would be the equivalent of about £50 today I would guess.

When I returned to the boarding house I hung up my coat, only later realising with a rush of horror that I had left the money in the gabardine's pocket. I rushed to find it, and - of course - it was no longer there!

Devastated, I reported the loss.

Rather than my receiving any kind of sympathy or support, everything then went from bad to worse, and I was subjected to a full interrogation.

"Why did you have the money?

"Why didn't you hand it in?

"Why did you need it?"

Then, as if it was *I* who was the culprit, I was paraded in front of all the other boys, when everyone was told that unless the money was returned *no* one would be going on holiday.

Now I had become even more 'the villain'.

This entire event was conducted by the housemaster, who to this day if I ever met I would 'sort out'!

On top of all that, he severely reprimanded me for having shown the money to the other boys. I had been in art class that day, which his wife taught, so no prizes for guessing where that tale came from!

Somehow or other the money was eventually retrieved and returned to me; well - £4.17s.6d - (four pounds, seventeen shillings and sixpence) of it was, the outstanding half-crown presumably having been spent already. Yes, of course I should have handed the money in for safekeeping, but this was a very cruel way to treat a timid, shy 12-year-old, or indeed any boy or girl of that age, particularly one who was already nervous and excited about an upcoming journey half-way round the world with his 13-year-old sister.

Our journey began.

I can't now remember who actually took us to the airport, but once there BOAC (The British Overseas Aircraft Corporation) operated a system for looking after children embarking on long journeys.

We reported to the check-in desk where we were given a badge and someone to look after us, both to ensure we made it to the plane.

After that we were treated pretty much like any other passenger.

I had flown once before on one of the very early package deals to Mallorca, on a family holiday. I remember that on that occasion the plane had propellers and was called, I seem to recall, a *Cavalier*. There had been a lot of turbulence on that flight, and a lady behind us had hysterics! So Kate and I were not seasoned flyers by any means. Few children were in those days; most people's holidays back then involving a cross-channel ferry and/or a car, not a plane.

This exciting, long-haul flight of ours out to Malaysia was in either a Boeing 707 or a VC10, I am not sure which, but BOAC being a British airline one would hope it was a VC10. Boeing wielded a lot of power though, and I know the VC10 - a superior aircraft - was not used as universally as it should have been. Later the USA would do its best to boycott *Concorde*, as it had done with the *Comet* previously, although the latter had its problems, like crashing a bit too often! In some ways though it was not surprising the Americans wanted to 'get their own back' at us. In the 1950s the Labour government had sold the secrets of the jet engine to the Russians, who then made a better version, which they put in their MiG fighter jets, which the Chinese used to pit against our own RAF and America's USAF planes during the Korean War!

Another less than clever Labour government decision of this era was the cancellation of the TSR2 project in the sixties. This was to have been the construction of an 'ahead of its time' multi-purpose fighter-bomber. Because of rising costs, but after much money and expertise had already been expended, the project was scrapped. This sounded the death-knell of our brilliant military aircraft industry, which since WWII had produced the awesome 'V-Bombers': the *Vulcan, Victor* and *Valiant*. The Harrier Jump Jet did arrive later, but again did not achieve the international acclaim that it should have done, I suspect once more because of the might and negative influence of our allies, the USA.

We flew via Rome, Bahrain, Karachi and Calcutta out to Singapore that Christmas of 1968, refuelling several times. I cannot remember if we deplaned and went into the terminals during the process or not. Eventually, after what seemed like an interminably long journey we arrived in Singapore, from whence - our trip not yet over - we had to get on up to Malacca, in Malaysia, where our parents were living, and there were no planes until the following day. So . . .

. . .we found ourselves being escorted to the Raffles Hotel. Yes.

The Raffles Hotel -

- Singapore's iconic 5-star establishment at 1, Beach Road, opened in 1897 with its 14-foot high ceilings, liveried Sikh doormen and home of the world famous gin-based *Singapore Sling* cocktail, first knocked-up by its Long Bar barman in 1915 - and this is where 12- and-13-year-old Crispin and Kate Swinhoe spent their first night in the Orient, which included a meal in the open central courtyard under the stars . . .

. . . but the whole meaningful experience was lost on us, really. We were hot, tired and just wanted to get 'home'.

Next day we flew in a small Malaysian Airways plane up to Malacca, and there - finally - were our parents, gleefully waiting to greet us.

Since Dad only served there for a year, we only ever had two holidays in Malacca.

During that Christmas holiday we lived in a house just outside the Army base, so we were reliant on either Mum or Dad to take us to the beach club, where there was a swimming pool. However, by the time of our Easter holiday they had moved into the army camp proper, so we were able to walk to the pool where every day was spent playing with the other children, swimming, and walking along the beach with short forays into the nearby jungle. The sea thereabouts was infested with jelly fish and sea snakes, so all swimming was confined strictly to the pool.

In our Easter holiday we spent a week over on the East Coast, where I remember lying on a beach at night waiting to see the giant turtles lay their eggs - but they never came! On the same trip I bought a lovely carved wooden spinning top and a blow pipe with very sharp and effective darts carved from wood. Back in Terendak Camp one ended up in the rump of a cat that was raiding our dustbins! Don't tell the RSPCA!

Before our Malaysia holidays my swimming wasn't up to much, but as a result of so much time spent in the water there it improved immensely. I was always grateful for this, because later in life I took up triathlon, by which time I had become well able to hold my own in the pool and sea.

Both those Far Eastern holidays were a fantastic experience for my sister and me. We were able to see and do so many things, which were rare for children in those days. The bustle of the Far East in general, markets and oriental food still spring readily to mind.

We British left Malaysia in 1969, and prior to that the country's elections were held. They were preceded by race riots, which started in Kuala Lumpar the very day we flew out from there at the end of our Easter holiday. We thought it a shame the event did not cause us to miss our flight home, become stranded in the country, and have to go to school there for the summer term - but we could only wish.

As the rest of 1969 went by I became more settled at school. The following year I would be going up to Public School as a boarder, but before that I had to take my Common Entrance examination.

I remember little about that exam.

What I do remember are my schoolmasters at Dulwich telling me that I would have little problem gaining sufficient marks to get a place in such an inferior school as Denstone College. Obviously they were not too impressed with a second rate public school in the Midlands, when many of my peers were going on to Dulwich College and others to Harrow,

Winchester, St. Paul's and Charterhouse - 'proper' schools in the south of England!

Before I left however, at the end of the summer term, there was the small matter of my final sports day and another 100-yards race in which to compete. (Incidentally, athletics was not my only sport; I loved my rugby in the winter).

This year being my last, there was not only a trophy for each race at sports day, but also a trophy for the boy winning the greatest number of events; 'the victor ludorum'. There was none of this newly contrived, politically correct socialist rubbish going on then, about it not being fair to reward the best and that no one should be allowed to lose in case their thus indicated lack of effort, or inadequacy should result in them becoming a psychologically scarred loser for life. Ours was a properly operated private school; winner took all. In fact, the ridiculous no competition business had not yet permeated even state education.

Life very often *is* unfair - *and* competitive.

During the dark days of pre-Thatcher socialist Britain, when and where could children ever be taught that fact, unless acquired through the lessons they learned from their experiences at school, imparted the way they had been for hundreds of years, successfully forging Britons of worth and global stature?

I knew I could win the 100-yards and the hurdles, but the 400-yards was the realm of Edward Waites, the scion of the eponymous building firm. Eddie and I were both boarders and quite good friends. He was much more confident than me, and one of the boarding house prefects.

I duly won the predicted races, but he beat me in the 400-yards, despite Mr Tanner giving me some individual coaching before the event.

This left just the high jump and long jump.

Eddie had started to receive and benefit from his internal testosterone boost, whereas I had not. He must have been four inches taller than me as well, and won both jumps.

The overall trophy was his.

And thus I learnt - yet again - that life is competitive, which I knew already a-hundredfold, of course.

But at least on this occasion I had been beaten fair and square.

Mum and Dad had still been in Malaysia for that final sports day of mine, so they'd asked my godfather to come along, to watch and cheer me on - which he did.

He was a doctor, who had been at medical school with Dad, and was a great godfather, never forgetting a present at Christmas or birthday until I reached 'manhood' at 18 - or perhaps it was 21-years in those days. I realise that the giving and receipt of presents are not the primary role of a godfather, but anything to do with religion would have been wasted on me anyway.

He had become a child psychiatrist by the time he attended my sports day, having moved on - like my father - from general practice. Many years later we were to meet again at my parents' golden wedding anniversary party. He remembered that final sports day of mine well apparently, and remarked: "You were such an *unhappy* child!" and I don't think he was referring to my reaction at not having won the overall trophy that day, but rather my general outlook and demeanour, an assessment with which I could only concur.

The end of term arrived, and still we had no parents in the UK.

I was due to go off on a sea-scout camp to Dover, where we lived in tents in the Castle grounds and sailed and canoed off the beach. Overall it was a good week, but my shyness was to haunt me again. No doubt attracted by our blue shorts and the rest of the uniform, a group of local girls seemed to take a bit of a fancy to us! For some reason they took a particular fancy to *me* in fact, and kept calling my name. Perhaps it was the name itself - *Crispin* - I ask you; why?

I was still unable to interact with the fairer sex without 'rigor mortis' setting in quicker than fast-setting Super Glue, along with an accompanying onset of dumbness. I found the thought of conducting any interaction with them petrifying. Every evening, I lived in fear of their arrival, not helped by the other guys all teasing me about my predicament. One day we returned from the beach to find them already there, waiting for us. One of the guys cried gleefully: "Oooh look, your girlfriends are here".

"Just . . . you . . . *Fuck Off*", I retorted furiously, but unfortunately my unseemly outburst had been unleashed within earshot of some of the masters.

It was the first time I had used such a word in front of any adults, who on this occasion were fortunately kind enough to see my distress and let it go. If I had managed to remain so fearful of girls for the rest of my life, I would probably be a wealthier man today - but not necessarily happier!

Whilst at Dover we saw the Moon-Landing, on a black and white television set somewhere up in the Castle. It seemed such an important and significant event at the time, but now nearly 50 years afterwards it hasn't taken us anywhere useful at all really. NASA would no doubt tell us of all the hidden benefits, but to me they are hard to see. Countries with millions of their citizens living in squalor now have space programs, and the USA itself still has many of its people living on the poverty line. What strange priorities we have, in the main - I suspect - driven by profit, power and greed.

Sea-scout camp was over, so I joined Kate in Weymouth to stay with my grandparents, until Mum arrived home. Even after our mother, at last returned from Malaysia's hot and steamy clime it was a nomadic holiday. We stayed with both sets of grandparents. Our home in England had been let and was unavailable, so the whole scenario of my existence that summer seemed a bit surreal, to be followed in September by my move to Denstone College.

4.

Formative Years

THE TIME CAME, AND MUM DROVE ME TO COLL, which I was quickly to learn, was the name that Denstone College was called by the boys and masters alike. All of us new boys had to arrive early to have tea with the housemaster, Mr Philip Smith.

There were nine houses, named after the founders and benefactors of the school: Heywood, Philips, Shrewsbury, Meynell, Woodard, and Selwyn, Lonsdale and Lowe - and, later, Talbot.

I was in Meynell, same as Dad had been.

There were about 320 boys in the school, all of us boarders.

The Captain of House was also at the tea, a duty that I myself would be performing in four years' time.

I felt very nervous and during tea could feel a few tears begin to well up, but I was determined not to let them show. In the main I had managed to conquer my homesickness by now, but joining a new school is still a daunting experience.

There were to be only four new boys in Meynell House that term, and as each of the other three arrived and I met them, I subconsciously began gauging them as potential friend material.

Colin Wood was the son of one of the school music teachers and didn't look to be at all sporty, so he was not going to be my cup of tea.

Richard Lamont (who had an older brother in the House already) looked like a mad professor and later turned out to be a funny guy, but wasn't my kind of bloke at that stage.

Then Duncan Watson arrived. I quickly learnt that he was a sportsman, and as it would turn out, better than me at ball sports. Duncan's sons now play rugby to a very high standard; Marcus playing seven-a-side for England, Anthony having just played in the Rugby World Cup, and - Duncan tells me - his youngest is the best of the three, but is yet to make his mark.

Duncan and I became the best of friends from that day on, and although we may not see each other for a number of years, we know that when we do meet it will be as if we had never been apart. Duncan's older brother, Mark, was a school prefect and in Meynell House.

After our introductory tea that day there was a tour of the House and the whole school, when we were inducted into a few ground rules. We were shown our dormitory and our basic, metal-framed, horse-hair mattress bed (which we had to make ourselves with our own sheets, pillowcases and blankets) beside which there was a small cupboard for our clothes. My blankets were the ones my dad had used many years before. They were not luxurious!

In my father's day the dormitory had been one long room for the whole house. Now it was divided into four; junior, middle, senior and the prefect's dorm, as they were called. The dorm's heating was rudimentary - just some pipes running along at floor level beneath the large windows. They were at best just warm! To give an idea of the standard of accommodation, if it was a 2015 prison it would abysmally fail an inspection undertaken by any appropriate body of prison inspectors; an observation that would have applied to all the facilities, not just the dormitories, and our parents were paying handsomely for the privilege of us being there!

Whether this comparison demonstrates that our prisons are now too soft, or perhaps in our best interest, 'for toughening-up purposes', we were treated this severely - who knows? Things did improve during the course of my five years there, but nowhere near up to modern prison standards, I suspect.

We weren't locked up at night, but silence was the rule after lights out!

During that 'Opening Grand Tour' on Day One we were also shown the House Common Room, where we had a desk, whereas older boys enjoyed shared studies in the study block.

There was one television in the school, which could be watched at weekends only.

The classroom block was effectively unheated. It was also in the process of sliding down the hill the school had been built on, in 1868. The subsiding block itself was circa 1920, and supposed to have been only a temporary construction even back then.

The sports changing-rooms had lockers in which we kept our kit. I don't think we washed it from one end of the term to the other, so it was just as well the changing-rooms were unheated or the stink would have been overpowering. The showers were cold and - surprise, surprise - ran at a trickle.

Juniors were not allowed to use the stronger and hotter showers in the dormitory bathroom and we had only two allocated bath nights a week, so personal hygiene was not optimal. It was left up to us when we decided to send our clothes to the laundry, so that was pretty much a hit or miss affair as well.

My memories of the first few days at my new school are sketchy with regard to anything in the classroom. Our lessons were forty-minutes long, in sets, depending on how bright one was. There were five-minute change-overs between lessons, when the masters would stand outside smoking. *Great* example this, when any *boy* caught smoking could expect 'six of the best' on his backside from his housemaster. *Don't do as I do, do as I say!*

In my first year food was served at sit-down meals, as opposed to the self-service system which came later. The food, not surprisingly, was poor, cooked and served (or so we reckoned with some justification perhaps) by 'trusties' from the local prisons and lunatic asylums. Judging by their finger-nails their personal hygiene was even worse than ours. They lived in worse conditions than us too, in the servant quarters, which stank, as did most of them. The highlight of our culinary repasts, therefore, was bread toasted in huge toasters by boys from the duty house for the week. Sometimes it was very pale, sometimes burnt, and occasionally just right, but whatever state it was in it was plentiful and kept us from starving.

So this was the world into which I arrived that September 1969.

In general I grew to be happy there at Denstone, made good friends, and enjoyed much of it. The school today has now become co-educational, and in retrospect I think the insular all-male, institutionalised and somewhat old-fashioned environment of my time was not a good preparation for later life. This is a view I have held for many years, but I did not make the association until I was in my late thirties.

Denstone's masters were mostly good people and generally kind and helpful, although quite a few were only pretty average teachers!

Sport was a very important part of our lives there.

The main sports afternoons were Monday, Wednesday Thursday and Saturday. Tuesday was set aside for other activities, in particular the Combined Cadet Force, adventure training, or Scouts, depending on whichever one chose. Each week every boy had to engage in at least two major sporting activities, and on the other days he could do major or minor sports, but not neither! Those in or competing for a place in a school team in a major sport did that activity all the time. In winter a major was rugby or cross-country running; minors were fives, squash and anything else. In summer athletics, cricket and swim-training were the recognised majors. On Fridays we could do different sports, like hockey, tennis, or other non-sporting activities in clubs; Richard Lamont, for example, having joined the Physics Club, seemed to spend his time building televisions!

In winter, after the clocks changed, sport took place in the early afternoon, in the light, and then we would return to the classroom for two lessons from 4.40pm.

I well remember my early sporting experiences at Denstone.

We had a rugby meeting, where we were asked what position we played, and were then 'tried-out' for it, so as to assess how good we really were.

I was a winger so was put into that position.

I was very keen on rugby, but over the first few weeks I became more and more aware of something that was soon going to lead me to seek my sporting recognition elsewhere.

All the boys heading for the under-14's First Team, like Edward Waites at Dulwich, seemed to have been issued a full set of hormones somewhere along the way. They were all developing into bigger, brawnier and stronger fellows than me. Concurrently, I was losing my confidence. I had been a fearless tackler at Dulwich, but now I just seemed to wimp out the whole time. Philip Smith was the under-14's backs coach as well as being my housemaster, and he gave me extra tackling lessons - but all to no avail.

I realised that I desperately needed to devise a new game plan.

After giving my situation much thought, knowing that I could run, or sprint at least, I decided that cross-country running was the answer.

I had never run more than 400-yards in anger before, but I remained undeterred. Our school cross-country was run by Mr 'Ratty' Williams, a lovely man, but a poor teacher who really did look a bit like a rat, so was understandably teased by the boys in class, and even to some degree I think by his colleagues.

But he was a great runner.

I was nowhere near as talented as 'Ratty' - but I was determined.

We spent the next five winters together, with the other boys who ran in the cross country teams. Wearing just our shorts and singlets we ran in all weathers, and I became the third or fourth best in my year.

Alex Lester and another lad were the regulars, who invariably beat me. Alex – I hope he won't mind me saying this - was a non-conformist, so when it came to our final season in the sixth form and I was made school cross-country captain he became a tad miffed, because I had been considered the more responsible and upright citizen. This is the same Alex Lester who today DJ's on BBC's Radio 2 in the small hours by the way; sorry Alex!

Another well-known boy in our year, who I left behind on the rugby field, was Alistair Hignell.

Alistair was a brilliant sportsman who later became a double blue at Cambridge. He went on to play rugby for England and first class county cricket. He then became a sports commentator for the BBC, before retiring early, sadly suffering from multiple sclerosis. None of us knows what lies ahead of us do we? It would have been a million miles from our perception at school that Alistair, of all people would ever suffer from such a crippling disease. There will be more on my thoughts about life and health later.

Every morning before the commencement of each day's lessons it was a requirement for us to attend a short 20-minute chapel service. On Sundays it was Eucharist at 10.00 am and Evensong at 6.30 pm, although the latter ceased in my second or third year because of the introduction of weekly boarders, who went home every weekend after Eucharist. I guess it was deemed unfair to put the permanent inmates through two lots of church, when the others would have got away with one, although I am sure the decision was not *really* made with those thoughts in mind.

I had never felt or been in any way religious, and school confirmed for me the seeming stupidity of the whole matter. There were our teachers drumming into us all day that we should believe in, learn and work with facts, and then on Sundays we were expected to unquestioningly accept, believe in and practise the fanciful precepts laid down by a string of 2,000-year-old Middle Eastern sheep-herders.

I can understand how the 'belief' held by an individual is a safe and comforting place to be, confident that when this life is over one will be going to somewhere better; in fact, so strong is the 'belief' of some that I am puzzled why more people don't take themselves off there earlier. Instead, there seems to be this universal desperation to cling on to life long after it can possibly be any use, or in any way an enjoyable or rewarding experience.

In my view religion has much to answer for with regard to the world's ills, and does more harm than good on a wider scale. It reinforces the belief that as individuals we are important. It generates the idea that we exist as an entity and possess this indefinably strange thing called a soul. This reinforces the ego, which produces conflict both between individuals and, on a larger scale, between nations, each intractable in the invariably erroneous belief that their take on the matter is the correct one. Some of the most selfish people I have met in life have either been highly religious, or vicars, which is hardly surprising since the priesthood must be the ultimate 'ego trip'.

However, the ego is simply a collection of thoughts and these thoughts are just thoughts and nothing more; implanted in our brains as a result of our experiences.

If we were to have a particular set of experiences today they would slightly alter or affect our thoughts and reactions tomorrow. If our today's experiences were *different* we would be affected in a different way tomorrow, and tomorrow, therefore, we would be a slightly different person to the one we would have been if we had had the first set of experiences. My premise is that there is no such thing as a person, or soul, just sets of thoughts, which create what we consider ourselves to be.

Our early experiences do a lot to mould our personality, so we tend to associate this with our own persona, thus feeling that we are this particular person. The ego and the importance of the individual are even more reinforced these days than they used to be, because of the way in which children are treated.

As already mentioned, in my own early days children generally came second to adults in the family. This was not true only of my own parents, who I admit were rather extreme in this way. Whereas today it seems to be believed that children should continuously be told how wonderful and important they are and family life revolves around *them*. Perhaps this approach is not such a bad one if it builds confidence etcetera, but every indication is that the practice has gone too far and leads to over-confident, over-exaggerated 'egos' with all the associated problems that they can bring.

For me this whole scenario is epitomised by those ridiculous signs we see in the rear windows of motor cars - *LITTLE PRINCESS ON BOARD*, - who no doubt will later turn out to be the same lovable (not) little miss we'll see having uncontrollable tantrums at the supermarket checkout, when being denied a packet of sweets, or some other such 'instant gratification, must-have' delight!

Life at school was very much a routine.

We got up, had our breakfast, went to chapel, attended our lessons, had lunch, returned for more lessons - or sport; sport or lessons, then supper, prep, bed and lights out. Generally, though, we had fun and my circle of friends widened.

One of the houses, Talbot, was added when the school expanded. Talbot was in the grounds, and not the main building.

Martyn Hughes and Martin Stark were in Talbot and were to become friends of mine.

Talbot then closed whilst we were at Denstone, when the school began to contract, and the Talbot boys were distributed amongst other houses. Martin and Martyn went to Selwyn, on the floor above Meynell in the main building. David Large, another friend, was also in Selwyn. He broke his leg in our first or second year at school and because there was no such technique for internally fixing legs in those days he had to lie in bed in the sanatorium for ages while it healed. Accordingly, David Large became quite enlarged, thanks to the longevity of his enforced incarceration and lack of exercise!

David and I were both in London at university, as was Martin, and we all shared a flat together for a year. David studied geology, and went into the oil business, which was an effective way to earn good money in those days. He ended up with his own business, and we still keep in touch. Martin studied zoology and later worked for various water companies. He is now retired and he and his wife Anne have a bed-and-breakfast place in Northumberland, and I stayed with them recently when walking Hadrian's Wall with my friend Jim and Charlie, the Dalmatian. Martyn (the one without the 'i') went to medical school in Bristol and became a GP. He is a lifelong Stoke City supporter and still attends matches. We met up at a school reunion just a few years ago.

In our first term at school my friend Duncan Watson was bottom of the bottom class! He managed to do alright with his 'O'-level examinations in the end, but fluffed his 'A'-levels. We lived together in London for several years, when I was a student and he was working there. The summer I qualified, he headed off to Scotland to pursue his dream of working in the petroleum industry and is now a very successful business man with interests in many parts of the world. So much for early academic success (or failure) being an indicator of future prosperity!

We are obsessed in this country with paper qualifications these days, and degrees have become two-a-penny, whereas it has been proved time after time that good practical skills, common sense and an entrepreneurial flair are far more important; all qualities which Duncan possessed in abundance. I suspect the Government welcomes the fact that so many *do* go to college and university, since it keeps the unemployment figures down.

In medicine I have never been able to understand why somebody decided a nurse should require a degree before being able to perform her/his job effectively. How ridiculous is that? It is not as though nurses have used this new-found academia to further their profession. Many of them, particularly the hierarchy, still live in Victorian times. I have misused the word 'profession' here, such use is a pet hate of mine. There are, in fact, only *three* 'professions': Law, Medicine, and the Church - oh, alright, four then, if we are to include prostitution! Now the word is used in connection with almost any job, along with such nomenclature as 'sales executive' (car salesman), 'beauty technician' (hair dresser) and so on; all quite absurd!

After this heated digression, perhaps we should get back to school . . .

. . . where, we were heading towards the summer term.

Athletics was to continue to be my summer sport, as it had been at Dulwich, but once again I discovered that being short on hormones was going to cause me problems. I had managed to sustain my 100-yards speed right through to the end of Prep School, but now I was no longer the fastest guy in town - although I could hold my own if there were hurdles in the way, and became the second-best in that event. Perhaps cross-country running's necessity to convert my fast-twitch fibres to slow-twitch hadn't helped.

Our athletics master was Henry Parker, whose son was in my year. Mr Parker decided that since I could hurdle and was a cross-country runner he would put me in the 2,000-metres (we had gone metric now) steeplechase, which I won at my first attempt in an athletics match against another school, unfortunately a performance that I never repeated. I was still a good all-rounder and did long-jump, high-jump and triple-jump as well, although I was hopeless at throwing events.

In the summer term two new boys arrived in Meynell, one of whom was Jeremy Riley, who my friend Duncan knew from prep school. Jerry did Duncan a massive favour that term by taking over the latter's baton and becoming bottom boy in the bottom class in school.

Another new boy arrived in the summer term. He ended up being teased a lot by everybody, the cause for which it seemed he brought upon himself by being the most contrary of people. On principle he often took the completely opposite point of view to the rest of us, which always got right up people's noses, although in some ways I admired him for 'sticking to his guns'. Duncan and I got ourselves into a lot of trouble with our housemaster, Philip Smith, over teasing him the way we did, although we were not by any means the worst perpetrators.

The third year at school, when we were in the Vth form, the same lad revealed a running ability, which beat me into fourth place in the junior cross-country championship; a four-mile course across proper muddy fields, which all of us had to do -we brooked no pussy-footing-about back then; it was the real McCoy and we 'did' mud - not like we see in World Cross-Country Championships today, which always seem to be run in a not very muddy park; better - presumably - for the spectators.

Luckily Alex Lester and a boy called Edwards decided it would be too much like hard work for them to race each other, so made a deal that they would contrive to cross-the-finishing-line first-equal. 'Ratty' Williams then fudged it and said that because they were first-equal there would be four of us in the winners' photograph; nice man.

Quite a few of our Coll masters had been there first as boys.

Linton Stocks was housemaster of Lowe (Alistair Hignell's House). Linton had been at school with my father, as had the housemaster of Shrewsbury, Michael Swales. Ralph Green was another. Even those masters, who had not been previous pupils there, had taught in the place for years. Mr Adamson had taught my father and although he was now retired he still lived in the school and taught games, staying there until he died . . . all very evocative of *Mr Chips*.

Terence Tookey and Ken Ryder were there when I was a boy, and still taught on for many years after that. Ken Ryder still lives in nearby Denstone Village itself, where he drinks in *The Tavern*. . . . some more of which later!

Philip Smith taught at the school from finishing his National Service, right through until he retired. He died living nearby, having smoked, drunk and eaten himself to death - guilt for all of which he would have admitted freely.

Philip was a happy fat guy, who lived life to the full. He was very kind to all us boys and loved his job. By the time I came to leave he had become like a surrogate father to me. The following summer holiday after I left he took me out to lunch at the ground floor restaurant at Simpson's in the Strand as a 'thank you' for being house captain. It was an all-male establishment where the massive roasts were brought to table on silver trolleys and carved there alongside the clientele.

Although Philip took me to Simpsons, I believe that public school masters generally were a pretty parochial bunch, and had probably been so for years. It is somewhat worrying, therefore, to realise that generations of future leaders of our land had traditionally been taught by a gentry who possessed such limited outlooks on life. In view of this, perhaps it is not surprising that I left school institutionalised, scared of girls and still generally timid and shy when outside my own close circle of friends.

Again, I have digressed.

Again, back to school . . .

A full year had now passed for me at Denstone.

Before we departed for that year's summer holiday, Philip Smith and Linton Stocks wrote a spoof play in which we had to star! My voice had still not yet broken, so I was put upon to play a Welsh girl. God knows now what the story-line was, but I was teased about it for a long time afterwards!

Whilst still at Dulwich, in 1967, I'd gone on a school cruise in the old British India ship *SS Uganda* (later used as a hospital ship in the Falkland's War). To render her 'fit for purpose' she had been converted, so as to have dormitories instead of cabin accommodation. Because one of her ports-of-call was scheduled to be Haifa (to enable us to visit Israel and the Holy Lands) we almost hadn't gone on that trip at all. The Six Day War was not long over, when Israel defeated mighty Egypt after the latter tried to wipe out the Jewish homeland once and for all, but to their surprise lost a large parcel of their own land instead. In the event we did go, and as well as Haifa visited Gibraltar, Venice, Malta and Beirut. We had a great time, both whilst at sea as well as on our visits to all the different and exciting places *en route*, which included Bethlehem and Jerusalem.

Before I left Dulwich another *SS Uganda* trip was being organised, this time to the Baltic and Russia. Some of the soon to be 'old-boys' were being allowed to go, and my parents agreed to me joining the trip.

Our first port of call was Copenhagen, although I am unable to recall which other Baltic ports we visited before reaching what was then Leningrad. From there we travelled by night-sleeper train on to Moscow, where amongst other highlights we saw the embalmed body of Vladimir Lenin lying in its glass-encased sarcophagus in his Red Square mausoleum. In Moscow we also bought cigarettes to smoke back on board ship! Bad lads!

Each evening there was a disco on board, when my hopeless and helpless state with girls reared its embarrassing head yet again. This condition was not aided by Edward Waites also telling me that my dancing was awful. Eddie - the swine - had already 'found' *his* hormones before the previous year's sports day, and in the meantime had since accumulated a whole lot more. His school, Westminster, must have been much more progressive than Denstone. Eddie had long hair, trendy clothes and his own cool dancing style. He was also capable of actually communicating with girls! I did manage to entice one nice young lady, who came from Devon up onto the back deck in the dark towards the end of our trip, but then found myself barely able even to converse (what I managed was in monosyllables) with her, because of my embarrassment; let alone try to kiss her - dammit. We did exchange addresses and wrote to each other briefly for a while afterwards, but then I received word that she would be visiting the Farnborough Air Show, just around the corner from where we lived, so I nipped our burgeoning relationship in the bud there and then, rather than have to endure the misery of any further embarrassment.

Back at Denstone College, from an academic point of view I was beginning to realise that science was my thing. I was not a particularly clever boy, but I worked hard, I had a good memory and I strove to understand things. Biology was my best subject, where there were no complicated formulæ to learn; next came chemistry - and I was least good at physics and mathematics.

Mr Nigel Green, a one-time notable triple-jumper was our biology teacher, who also coached rugby and athletics. Tall and scary-looking he liked to play on these features and had no problem with discipline in class. I got on well with him and he became my tutor - a kind of mentor separate from a boy's housemaster.

He expected all of our work to be neat, and it was he who was responsible for me developing what is today recognised as being obsessive-compulsive disorder (OCD). Because of his expectations I would write out my pieces of work for him as perfectly as possible, and this obsession spread to include all my other subjects. It reached the point where, if I made one error, even if it was the last word on the page I would feel compelled to start the whole exercise all over again. This began to become a problem at home too, where I had to check several times that I had shut all the doors, turned off the taps or flushed the toilet. I cured myself of the disorder eventually by simply refusing to acknowledge it, or perform the tasks it demanded. If I turned off a tap, I would stare at it and count to ten, by which time I successfully managed to convince myself that it was off and so was able to walk away and leave it. In each repetitive instance I counted to lower and lower numbers until at last I was able to be 'normal', or as normal as I have ever been. But then what is normal?

Society decides what should be perceived as normal, and different cultures set different values on things. The word 'values' is much overused and misused as being a word synonymous with goodness, which is incorrect. We all have values, but this does not necessarily make them good. A criminal's values might be that it is alright to steal, because other people possess more material items than he or she. A social security fraudster perhaps believes the 'value' that what they are doing is fine, because they are eligible, so have a 'right' to the tax-payers' money they receive. So we should more properly refer to 'principles' rather than 'values'. Principles include honesty, integrity, kindness and decency, the meaning of which are universally the same and do not change with an individual's personal interpretation.

Let us return to what is normal.

It is potentially dangerous ground.

In the past, homosexuality was illegal, the age of consent was 13 and women could not vote. Few of us now would take the view that any of those mores are acceptable. Is 'normal' what the majority of us does? Clearly not, otherwise all minority activities would have to be considered 'abnormal'. Generally speaking society needs to take the broader view that accepts all manner of standards, opinions and activities. Unacceptable behaviour is that which impinges on the well-being of others. There are some aspects of social behaviour that do affect the well-being of others and little or nothing useful seems to be done about some of them. The deleterious effect that alcohol abuse has is one such problem, which I shall discuss in the next chapter.

Reference to well-being leads me to an incident that occurred in one of our IVth Form chemistry lessons once. The science block at school was separate from the classrooms, those decrepit affairs we left sliding down the hill a few pages back.

During this particular chemistry lesson we were heating something up in a test tube over a Bunsen burner. There was only one fume-cupboard in the lab and we weren't using it, so noxious fumes were being allowed to emit freely from my test tube. This was a kind of yellow-green gas, (used by the Germans in the First World War!), of which I inhaled a lungful, thereafter spending the rest of the class sitting with my head out of the window, spluttering and fighting off potentially lethal pulmonary oedema (fluid on the lungs) . . . *erm*, well, perhaps I might be exaggerating just a bit, but still it was not a very pleasant experience.

Health and Safety is now a national obsession, indeed a European obsession. I came to no harm as a result of my experience in the laboratory, and learnt a sound lesson from it. Don't put your head over and inhale from a test tube producing chlorine gas: *simple*! I would be the first to concede that conditions at work, or anywhere else too for that matter should not be overtly dangerous, but today the entire safety culture would seem to have gone overboard with absurdity.

The 'nanny state' in which we live is exasperating.

Earlier I referred to the majority being the ones who make the rules. This is not necessarily true, and certainly not in the case of health and safety legislation. One only has to ask around to have it confirmed that the vast majority of the population believes it has all 'gone too far' - unless those polled are greedy solicitors feeding from it of course. However, despite the views of most of us, more and more ridiculous health and safety legislation is being made up by the minority in places like Westminster and Brussels. The fatuous decisions made are then compounded by organisations' unimaginative, unintelligent middle-managers, particularly in the public service sector, insisting that we follow the dictates. These people are surely the subject-matter referred to in this old adage. *Rules are made for the guidance of wise men and the blind obedience of fools.* They are obedient it seems, but certainly not wise.

For those middle-managers now bristling with indignation, I would only say this.

"If the cap fits - wear it."

If it does not fit and you *are* a good, very good or excellent middle-manager, especially in the NHS or some other public body, then I applaud you and thank the Lord you exist, whilst sadly suspecting that you might be the exception that proves the rule!

Not long before retiring from the NHS I walked up the stairs and onto a landing at Barnsley Hospital one day to find two women operating what looked like a swingometer in the middle of the linoleum'd floor area.

"What on earth are you doing"? I asked.

"Measuring how slippery the floor is", they told me.

Their machine consisted of a pendulum with a pad on the bottom being moved across the floor to have the degree of resistance it met recorded on a tension gauge.

I would have been less bothered by this initiative if I thought the degree of resistance recorded was to see whether preventive measures needed taking to save members of the public slipping and hurting themselves. But such was not the case I strongly suspect. The degree of resistance was being recorded as an advance support-aid to help fend off culpability in the event that some member of the public *did* slip and decided to pursue the matter legally.

By the way, on the subject of slipping; why from a health and safety perspective is it not alright to slip on a wet floor, but apparently ok to fall over the yellow boards that declare the floor wet? I say this, because I have nearly tripped over such items on many occasions and they often seem to be hidden round corners and behind doors to make them much more likely to cause such an event! The madness of it all is often too much to contemplate, let alone understand.

There will be more on these matters, I am sure, when my story moves on to my time in the NHS, where the middle-managers to whom I referred earlier, exist in abundance.

Their numbers have multiplied exponentially over the years, which is even worse than it sounds. Why? Because having ensured lower unemployment, by creating more and more unnecessary jobs, the 'Powers-That-Be' then employ yet *more* people just to check that the *former* people they have employed are doing their jobs properly - and never-endingly so on.

This NHS 'checking culture' takes the form of such organisations as **Monitor,** and the **Care Quality Commission** (CQC). All the country's over-pressed doctors and nurses, meanwhile, stoically struggle on striving to do their, at times difficult jobs, as well as they can in an increasingly frustrating and trying environment.

There are also private sector bodies monitoring what companies do, such as Ofgem, which is for different reasons and indeed necessary, because private companies answer to their shareholders, making *their* driving forces those of money and profit. The customer is only important in the sense that the greater number there is of them, the more money the company makes for its shareholders and senior staff's bonuses.

I am no socialist, but utility companies should never have been privatised. It is quite wrong that people should be able to profit so outrageously from providing such essentials in life as power and water. It is even zanier that these companies and their shareholders can make such outlandish profits, only for the Government then to have to hand money out to the elderly and poor to help subsidise payment of the over-inflated winter fuel bills they receive from those profiteers.

To re-nationalise these companies now would be very expensive in terms of buying out their shareholders, and I fear that in the event of such steps being taken the Unions would highjack the process by ever-increasing wage demands. The same is true of the railways and the rest of our public transport system. This digression aside, meanwhile . . .

. . . what was happening during the rest of the fourth year back at Denstone College . . . ?

Much of the same, really.

It may be recalled that on Tuesday afternoons we did not have sport, but pursued various other activities.

In the past, this had been the time when everyone did something military, in the Combined Cadet Force (CCF), parading, clad in navy blue, khaki or light blue.

When my intake arrived at Coll in 1969 the CCF was no longer popular, because it meant always being shouted at and having to march about wearing itchy old-fashioned uniforms and boots with gaiters.

Our CCF's Army section was run by a Captain Hunt, who was not one of our masters, but lived in nearby Denstone village and I assume did it either because he liked dressing up, shouting, or for love. He certainly found a necessity to shout much of the time, but was a decent enough bloke, whose 'partner-in-crime' happened to be our French and athletics master, Henry Parker, who one day played a blinder on us all.

When we made our first-term choice between Navy, Air Force or Army, or the softer options of the Scouts, run by

'Ratty' Williams and adventure training organised by Ken Clark, another easy-going guy, which were, therefore both a laugh, we were told a few fibs. To clarify, I am not sure adventure training is the correct title that activity should have been given.

Those of us who elected to choose that option were to be able to do all sorts of stuff in our civilian clothes, and not those itchy old-fashioned uniforms. A lot of what we would get to do would be good and exciting, some of it less so, like visiting and helping old ladies; commendable, I concede, but not what the average 13-year old lad would want to do on a Tuesday afternoon! (Or any other time either, for that matter).

Mr *Parker* then told us that if we joined the Army, we would be issued new uniforms, consisting of modern army jumpers and green cotton non-itchy trousers, and would have all sorts of adventures; not just marching up and down and being shouted at.

Duly thus conned, my friends and I signed up.

At least we weren't off to the trenches, and in fact we had a great deal of fun on Tuesday afternoons, as well as at CCF camp in the summer holiday.

Writing of uniforms reminds me that I have not yet described our school uniform, which along with all our other possessions was transported by train in a big trunk at the start of each year.

During the week we wore long grey trousers, an easily washable nylon shirt, the school or house tie, and either a blazer or tweed jacket, of which there was a choice of unexciting colours!

The school tie was red and silver, while silver and green diagonal stripes adorned my Meynell House tie. Other houses had their own different colours, of course.

Our house rugby shirts sported the same colours, although the silver was white on them.

There was also a VIth Form tie; red with school crests on, *and* a school prefects' tie - green with the same crests. If one had been awarded school 'sports-colours', our parents could buy us a blazer in the appropriate colour; rugby, for example, was green. Or we could more economically simply have a 'school-colours' badge sewn onto our standard navy blue blazer, which is what I did.

If awarded 'school-colours' one was allowed the swank of wearing an open-neck shirt in the evening, with a cravat. This privilege became superseded when I was there by us becoming allowed to wear clothes of our choice out of school hours, in line with whatever the latest fashion was. I remember loon pants to be one! These were hipster trousers with very large bell bottoms that completely engulfed one's footwear, which might have been boots with very high platforms!

Possessing a 'school-colour' afforded a few other privileges as well, such as being able to use the rather more civilised pavilion changing-rooms, and walk where mere mortals could not tread; like in front of the cricket pavilion rather than around it! *Wow!* I mock - but to us young men at the time these privileges were perceived as bestowing considerable status and seemed important!

So - back to the CCF.

When the summer term ended we all headed off to Sennybridge, in Brecon, for the annual CCF camp; at least the Army part of it did. I don't seem to recall the Navy or RAF boys doing anything at all very much really, except going straight off home on their holidays.

We were billeted in old WWII Mizzen huts. I cannot remember a lot about what we did whilst there, except for two interludes:

. . . one very hot day we were sent off in groups of three with just an Ordnance Survey map and compass to navigate ourselves in a march from point A to point B across the Brecon Beacons.

Our Army rig of the day was 'belt order' (there will more about this later).

Talk about character-building!

Aged 15, (not quite yet in my case) we had never done anything as bold or as adventurous as this before. Fortunately my threesome had Henry Parker's son, Chris, in it, who was into orienteering, so he was good with a map and compass.

I remember it was very hot and there were lots of flies swarming about, and they invaded my water bottle, so I ditched its contents and became very thirsty by the end of the day, but we all survived the ordeal, reached our destination, and in due course arrived back at camp blistered and content.

The other event I remember was going to the cinema.

In those days even small places like Sennybridge had a cinema, and it was clearly not too bothered regarding certification laws. We managed a double-bill - *The Vampire Lovers* (about lesbian vampires) and *The Buttercup Chain* (involving hippies and a lot of sex). Both films were X-rated, but pretty tame by modern standards!

Where were our supervising masters at the time?

In the pub!

Then it was off home for the summer holiday.

We now lived in Netley Street, in Farnborough; the year was 1971.

As a school boarder, away from home, holidays always seemed a little strange. My school friends were spread all across the country, so a lot of time had to be spent entertaining myself. Kate, my sister, and I were not particularly close and had completely different interests, so didn't do much together.

I remember once when our parents were living in Germany some years later and Mum had occasion to describe me to someone as being 'a loner'. I became very angry, but declined to explain to her the reason. What other choice did I have *but* to be 'a loner', when all my friends were from school and I was spending my holiday miles away from them, in Germany? My parents also had a habit of taking holidays together during term time and not with us in the summer, so the break from school did not even involve us having a trip away.

The next year at school was GCE (General Certificate of Education) 'O'-level time. I had already taken elementary maths (advanced would follow) and Latin at the end of the IVth Form and passed the maths well enough, although having failed the Latin, I received extra tutorials from John Adamson (the retired teacher) during the winter term, and passed it then. I only took the subject because someone thought I should aspire to going up to Cambridge, and in those days Latin was an entry requirement.

During the course of that year, I became increasingly obsessive about work and revision - yet another demonstration of my OCD in action. I know I have only ever teetered on the edge of 'real' OCD, but feel deeply for those who suffer the whole shebang! It spoils one's enjoyment of life, and particularly in my experience - possessions. One of the manifestations at my level of OCD was that things I owned had to be perfect in every way; if they were not I would obsess over trying to make them 'right', which was not usually possible, so to me they seemed spoilt. Let me give some examples of this, with which I imagine quite a few of my readers will relate, because I know I am far from being alone in this way. I suppose many would recognise the condition as being a striving for perfection, which of course it is. I am no psychologist, but certainly believe it to be a type of OCD.

When I was 15 my parents bought me a cassette recorder for my birthday; all the rage in 1971 . . .

. . . that summer we went on holiday to the River Shannon, in Ireland, where we hired a four-berth motor boat. On our ferry ride across the Irish Sea I put sixpence into a one-arm-bandit, and - amazingly - out spewed £5's worth of pre-decimalisation cupronickel sixpences. My win excitedly allowed me to buy some pre-recorded cassettes for my new pride and joy; one of the cassettes being by *John Mayall*, and the other - *Deep Purple*.

Upon our arrival at the four-berth motor boat we humped all our stuff from the car to stash on board. When shortly afterwards I came to check my beloved cassette recorder it was to discover that some inexplicable damage had occurred to the battery charge and volume and recording meter. I then spent the rest of the machine's life trying to find ways to cover up this damage without it appearing that I'd done so, but the whole fruitless endeavour was a hiding to nothing and I was never able to covet the thing again. Sad!

A sudden afterthought:

Sister Kate; you didn't by any chance accidentally happen to drop my cassette recorder on the way to our boat that day, did you . . . and then forget to mention it to me?

When I was a medical student I owned a series of motorbikes - more of which later.

However, for now I can tell you that one of them was a Yamaha RD 400.

In my final three student-years I was a Royal Navy Medical Cadet, earning a salary that enabled me to afford such luxuries.

The Yamaha was my pride and joy, but I made a mark on the top of one of its side panels, which barely showed, but still I fussed and fussed over it for as long as I had the bike.

More recently, I owned a couple of Alfa Romeo cars, with low profile tyres and lovely sports wheels. The trouble with this combination, as many of you will know, is that the tyres' sidewalls are lower than many of the curbs they encounter, so any contact scratches the wheels. I became completely paranoid in trying to avoid having this happen, but inevitably eventually scratched my special wheels, and thence to some degree my enjoyment of each of the cars. How ridiculous is that? As a result, when I had a choice of wheel sizes for my present car I bought the smaller wheels, with taller tyres!

I am also fussy about parking, and will only park in a space which has plenty of room on each side - or preferably an end space, so that I can leave a big gap, because I do not trust others not to mindlessly bash my car when they open their doors.

Whilst on parking, I have another message.

There will often be found spaces in supermarket car parks which back onto each other - so why do people *reverse* into them? Their doing so results in their boot being bang up against the bonnet of the car in the space behind. When they return to their car to offload their laden trolley they then can't reach or open their boot without difficulty. This leaves them several options, any one of which is likely to scratch someone else's car. Whatever option they choose will necessitate wheeling their trolley between their own car and the one parked beside it. Being naturally disinclined to scrape their trolley along the side of their *own* car, there are no prizes for guessing . . .

If because of this lack of foresight their boot is completely inaccessible, they may then decide to load their shopping from the side, thereby even further increasing the almost inevitable likelihood of inflicting scratches to their innocent neighbour's vehicle . . . *or* they may still determinedly persevere, still opting to force access to their boot, and scratch the car behind that way. Better by far for everyone's peace of mind *not* to reverse into such spaces in the first place, and if not capable of going in forwards then have the kindness to park somewhere else instead!

Now back to my GCE 'O'-levels.

During the summer term my obsessive hours of revision reached their zenith.

Sports day then approached, and the House Captain of Athletics entered me for several of the events. Most of his choices I was alright with - but not the pentathlon. I was not half-bad as an all-round athlete, but I could not throw, so knew it would be hopeless for me to enter this event. The pentathlon was held before the actual main day and I had revision to do, so I simply did not turn up. The House Captain obviously found out about this and reported me to Philip Smith, who was not happy. I had let Meynell House down and thereby lost them team points.

I was given a choice of punishments, most of which involved not being able to do things I wanted to do, so I opted for a few strokes of the cane instead. Those of us who received early-warning of a forthcoming beating might have donned two pairs of pants, or packed blotting paper in them - or both. However, if discovered employing this crafty defensive ploy we would end up getting the traditional six with an additional six for luck, with the aforementioned defences having been removed! My punishment was administered there and then, so there was no time for taking any preventive measures. In fact, Masters' canes were whippy and swung round the side of the thigh, where a lot of the bruising occurred, so any defence was only partially effective.

I was only beaten twice whilst at school, though in truth it should have been thrice.

Our routine punishment was the writing-out of lines. This involved writing a passage copied from a book, with a dip pen using a bottle of black ink on that paper which has lines where the large and small letters should touch. It was a tedious task. Masters, and mostly prefects, gave out lines for such offences as talking after lights-out or in prep, walking off the designated paths and other pretty minor misdemeanours. They were usually dished out as 25 or 50 lines. There were 25 lines per page of the paper. If a boy received 400 lines in a term he was then beaten as an unwanted bonus and his total returned to zero.

I reached 400 on one occasion.

In these circumstances, we were collected from the common room during prep by the House Captain and taken to the Housemaster's sitting room for receipt of our punishment. In the event I sat in the common room awaiting my fate, but no one came for me. It was about a week before the end of term, so I waited in trepidation every night for 'the call', but still nothing happened. To reduce the anxiety it would have been much better to have had my 'six' on day one and been done with it. Still to this day I have no idea how I managed to get away on holiday with an unbruised backside; possibly because although I'd hit the magic 400, I had refrained from exceeding it. Or perhaps the House Captain was kind and did not tell Philip Smith I had reached the magic number!

The other occasion I was beaten was a bit of a joke really; the result of us all being in the dormitory pillow-fighting after lights-out. Philip Smith came in and warned us to stop - 'or else'. Needless to say we carried on, so he returned and warned us yet again; can't say fairer than that, but we were still not prepared to desist, so finally he marched us all down to his room for a communal beating. He went inside and we stood in the corridor outside waiting, arguing about who was prepared to go in first. The door opened and we pushed forward Richard Lamont so forcefully that he stumbled and nearly fell over. Philip Smith later told us that he nearly started laughing at this point. The rest of us followed in turn, with Jerry Riley going in last. Mr Smith always had us bend down in front of the fireplace, but on this occasion Jerry actually fell into it (it was not lit at the time), at which point the evening became even more farcical. I am sure we must have made more noise laughing about the whole absurd experience in our dorm afterwards than we had having the pillow-fight in the first place. Mr Smith had not hit any of us hard, and the whole episode took much less time than it would have done for us to write-out 50 lines, or even the 100 he might otherwise have given us. Good result all in all!

Our 'O'-levels came and went, and then it was time for us to go home for summer holidays.

Accompanied by Mum, Dad had now been posted to BAOR (British Army of the Rhine), in Germany.

Our family had also acquired a Dalmatian dog, called Chum.

'Cholmondeley' actually, pronounced 'Chumley'.

My parents had always been rather pretentious in their selection of names.

As mentioned before to wit: Crispin Francis Swinhoe.

Now aged 16, I spent many hours walking in the woods with Chum, and soon a 13-year-old German girl, called Gaby, started to accompany me. Nothing improper happened in the woods I hasten to add! Gaby spoke a little English, but I (typically) no German. We used to play the card game 'Top Trumps' together. In those early days, before its popularity increased I recall it only had a version relating to cars.

Without fanfare, my 'O'-level results then arrived in the post one day.

Is it possible for me to be enlightened as to why the annual arrival of pupils' GCSE and 'A'-level results have now become 'mega news' of such national importance?

Just kids taking their exams. Why?

Which, whatever anyone says, are far easier today than ours or those of previous generations *ever* were. In our day the whole result for each subject we took rested on how well we'd done in one or two three-hour papers, for which we had to know virtually everything we'd been taught about the subjects. We didn't receive continuous assessments along the way. They were a thing of the future.

My results were satisfactory enough to enable me to then go ahead and set myself up to follow on by taking three science 'A'-level subjects: biology, chemistry and physics, which would, as it turned out, have huge consequences for the rest of my life.

My parents were pleased with me, but there was no great fuss; it was expected. After all they were paying for my education and - quite rightly - expected my masters, the system and me to deliver the required results, not a string of excuses for failing to have done so.

The next year at school was lower sixth - called Divisions.

It was a strange year. There were no AS levels then, so there was no good reason to do any work, so I didn't - just enough to get by.

We had now moved out of the common room and into shared studies. Duncan and I were in Chapel Study with another boy called Paul Davenport; yes - near the Chapel.

Chapel Study had a reputation for housing the school's more unruly element; a reputation, which in many ways we strove to maintain.

Paul Davenport was a nice lad, but for some reason Duncan and I were not very kind to him, so he requested a move elsewhere - and Jerry Riley joined us.

We had different teachers now. Mr Nigel Green had left, and we had a female biology teacher, who was the wife of one of our new masters. Denstone had never seen anything like it before: a *woman?* Teaching? **Biology!**

We gave her rather a difficult time of it.

Duncan in particular considered that causing as much disruption as possible was fair sport.

We did a lot of dissection in biology lessons in those days, with rats and dogfish in particular. The fish came already preserved in formalin, but the rats we killed: fresh. It is hard now to believe this would have been an acceptable practice, even back then. The rats were bred in a room, where they were kept in cages and there was a rota for cleaning them out - not unnaturally, a job we hated. When the whole class was dissecting, our teachers killed one each for us with ether, but if we then wanted to do any additional dissection this would necessitate us killing our own!

I think Duncan's parents must have been out in the Middle East somewhere, so that year he came over to Germany with me for the Christmas term, half-term holiday. We had to get there by train and North Sea Ferry, but for some reason Mr Smith would not allow us to get away for the earlier train we wanted. This meant we missed the connection in London for the boat train to Harwich. We managed to get a train to Colchester and a taxi to the ferry. We, two unleashed 16-year-olds, then consumed a large amount of beer. We did not have a cabin to sleep in, so crashed-out in the bar. My parents were there to meet us upon our arrival in Germany, and it was two very pale and sickly boys, who had to endure the car journey home. There seemed to be a lot of bumpy cobbled streets, which didn't help our condition too much.

I did not want my time there in Germany with my mate to be curtailed in any way by a young girl, so when opportunity presented itself poor Gaby was unceremoniously and unkindly dumped. I regretted this deed when I was there alone on future holidays and would see her about the place growing into an extremely attractive and exciting looking young woman; served me right!

Our ferry episode was not Duncan's and my first alcoholic encounter. Sometime earlier, he had managed to bring a half-bottle of whiskey and a half-bottle of brandy back to school from holiday. We'd drunk these on the first night, as a result of which neither of us could walk down the dormitory to our beds and had to crawl. I don't know how we got away with it, but we did. I suppose I started drinking at about age 14, whenever we had a chance to escape to a pub from school. No one bothered checking one's age back then. My parents, who had never been big drinkers, would offer me the odd can or so at home as well. Later, when I became the House Captain, Philip Smith and I would share a chat about House matters and a few cans of an evening in his room. In fact, his favourite drink was gin and Punt E Mes. Heard of that? It is a type of vermouth I think.

There will be a bit more about my less than healthy relationship with alcohol coming up later.

So the rest of the year passed and we came to the summer term. Having done very little work at all that year I was a little shocked when the biology department decided to have an end of year exam. We duly sat it, and to my surprise I came top - saved by my knowledge of the habits of honey bees and ants, and much to the disgust of Paul Davenport, who knew how little work I had done, I was awarded that year's biology prize. What's more, we prize-winners also won a trip to Oxford to go to a famous book shop there to choose our own prizes. I still have my book up in the loft somewhere - *The Body* - a suitable biology prize, which has the Denstone crest imprinted on the front in gold. Again, I remember going to the pub as well as the book shop!

The summer holiday had duly come round again, and it was back to Germany once more for me.

During the first part of the holiday my sister had a friend staying with us, called Caroline. I can't remember whether they fell out, or something, but somehow or other I got to go off on walks with Caroline in the woods, where we talked and held hands; not much else, but this was a considerable advance for me on the girl-front. Caroline was a year older than me and going up to university! She wrote to me from York, when I was back at school, and invited me to go and stay there with her, but my embarrassment with girls kicked back in again and I couldn't bear the thought of telling Philip Smith I wanted a weekend away with her! In retrospect this was such a shame, because if I had gone perhaps I would have lost both my virginity and female phobia sooner, either of which might just be wishful thinking of course, but one never knows . . .!

For the final two weeks of that holiday we went by car to Yugoslavia for a fortnight by the sea, the first such holiday as a family we'd had since 1963. It was a long trip, the last part of which was along a cliff-side road where my sister, Kate, had a complete sense of humour failure and was convinced we were going to plunge to our deaths.

When we returned it was to find that Philip Smith had been trying to get in touch to tell me I was to be House Captain for my final year, and therefore automatically a school prefect as well. Other than the eight house captains, there were other school prefects nominated by the Headmaster, as well as a Head Boy and his Deputy. There were House prefects to support me, but they had no school-wide powers.

So I had to return to school early in order to be there for the new boys' induction tea party. I had gone full circle!

My final year revolved around my duties as House Captain and as a School Prefect, sport, and - of course - 'A'-levels and submitting a university application.

The other thing there seemed to be a lot of was alcohol.

The school prefects were called 'screws', as are prison officers in prisons, and on Saturday night after prep we had 'Screws' Booze' for which we were given a number of 'Party Sevens', although being almost 8-pint cans I don't know why they were called 'Sevens'. It was good training though, because I later found them to be very useful accompaniments for watching England rugby matches. One could drink their content, then stand on them to have a better view (terraces in those days) and even pee in them if desperate.

I always drank too much on those Saturday nights. I would go to bed, then awake later with the 'whirlies' and spew-up in the sink.

I was now sharing a bed-sit with Duncan, who had to put up with all of this. Undeterred, we would all head to *The Tavern* after attending Chapel on Sundays, for the 12pm to 2pm session, which is all the licensing laws allowed in those days, before the arrival of all-day drinking. The masters didn't seem to mind. A rule was brought in that we could only go pubbing if aged over eighteen, but it was a rule enforced by no one. I would not be that age until after leaving school - and, there, my bad relationship with alcohol had begun already!

Besides Caroline, I managed to enjoy very short relationships with two other girls around this time.

Abbots Bromley was a girls' boarding school ten miles away, attended by Kate before she'd gone up to university. In fact it was a more pretentiously named establishment than that, being known formally as The School of St. Mary and St. Anne, which just happened to be located at a place called Abbots Bromley, and it was with some of their girls that we were to have a sixth form 'social evening' (as they were called). I found myself chatting the whole time to a particular girl, sensing that I was doing quite well and that she rather liked me. How wrong I was! We also performed our school plays in concert with the Abbots Bromley school, so when along with others the same young lady came over to us to rehearse, I thought I would be 'in'. However, I was not in the play and the fickle creature was quickly taken up by and tabbed-off with one of the actors; the lad from my first year, the 'always contrary' guy, and better runner than me.

My relationship with him, still far from good, had now become even further soured by the behaviour of this frivolous bloody actress. That was all I needed, to boost my limited confidence with the fairer sex. Oh, we're not supposed to call them 'actresses' any more though, are we; now male, female or in between all 'luvvies' are actors!

Equality?

What *is* it all about?

Of course women should have the vote and equal pay for doing the same job as men. However, men and women are not the same, and therefore are not and cannot be equal in *every* thing. Men, for example, use one side of their brain more than women; that concerning logic and fact and matters of that nature, while women employ the opposite, the more conceptual side, which is good at understanding more esoteric stuff. It is pretty obvious that we are not the same in other ways as well!

However, the idea that women should have the same rights as men, which I support, has been expanded into this idea that we are all equal and all the same, which is obviously rubbish. With no prompting to do so at all my wife Julie recently supported my view. There had been a piece on the news about 32-year-old Susie Wolff, the Williams Formula One test driver, who said: *'My progression into Formula One came to represent so much more than a racing driver simply trying to reach the pinnacle of the sport. It was also the hope that finally there may again be a female on the starting grid.*

'I rode the wave, was energised by all the support and fought hard. There were those who wanted it to happen. Those who didn't.

'I can only tell you, I gave it my all. Do I think F1 is ready for a competitive female racing driver that can perform at the highest level? Yes. Do I think it is achievable as a woman? Most definitely. Do I think it will happen soon? Sadly no.

'We have two issues: not enough young girls starting in karting at a young age and no clear role model. Sometimes you just have to see it to believe it.

'My gut feeling tells me it is time to move on.'

My wife's response was.

"Well, perhaps women are just not as good at racing fast cars as men".

She'd got the point . . .

. . . which doesn't necessarily mean that women are being discriminated against, somewhat the implication of the news item.

If one considers any situation where one group of people seems to dominate, the same thing applies. There *may* be discrimination, but equally there may be many other decent and perfectly sensible reasons, but the news always seems to report it as being the former - probably because bad news gets more viewers and sells more papers!

On the subject of equal pay and returning to sport, there was for a long time a fuss that lady tennis champions at Wimbledon won less money than the men. The women, however, only play best of three sets, not five, so it is *not* the same job, *ergo* they should not receive equal pay.

Back to my short-lived relationships:

The second encounter took place in a Norwich cinema.

Duncan and I were on half-term holiday in Norfolk, where his parents lived, who were away at the time.

We met up with Jerry Riley in Norwich to go to see *Love Story*, would you believe. In the cinema Jerry decided to 'move in' on a couple of local 'scrubbers' sitting near us. Duncan wisely kept out of it, but 'in like Flynn' the heroic Swinhoe took the opportunity to edge up, grope and snog one of them. It was pretty apparent that they would have been fully prepared to have gone further there and then in the cinema (or anywhere else for that matter), but common sense prevailed and we parted company at the end of the film.

This adventure led to me experiencing the second hypochondriacal episode in my life, in convincing myself that I must have caught some awful disease from this mucky girl; syphilis probably. I'd not engaged in anything likely to have allowed the transmission of that horrendous bacteria, but rumours abounded that it could be caught bouncing off toilet seats, let alone playing tonsil-hockey and swapping spit with someone. The fear of copping such an inexplicable dose remained with me for years, becoming even more ingrained by my going to medical school where I had easy access to books telling me all about the signs and symptoms of the horrid thing in graphic detail.

Syphilis is the old-fashioned HIV, which can produce any sign or symptom one wants to imagine, so I conjured up more and more reasons why I was certain I had it. This made me quite unhappy at times, until eventually I was able to sort myself out.

The previous phobia I had was related to the fact that I smoked at school in the sixth form.

Again, that was Jerry's fault!

The bed in my bed-sit was set up on a sort of shelf in the wall, with a ladder to climb up to it in an area that could not be viewed from below. We reckoned that Philip Smith was much too fat to climb the ladder and *he* smoked like a chimney so would not smell the incriminating evidence in any case. So I let Jerry use my space up there in which to smoke; soon, inevitably, joining him. It was not really Jerry's fault; I had smoked before, earlier on at Denstone. *But . . .*

. . . as a consequence I developed the idea that I had lung cancer! My hypochondriasis at this stage in life would seem to be related to guilt perhaps.

The first time I ever smoked I must have been aged about ten. In those days ten cigarettes could be bought outside shops from a cigarette machine for two shillings (10p), so there was no problem getting hold of them.

The remainder of my final year at school went well enough, I suppose. I applied to medical school, and after what felt like a very poor performance at interview - attended the day after the snogging episode in Norwich, so perhaps I was a tad preoccupied with the encroaching syphilis - was pleased to be offered a place at St. Mary's Hospital, Paddington, thereby following in my father's footsteps. I had to travel on my own to this important moment in my life, by bus, train and tube from Duncan's parents' house. There were no supportive parents in sight, whereas today there almost certainly would be, but I was used to that. The offer was three 'C's.

Fortunately, in those days it was not considered that only those with three 'A'-grades at 'A'-level would make good doctors. Some boys in my year at medical school even had offers of three 'E's. They also obviously had some particular other compensatory talent; an ability at rugby perhaps, a very important part of London medical school life. I do not see anything wrong with this, because often people very good at one thing turn out to be multi-talented. For example, the Formula-One driver, Jenson Button, is also a very good triathlete; James Toseland, the World Superbike Champion is a concert-standard pianist, and what about the Isle of Man TT motorcycle rider, Guy Martin, who also works as a motor mechanic and TV presenter, and is also a very strong cyclist.

In fact, in some ways it was a shame, because later I discovered that I didn't really want to be a doctor after all!

A colleague of mine with whom I worked in my final five years in the NHS, Rachael Snyder, was an anaesthetic assistant. She was allowed to administer an anaesthetic under the supervision of a consultant anaesthetist, and was very good at it, indeed much better than a lot of the trainee anaesthetists who are qualified doctors. She also had a first class honours degree in astrophysics, grade-eight piano and violin, did all her own DIY at home *and* baked great cakes.

By comparison, consider the uni-dimensional young doctors we have these days, but of course they *do* have three 'A'-grades at 'A'-level; great! It is a limited view that selection of doctors now relies so heavily on such results.

They are, in fact, selected on other criteria as well, but these are known by the applicants to be a requirement beforehand, so they make sure they have completed the necessary task and have it included in their CV, which actually makes these criteria non-selective.

One of these pre-selection requirements is the ability to indicate the possession of 'caring awareness and skill', which is generally interpreted as having worked in a care home. Doctors do not become good practitioners because they are interested or not in that kind of caring. Doctors are interested in the application of science to the human condition, and caring as a result of treating and curing disease. This may well still not be their most important motivator; doing their job well and to a high standard is the key. Helping others is a bi-product of this, often not the primary goal.

I was shy and did not like communicating, particularly when I started out in medicine, which is probably why I preferred dealing with patients I'd put to sleep! I was a good anaesthetist because I was a perfectionist and couldn't abide things going wrong, so my patients did very well. Perhaps blowing my own trumpet, but any anaesthetist in Barnsley, where I worked for 19 years, would confirm this fact, even those who didn't like me. My communication skills were to improve over time of course, and I was often complimented on the way I spoke to relatives of patients in intensive care where I also worked. I did care, but success was my primary motivator.

Whilst at school that final year I also applied for Cambridge and did the Oxbridge examination, but I could barely understand the questions, let alone answer them. I could have gone back to school after my 'A'-levels and tried again, but I wanted to move on.

I was relieved in the final year when the school cross-country championship races were cancelled, because of a foot and mouth disease outbreak. As school captain of the sport I did not want it to be obvious that I was not the best runner. I have since learned that captains do not necessarily have to be the best. I had been a good one, and supported 'Ratty' Williams, and I received my cross-country and athletics school colours that year, which was an honour.

At my final school sports day I did alright, but didn't win anything, and my interest in athletics was on the wane. There was an event called the *parlauf*, which must be a Scandinavian name, which involves a team of two running, in a continuous relay. One runs 200-metres, hands over to the other, and then crosses the middle of the track to take over again. This lasted for ten laps, I think. Another boy in Meynell, who was a good runner (yes you've guessed who) and I would have won it, but he refused to run, and - interestingly - was not beaten for this misdemeanour! I did it with Paul Davenport, and despite running my socks off – as a result of which Henry Parker told me, he had never seen anybody try so hard – even then we did not win.

So we all took our 'A'-levels, had a final celebration at the village pub, and then it was off home for the summer holiday.

Thus was marked the end of this era of my life.

5

Student Life

THAT SUMMER HOLIDAY MY PARENTS WERE BACK from Germany, but had no house, so we stayed in my Great Uncle Albert's London flat in Knightsbridge, just behind Harrods.

Uncle Albert was my favourite relative.

He was a self-made man, who when he retired owned a chain of men's clothing stores.

He now lived in Sussex with Auntie Betty, but owned the flat in London as well.

What Uncle Albert did with his life is what I would like to have done; been my own man with my own business, but it was not to be. At this time, I was too conformist to not go down the planned academic route.

I wonder how many of us this happens to?

I have met those in life who make up their mind exactly what they want to do and follow that dream successfully, remaining constantly focused on achieving their final goal. I was focussed and driven, but only ever on the next goal. This leads one to a much more haphazard life, which goes down many routes.

In my case I had decided that the cleverest thing to do with science 'A'-levels was to go to medical school. Note that the goal was to go to medical school, not to be a doctor. That is how it was. During the course of that summer I began to hope I had not achieved the necessary grades for St. Mary's, Paddington, so I could do something else without having to front up to my parents. I was not a rebel then, and tended to do what I believed was expected of me, not necessarily what *I* wanted to do - so if any reader recognises himself or herself in that, please take note. Follow your dream and not anyone else's.

I can also recommend not being driven.

Material success and money alone certainly don't lead to happiness. I believe that nothing 'external' will make you happy; true happiness can only be generated from within. Of course our gleaming new car makes us smile, for a while, but shortly afterwards our happiness will default back to our usual level, a topic I will re-visit later.

So there we were, living in a flat next to the world's greatest department store - Harrods - so surely the obvious thing for me to do was find a job there, which I did, working in the Fruit and Vegetable Department, earning the princely sum of £12 a week after deductions. By the end of the holiday, when the regular member of staff was away I was allowed to set up my own show of soft fruit. I enjoyed the work and interacting with different sorts of people; the customers and my colleagues. The staff were mostly cockneys, who were a laugh to work with. The customers? *All* sorts, including actors and 'actresses', from whom, for helping them with their bags I used to receive fairly good tips.

It was at about this time that I had another short-lived romance, with a girl called Louise.

We got along well at work and I took her out a couple of times, but then soon found myself dumped. She told me she had a boyfriend who was abroad, but was shortly due to return, so there was to be no progress for me on that front, just another blow to my limited confidence on the girl-front.

My first year at St. Mary's was devoid of female activity, but in fact that was no bad thing because it allowed me to have plenty of fun with the lads! Medical students at that time were still predominantly male, and in the first two years there was no day-to-day contact with nurses, so romantic opportunities were limited.

I received my 'A'-level results from Philip Smith on a pay-phone in the basement of Harrods and, quite rightly, in those days the national news didn't give a s**t whether I had passed or not. I had done enough though; an 'A', 'B' and a 'C'.

Another blow to any aspirations I had to break my 'duck' as a successful Casanova was that I did not get a place in one of the London Universities' (of which St. Mary's was part) Halls of Residence, where I would have met students doing courses other than medicine and there would have been a much greater female presence. These Halls had their own social life, but I had been found digs in a house in north London.

The landlady was not a cheerful soul and grew to dislike me and my late returns home, usually the worse for wear.

I shared a room with Rob Deery, another first-year at Mary's. Our landlady's idea of the model student was the young man in the other small single room, who never went out, was not a rowdy medical student and to me, seemed thoroughly boring.

Rob and I got along well.

He was a quiet lad, but with a dry sense of humour.

He was Welsh, but played football - not rugby, and happened to be a very good goalkeeper, who had been previously watched by scouts from professional teams.

There was a register in most of the sessions and lectures, so it was difficult not to attend, and we had quite a lot of homework, but neither stopped us having plenty of time for fun. I despair when I hear modern day students complaining they are over-worked and far too busy; surely not!

In those days one's first two years at medical school involved science work, consisting of lectures on anatomy, biochemistry and physiology, there being no patient contact at all. Additionally, we had a body to be dissected between eight of us, generously donated to medical science by its lately vacated owner. If only he'd known!

Theoretically we spent 13 hours a week performing this grisly task under instruction, but in reality wasted most of the time chatting and messing around until the end of the week, when we then frantically tried to catch up by cutting and slicing most of the muscles, arteries, veins and nerves, along with anything and everything else we were supposed to discover.

Our busy social life revolved around the bar in the medical school, discos there and elsewhere, and drinking sessions at other establishments.

Dave Large and Martin Stark, from school, were studying at Chelsea College in the King's Road and I spent many a weekend there. Dave had a room in the College where often four of us would sleep at weekends; Dave in the bed, two of us on the floor and another on the desk. Increasingly my fun seemed to revolve around drinking, which became a cure for my shyness in large groups.

Towards the end of the spring term, all the London hospitals competed in the inter-hospitals rugby cup. This was a long established contest, quite a big deal, and the reason why good rugby players received good offers at 'A'-level. There were a lot of Welsh players at Mary's. It was said, because trains to London from South Wales arrived at Paddington, where the hospital is located; it was therefore easy for them to find! With his long sideburns and socks round his ankles the Golden Era's aggressive rugby-union fullback JPR Williams (and all his brothers) trained at Mary's. (Professionally JPR was to become an orthopaedic surgeon).

That year's inter-hospital rugby cup was the last straw as far as my landlady was concerned. Mary's had reached the final and Rob and I supported and drank avidly. Mary's lost, Rob vomited repeatedly on the way home, and I argued with the landlady the next day, who accused me (maybe she had a point) of making too much noise when we'd returned.

She threw me out!

I know I wasn't *nearly* as bad as she claimed, and she did seem rather naïve about the ways of students. So I spent the summer term living with my parents (now living in Farnborough again) and commuted daily. This allowed more time for revision, enabling me to pass the end-of-year exams fairly easily. This was not to be the case the following year. Those who failed had to retake in September, and a failure then meant the end of one's medical aspirations, as a result of being 'thrown out'! A friend of mine who was forced to leave the following year went on to become a professor of genetics; so much for 'the system'!

I wanted a motorbike.

I had passed my driving test a while back, but had no bike licence.

I had become interested in owning a motorbike in my last year at school, following the scooter episode at prep school. I am not entirely sure why my interest was reignited. The whole motor-cycling ethos excited me and it was something I wanted to experience.

In my first year at Mary's I became friends with Roger Parke whose home in Guildford was not far from Farnborough, and - like me - he was living at home. Roger took me pillion on his 350cc Yamaha one day and nearly scared me to death, but I was hooked. My parents weren't keen on the idea, but that didn't stop me, only there now arose the matter of finding enough money to finance the purchase of my first bike Any savings from my job in Harrods the previous year having long-since been squandered on boozy weekends and other such stuff.

So I found a job in a laundry for the summer.

It was not that well paid and the work was boring and hot, but beggars couldn't be choosers.

A major part of the laundry's work was fading jeans for two premier retail outlets of the day: *Jean Machine* and *Jean Junction*. Dark blue jeans at the shops in those days cost £10, but the *faded* item £11. I cannot imagine why anyone should want to spend an extra £1 just to have their jeans boiled in bleach before buying them, which must have impaired their longevity, but they did. We all did. Now people pay to have holes put in them too, and their knees and thighs slashed and shredded as though they've been attacked by a razor-wielding lunatic. Madness! So I suppose, merely bleaching them was nothing in comparison.

My first job in the laundry was pressing the jeans after washing. I worked long hours and did extra night shifts. The head laundryman was away for a while during the summer and I was promoted to his job of filling the washing machines. I had a bit of a disaster once when I mixed some coloured clothes and white sheets by mistake, producing rainbow coloured sheets!

My hard-earned money was mounting up, but I did have one major setback when having been paid for the longest set of hours I had worked I lost my pay-packet, which must have fallen out of my pocket whilst cycling home!

Finally, I managed to accumulate enough money to go out and buy myself a motorbike.

For some reason a new one.

A Yamaha RS 125, from Ken Heanes in Fleet, near where we lived.

It cost £300.

I went to the shop to pick it up, having never ridden a motorbike in my life before, and rode it home - that kind of thing was possible back then - and soon taught myself to ride it properly and proficiently enough to take it to London with me for my second year there.

Dave Large had found a flat in Acton that Martin and I shared with him, along with Rob Deery and another guy, from Chelsea College, called Andy McGrandle. Rob and I shared a room again, as did Martin and Andy, while Dave had his own - a privilege we felt he deserved for having found the place and done all the hard work. Dave was also the only one with a regular girlfriend, so needed his privacy!

The flat was not smart, but then it cost us only £8 a week each. That left me about another £10 a week to spend from my university grant. It may not sound much today, but it should be borne in mind that one could get five pints of beer, a packet of crisps and change for the jukebox in a pub in those days - all for a quid (£1). Conscious of the cost, we refrained from using the electric heaters in the flat, heating it instead with paraffin heaters, which my parents had given us. It was still freezing and would have failed the most rudimentary health and safety inspection these days, but it was home and we had a lot of fun there. We held one party at the flat in the spring.

Deciding to keep it cheap, we produced home-brewed beer.

Because the flat was so cold the beer did not ferment well, but we served it anyway, resulting in one of our guests vomiting on the outside stairs up to the flat's front door (that was his excuse anyway; not the quantity!). We were quite chuffed later that this solidified pile of memorial up-chuck was still there when we moved out!

Rob decided that he wanted a motorbike too, and went down the more sensible route of acquiring a second-hand machine.

A 250cc Suzuki Hustler.

One could ride anything up to 250cc on 'L'- plates in those days. Rob's new pride and joy was reputed to do a ton, but probably only downhill with the wind behind and its rider's chin on the tank. Fast enough for a learner anyway!

Me? Already I was hankering after a bigger machine.

I will not mention academic work too much at this juncture, simply because I was doing only the minimum to get by.

Pharmacology had now been added as a subject to our curriculum. We also had statistics to study, and other minor subjects I no longer recall, upon all of which we were tested at the end of the year under the heading of 'Paper 4'.

'Paper 4' was to be my undoing!

Early, in the spring term I had my final abortive romance, with a girl called Kathy.

Kathy came to a disco at Mary's with a friend from the first year. I liked her and visited her in Welwyn Garden City, where she lived, but as usual in my case, nothing blossomed.

On our way home from that disco Rob crashed his bike, probably, (almost certainly, I'd wager), whilst over the legal limit. I am not sure what my own status would have been on that score either! He bent the front forks and could not afford to repair them, so his biking days had been short-lived. Mine, however, were on the up.

I passed my test, which was rudimentary in those days to say the least. Roger had decided to sell his 350cc Yamaha and I was desperate to buy it. I had been working in Harrods again over Christmas and had earned a bit of extra money for myself. I was on my own in the flat at that time, which was freezing. I would ride from Harrods home to Acton and keep nearly all my bike kit on in the flat, because I could not get warm! Impetuous, as I still am today, despite not yet having sold my current machine, I went ahead and bought Roger's bike, giving him £300 for it, which in retrospect I considered a bit of a rip-off, because there was a dent in the tank, and not long afterwards both exhausts fell off and I had to buy new ones. When I did eventually sell my 125cc I did not receive as much as I thought I would for it, so with all that expense I found myself completely broke for the rest of the year!

For the summer exams I did the minimum amount of work, expecting to scrape through, but I miscalculated, and although my overall average was above the required 50%, I failed two papers - pharmacology and Paper 4. This meant my having to re-sit them both in September. I protested, but was told I was lucky not to be having to take all of them again. Thus the whole of that historic hottest-ever summer of 1976 found me revising. In truth, I am not sure that I did really work that hard, because at some point during the process, I rebelled. As touched on earlier, I had come to realise that I didn't really want to be a doctor after all, so I told my parents I was going to quit.

They persuaded me to at least complete medical school and then think about it.

So here I sit writing this now, recently retired aged fifty-nine, having spent the past thirty-six years thinking about it, whilst working as a doctor. So yet again I say to one and all - follow your heart!

That summer I moved into a new flat in Queen's Drive, Finsbury Park.

My new flat-mates were Duncan from school, and – are you ready for this . . .? *my girlfriend, Jackie;* more of whom in a later chapter.

I successfully managed to pass my September re-sits - obviously - otherwise I wouldn't have spent the following thirty-six years a doctor, and then . . .

. . . our next three years were spent in clinical studies, which I disliked.

We had to meet and talk to patients, take medical histories, and examine them. I was still shy with strangers, and also found the doctors and nurses on the wards intimidating.

I did not mind ward rounds, when there would be a whole group of doctors and students together, but I rarely ventured onto the wards on my own. I can truthfully say that I only took a 'full history' and did a 'thorough examination' on fewer than a handful of patients before my final exams. I missed a lot of days doing more interesting things, and on some attachments I would miss weeks at a time - notably paediatrics; if adults scared me, children with their parents in tow were even worse.

I did enjoy obstetrics – which sounds odd in view of my frequently referred-to inadequacies with women – however childbirth involves the student carrying out a lot of practical stuff, which I liked. During the 'labours' that we attended, the midwife was there as well, so she could do all the communicating, and if she left the room one could always strike up a conversation with the soon-to-be new dad.

We were required to deliver eight babies each, as a minimum.

The midwives made sure that we would only be allowed to do the delivery if we sat in the room the whole time during the labour. In those days labour was allowed to continue a lot longer before any intervention, so sometimes I would sit for eighteen hours, only to have the poor woman eventually undergo a Caesarean section, which would mean me being unable to record a delivery for my time spent in attendance.

The midwives were a contrary breed, not averse to telephoning the night duty-student to turn out to sew up the episiotomy that had been cut at the mouth of the mother's vagina to assist delivery of the baby's head. This, despite not having informed them earlier of the mother's labour, so that the student could attend the delivery.

120

I remember us being given one, and only one, demonstration of how to suture an episiotomy.

That same night I was the duty-student and was called by the midwife to perform the deed. I remember sitting between the poor mother's legs trying to remember which piece I should suture to which, while sweating profusely under the light. Occasionally the young mum would ask how it was going, and I would lie that all was well. Eventually I completed the task and returned to my bed.

The following morning we had a ward round with Mr Fraser, the consultant.

To my horror we headed towards the very same lady, after whose well-being he enquired. "A bit sore," she said, pointing at me. "That young man there, stitched-me-up last night."

I am sure I went puce and the sweating returned.

"Let's have a look for you, shall we?" Mr Fraser suggested, and sister assisted with exposing the part in question.

I was in complete panic by now, thinking that before I was even on it I was about to be struck-off the medical register for gross negligence.

"A very neat job, Swinhoe," Mr Fraser intoned as we moved on to the next bed.

Medical-school life continued.

There were various cliques amongst the students and I was actually one of the few people to have friends in a number of them, and this became increasingly to be the case as time went on. There was the rugby lot in particular many of whom now lived in the medical school's own accommodation, Wilson House, just around the corner from the hospital. One of them was Neil Butterfield, who like me later joined the Royal Navy. Neil now lives in Spain, but we continue to remain in touch.

By now, I had taken up rowing, so had several friends in the rowing club, who spanned a number of academic years.

Then there were my motor-biking friends, Roger Parke and Martin Schwarz, and a friend of Roger's called Richard, who spent a lot of time with us. Neil Butterfield also had a motorbike.

Martin Schwarz had been kicked out of Mary's by now, but still lived in London. He was the one later to become the professor of genetics!

Dave Large and Martin Stark were still in London, and I lived with Duncan, so my social life was busy. On occasion Roger, Neil and I would simply bunk off and take a ride down to Brighton together. I think we fancied ourselves as modern day Rockers. *Quadrophenia* was a recently released film that would later achieve the cult status it did.

There were no exams for us to stumble over at the end of the third year, so no need for us to do any work at all.

I stayed on in the same flat with Duncan, and we acquired a new flatmate, Kim Wagstaffe, who we found by using the Capital Radio flat-share line.

Kim was a humorous guy with a lovely French girlfriend called Nicole, who we all loved to bits, but then much to our disgust he dumped her. Kim came from Chesterfield, and apart from anything else was frequently rude about his home in the north and also his mum's cooking!

By this point Jackie and I had split up. Martin Stark later came to live with us, and I slept in the sitting room to make room for him, often with my then new girlfriend.

Kim got himself a job in our local, *The Queen's Arms*, which meant the provision of a few free beers for us. Duncan and I had a particularly drunken night at *The Queen's* one time when we'd gone out for a few beers at about 9.30 pm, thinking the pub would be shutting at 11.00pm, when in fact in celebration of the Queen's Silver Jubilee it didn't close until 12-midnight. We neither knew that it was the Jubilee, nor that there was an extension of hours! By closing time we were both in a pretty poor condition and as a result, for no good reason decided to climb the railings into Finsbury Park. The things I have done 'in the name of fun and alcohol'.

In celebration of St George's Day on 23rd April, another of our favourite hostelries, Paddington's *The Fountain's Abbey* decided that a pint could be bought for a shilling. At that time the old shillings were still in circulation, effectively five-pence coins and of the same size and shape. A new five-pence coin was not part of the deal, so a lot of us went along to the bank and bought five-pounds worth of coins and extracted the shillings. Just one bag held more than enough for the purchase of far too much beer. One of the resulting japes was that at the end of the night I removed the St. George's Cross from above the door, which I still possessed until relatively recently.

The nearest curry-house to St. Mary's was called the Dilshad. We frequented it often, and took great delight in running out at the end of the meal, and not paying the bill. It was a silly game and completely pointless since everyone knew exactly who we were, and when we arrived at the door of the medical school the next day, the porter on duty would duly present us with our bill and ensure that we paid it.

Other culinary delights were fish-and-chips for lunch from the nearby chip shop. My favourite was fried battered cod's roe and chips, all for thirty-seven pence. Recently I found some of the same at the Sheffield Meadowhall shopping centre's food emporium, and indulged myself . . . but this time it cost £3.79.

When we'd all first moved into Acton we had a rota and someone cooked every night, but this had long since been discontinued and we subsisted off peanut butter sandwiches, egg sandwiches and other such delicacies. However, we did throw the occasional dinner party, including one to which Duncan and I invited our parents. God only knows what we served them! Lots of booze I expect.

Third year moved into fourth year and life carried on pretty much the same.

My parents had now moved back to Germany and I made two trips over there on my current motorbike, on one occasion with a girlfriend, Christine, later to be my wife, on the back. It was a long, cold journey, when it snowed and we got lost.

At the end of the year there was a pathology exam, which I passed without trouble having swotted intensely for about six weeks before.

I enjoyed rowing very much, and this became my main sport for most of my time at Mary's. I also ran and did 'weight' and 'circuit' training to keep fit. So much weight-training in fact that I became sufficiently muscular for someone to ask if I would play prop for the 3rd XV rugby team. I declined the offer of prop, but rekindled my love of rugby by playing either flanker or centre. With my increased weight and stature, I tackled happily now and became closer friends with many in the rugby club.

There was one particular game held between our year and the doctors. I had a grudge against a urologist who had belittled me on a ward round. Wherever we were in our training us students were allocated patients that we were supposed to see. At the time in question my group was doing urology; men's bits and pieces in other words. We did a ward round with Mr C, the urology senior registrar, and were standing beside the bed of one of the patients.

"Whose patient is this?" asked Mr C.

I owned up, although of course, as usual, I had never actually got around to seeing 'my patient'.

"Well, what did you find when you examined his genitalia?"

"They were normal", I said.

Mr C looked round, stared at me askance, and to everyone's hilarity, cried; "Well, you obviously haven't got a set of balls either then".

So I was able to get my own back on him out there on the rugby field, glad to be back in the game. Having done all that weight-training and rowing I was by then very fit and absolutely loved tackling overweight urologists!

For the final term of my final year, I decided to move into Wilson House, believing that I would be able to work harder there. We all of us developed the habit of revising till 9.45pm and then rushing off to the pub just for a few beers - which was never enough. Fortunately, at 11.00pm two options remained. A lock-in, courtesy of the landlord Sean, with whom we were very friendly, or returning to our accommodation to break open the Wilson House bar, a ritual in which we were well-versed.

Because I had seen very few patients as a student, I relied for my revision upon book illustrations of the various conditions. My father had given me quite a few of his old texts, which were excellent, because in his 1950s era the conditions had been much more florid, and the illustrations more graphic.

Finals consisted of multiple-choice and written papers, oral examinations (with lots of questions from clever doctors) and clinical history taking and examination of patients, from which one had to find the correct diagnosis.

My final examination was my psychiatric clinical, at the end of which the patient enquired of the avuncular examiner; "Is he (meaning me) a doctor?" The examiner replied no, but affirmed that I would be fairly soon!

My life as a medical student was now drawing to its close.

My friend Neil Butterfield suggested to me recently that this period of someone's life is a very formative time.

I did not find it to be particularly so.

I have pondered this and think that is because for me there was no real change. I had left home at 11-years-old and since then had become accustomed to looking after and doing things for myself. I was used to being separated from my parents, so that issue was nothing new to me. Indeed, when I started at medical school Mum and Dad were still living in Knightsbridge, so geographically they were closer to me than they had been for seven years.

A London medical school at the time was a rather parochial institution, so I had simply moved from one such establishment (Denstone College) to another; the only real difference being that there were women around. That was a significant change, discussed elsewhere. Another difference was that I could live independently, which again was no big deal to me.

I believe that the most important formative period for me was between the ages of 12 and 18, although I feel my path would have been more straightforward had it been between 18 and 23, when I was at medical school. I also believe that university would have had much more impact on me, if I had attended a 'proper university', not a London medical school, and preferably pursuing a subject other than medicine.

Both our personality and outlook are massively influenced by our early years, and for a considerable period mine were those of a middle-class boy who went to public school and joined the Forces. As will be seen later, eventually I was able to break away from that persona, but it took me a long time and much heartache to achieve.

Now back to St. Mary's.

The night before our exam results came out a lot of beer was consumed, a practice at which, as usual, I excelled.

We drank in the pub, we drank in Wilson House bar, and we drank on the balcony of Rob Deery's room.

The police appeared several times to shut us up.

We swam in the Serpentine and played football in Hyde Park at dawn.

We then drank some more somewhere else.

The results were announced in the medical school at 11am.

We had been up all night.

In a noticeably dishevelled state, we walked through the streets of Paddington, with me still wearing just my swimming trunks.

I had passed.

I was one very drunken doctor, who had to return later in the day to re-check and confirm the results on the notice board, just in case I had misheard.

Unable to focus properly I had to squint to read the notice!

Everything was A-OK, above-board and kosher.

I could now put MB.BS after my name.

6

Alcohol

I HAVE DRUNK A LOT OF ALCOHOL IN MY LIFE.

I have read loads of books about how to give it up, and books written by people who *have* given it up.

I am a doctor, a doctor who has seen the ravages alcohol can cause, so I do know a bit about it and here would like to discuss the subject a little.

I have not had a particularly healthy relationship in life with the substance. I have never been a down and out alcoholic, and have never drunk alcohol either immediately before, or at work; nor have I ever been convicted of drink-driving, but I do confess to having had a problem with the stuff.

Let me discuss the term alcoholic.

The classic picture the word conjures up is what I have called a 'down and out' alcoholic - the unfortunate person who drinks and as his or her tolerance increases, drinks more and more. They drink to the point of coma, and when they awake - drink some more. The process destroys their *lives* and their *livers* and often they die of liver failure and bleeding from engorged blood vessels at the bottom of their oesophagus.

I am sure there is genetic variation, in terms of how tolerant or not different people are to this level of drinking, but generally speaking a person does not reach this desperate condition just by drinking six pints a night or a bottle of wine a day. It is not healthy to drink even that much however, and those who do, certainly *do* have an alcohol problem. Fortunately, though, these people have an off-switch, and can often muddle along without things becoming completely out of control. I became one of those people.

Many of those who reach this stage in their drinking habit have been shy and unconfident children, who have found the benefit of alcohol and the relaxation and numbing of inhibition it provides to be of benefit when confronted by otherwise daunting social situations.

My drinking started when I was at school and continued into university. I then joined the Royal Navy, where the 'work hard, play hard' ethos was prevalent. However, significant periods arose where work prevented my taking alcohol, which was also true in medicine. In my day, junior doctors were on call every other, or every third night and weekend, and at best, towards the end of my training, every fourth. Even when I was a young consultant, the on-calls were quite frequent, but in any case it is not good, sensible or appropriate to drink heavily the night before going to work.

That is not to say that I, and other doctors, did not indulge on occasion; we did, and indeed in the past it was not considered a crime. It is ironic that as society has made alcohol more and more available, it has made its use, in some circumstances, more and more frowned upon. When I started in medicine it was acceptable, when on call, to go to the Mess and have a couple of pints before going to bed. In the Royal Navy I saw senior hospital doctors have a few pints at lunch time before going on to an out-patient clinic in the afternoon. One may also be interested to know that despite a rule that they should not drink for eight hours before flying, many a Royal Navy pilot has flown off an aircraft carrier with their blood alcohol level well over the legal driving limit from the night before! They used to say that breathing 100% oxygen from their mask was a great cure for a hang-over!

As my on-call commitment decreased, that brake disappeared and I found myself drinking more and more regularly. I believe that over the years I have also managed to keep a cap on my drinking, not only because of my work, but also because I am a fitness fanatic and did not want this pursuit to be jeopardised. I would also use my training session as a punishment if I had drunk too much the night before.

In 2008 I stopped drinking, because I knew it had been out of hand at times in the past and seemed to be getting so again.

I had stopped on previous occasions for several months at a time; the first back in 1990. However, this time I was much more determined and stopped for over two years.

Foolishly, I then started again, as a celebration for having completed an Ironman triathlon in Nice, France, in 2010.

I have stopped on numerous occasions since, for periods of up to eight months.

Now, I no longer drink alcohol anymore.

The problem with someone like me, is that as soon as I start again, thinking it will not escalate, it always does, and to a level slightly worse than before. It is interesting that one's tolerance does not seem to wane during the interim periods of abstinence. When I restarted in 2010 it took the same amount of alcohol to have the same effect as it had before.

I have done things that I subsequently regret whilst under the influence; mostly saying things I shouldn't have said, and arguing and upsetting people, including my friends and the wives of those friends. I have even injured myself because of alcohol, and done other stupid stuff as well. Sometimes, possibly often, the stupidity seemed funny the next day, particularly when I was younger, and everyone around me was being foolish too, but all too often there would be remorse afterwards.

Alcohol is a drug, like heroin, cocaine or marijuana. The only difference is that it is legal. Having been such a culprit myself I do not, *per se*, object to people drinking alcohol as long as they accept they are using a drug. It is interesting that the term 'recreational drug' has been coined to describe all the illegal drugs, but has not been applied to alcohol – the most widely used recreational drug of them all; and the term fits it so well, even better than to the other substances to which it refers. Smoking is now vilified in our society. I am of course pleased that I no longer have to passively smoke in pubs and restaurants, and no longer need to wash my clothes because of the stink of smoke. However, leaving that issue aside and others such as smoking in cars with children, the people who smoke are essentially only doing themselves harm.

I consider smoking to be a ridiculous addiction.

Once a person is addicted to nicotine, smoking a cigarette simply takes away the craving, and thereby the individual perceives pleasure. There is no extra feeling, just the removal of craving. If they did not smoke at all they would feel equally as good. The use of alcohol makes some sense, since unlike smoking it has perceivable effects. It changes one's mood, and perception, and we believe that it enhances our enjoyment and the party spirit, albeit as one becomes more and more addicted larger and larger quantities of the stuff are needed to create the same effect.

However, the cost to society of drinking exceeds that of smoking many times over, and yet it is encouraged, and the supposed good aspects of alcohol (in fact there are none) are promoted. Cigarette advertising was banned many years ago, and yet alcohol is touted everywhere as something that improves enjoyment of whatever one is doing. Increasingly, on television, scenes in the home include a glass of wine. Even in dramas set in the sixties and seventies couples are shown enjoying a bottle of wine with their meal. Drinking wine at home was an unusual practice in those days; there is no reason to include such activity in these scenes.

When we take our first sip of alcohol we do not enjoy it, and yet we persist in drinking it until we teach ourselves that it tastes nice. It is the drug in the drink that makes us do that, plus the indoctrination that alcohol is something special; that it is 'grown-up' to drink it. Traditionally, in the past, young people have mixed alcohol with sweet things to mask the bad taste; lager and lime being a classic example. This is no longer required because the manufacturers do it for them by producing sweet-tasting 'alcopops'. The manufacturers then sign up for 'Drinkaware' the alcohol advisory service, as if this offsets the criticism of them selling an addictive poison; a poison that once you drink one glass makes you feel like having another; having three makes it more likely that you will have four - and so on. The suppliers of these drugs are limited companies, who answer to their shareholders, so they want as much to be drunk as possible to boost their profits. What an absolute nonsense. I am not on a crusade against alcohol, although it may sound like it, but I hate double standards, lies and hypocrisy.

Recently, there has been this idea of setting minimum prices for alcohol in supermarkets. As far as I could work out the supermarkets would have simply made more money and it would have made no difference, except perhaps moving people back into the pubs if the price-differences were less. If it is considered effective why not raise the tax on alcohol and use the revenue to do something good and useful? No government will do that, because politicians' main consideration in policy-making is whether it will increase their chances of re-election. Such a policy clearly would not.

Another problem is that in countries like Norway, where tax on alcohol is very high, the population simply make their own, and in fact Norway has a high rate of alcoholic liver disease. Talking of politicians, how pathetic it is that on a number of occasions in the budget the Chancellor has cut the tax on a pint of beer by a penny. As if that makes a blind bit of difference to anyone, and only serves to reduce the money available to spend on something useful. How shallow can a human being become?

The main factors influencing how much alcohol is consumed in a country are culture - including attitudes to alcohol and drunkenness - affluence and availability.

Alcohol has become relatively, significantly cheaper as wealth has improved over the years. As a student my consumption was often influenced by limited funds.

The Government, quite a few years ago, made an astonishing decision. Their premise was that the French drink in a more civilised fashion than us, because they can do so at any time of day. They did not recognise that the real reason for the French people's drinking habits is that the French have a more sensible and mature attitude to alcohol. Although, they have a high incidence of alcoholic liver disease they do not have the same problem we do, with public drunkenness.

So the Government made the insane decision to make alcohol readily available twenty-four hours a day. Surprise, surprise - alcohol related problems, including crime and public drunkenness are now worse than ever. In the 1970s, the pubs were open for limited hours, supermarkets did not sell alcohol, off-licenses shut before the pubs, and alcohol was much more expensive compared with income, so we drank less.

Although this is not a self-help book, might I suggest the following . . .

If you are someone who repeatedly drinks to the point of coma, then wakes up and starts again, then I suspect you will probably not be reading this, but if you are, I suggest you really should seek medical advice and stop drinking.

If you are someone who drinks a significant amount every day (a-bottle-of-wine-a-day-type) then the best plan would be to stop drinking, because it is bad for your mental and physical well-being. However, only give up if you really want to, not because anyone else says you should (like I am!), because otherwise you will fail. The reason could be because you want to improve your family life, but not if you don't want to and you are doing it only because your family is telling you to. Of course, if your family are telling you to, then really you should want to, don't you think?

Giving up is not necessarily easy, but is *simply* a matter of will power; there are three phases to be aware of. For the first few days you will crave a drink as a result of the addiction. You may get some mild physical symptoms like nausea, sweats and a general feeling of unease. Keep yourself occupied and find new things to enjoy.

This stage will fade. It will be more severe in the first few days and will take up to two weeks to get through.

You now move into a period where you will have urges to drink because of triggers. For example, if you are used to going to the pub on Sunday lunchtime, that will be a big trigger. You must deal with these triggers as they occur. Always keep in mind in these situations that when the next morning arrives, if you have had a drink, you will be very fed up. If the next morning arrives and you have not had a drink you will be very pleased with yourself and have no hang-over. Which of the two is better?

I have my own mnemonic to help me remember and be aware of the triggers. It is *THEMES* (T.H.E.M.E.S). There are others.

- Thirst (T) may be confused as a need for alcohol, as may -
- Hunger (H) drink water, or eat
- Emotions (E) such as anxiety or anger may be a problem
- Manipulation (M) by others: "Oh go on, have just one drink, it won't do you any harm"
- Exhaustion (E) is a strong trigger because tiredness reduces willpower. Finally -
- Situation (S); there will be events where you would normally drink and some may already be planned. In the early days it may be best not to go.

It should be announced to everyone that an 'alcohol withdrawal programme' is underway, so that they know where they stand with the issue. Some erstwhile drinking buddies may not be at all happy, so perhaps it would be a good time to reappraise upon what their friendship was based - alcohol . . . or mutual respect.

In this phase, you might find yourself looking ahead to events like Christmas and wondering how you are going to manage. Those days should not be thought about yet. Stay in the moment, and deal with the future when it comes.

Finally, the third phase is where you have not had a drink for quite a few months and might say to yourself "I am fine now; I could just have a few drinks tonight, then stop again tomorrow." It's not fine, and you will not stop again tomorrow. You will, in fact, think to yourself: "I have ruined my record, so what is the point? I might as well carry on drinking." And thus the whole vicious circle will start all over again. Think how angry you will be in the morning after you have let yourself down by such a relapse?

There are whole books written on this subject, but the foregoing is the essence of it.

You may be someone who has a lot to drink a few, or perhaps several nights a week; something like most Friday and Saturday nights and, not infrequently, a couple of evenings in the week as well. If you are, then carry on if you want, but be aware that you may be heading for a problem. I was there once!

If you have one gin-and-tonic a night and have done so all your life, like my mum, then you should feel free to carry on, but I personally am not sure why you bother. Why take a drug in a quantity that will have no noticeable effect, but then I suppose some people believe in homeopathy as well.

That's it, enough said, don't let me spoil the party. Having enjoyed the stuff myself for so long and only just having realised the effects it was having on me relatively recently, who am I to spout?

Today is Tuesday 22nd December 2015.

I have returned to this chapter because of something I heard on the news this morning. It was reported that a study had shown that admissions to accident and emergency departments with alcohol poisoning had doubled in the last few years, and that a certain age-group of women were at particular *risk*.

Risk?

This demonstrates the 'kid gloves' approach used by our 'nanny state' whenever the devastating effects of alcohol on society are reported.

Did someone force the alcohol down those women's throats?

A better word to have used might have been *'culprits'!*

It is now after Christmas.

The Chief Medical Officer, Professor Dame Sally Davies, has just decided to pitch in with the 'intelligence' that any alcohol increases the risk of disease. What a surprise! It is a mind-bending alien substance to the body. However, instead of stating that ideally it should not be drunk at all, Dame Sally set some new limits that no one, who wants to feel the effects will follow, unless they demolish all 14 units on one night of each week, which she has told them not to do anyway.

No wonder everyone is confused.

Anyone is perfectly entitled to drink the stuff if they want, but should recognise that by so doing they may hasten their demise.

Mine, I am quite sure, must have already been hastened considerably!

7

Her Majesty's Royal Navy

IT WAS SUMMER 1979 AND I HAD QUALIFIED AS A doctor.

Mission accomplished.

The time had now come for me to be one.

Realising as a student that I was not particularly keen on the idea, I had decided that if I joined the Forces as a medical officer I could do lots of other stuff as well, and not just medicine.

As you know, my father was in the Royal Army Medical Corps (RAMC) and I did not want to follow in his footsteps yet again. I have never understood why anyone would want to join the RAF other than to be a pilot, so that was out. *Hence . .*

. . . . . as a student I'd become a Royal Naval Medical Cadet; the express aim of which was to undertake the Commando Course and serve with the Royal Marines - another target set!

However, before any of that, to complete my medical training I had to work two periods of six months in a hospital, as what was then called a 'House Officer'; colloquially known as 'house jobs'. Back then, one worked as one of the junior doctors during this year, clocked-up a lot of hours and learnt by experience, rather than receiving specific training. The equivalent today is very different, and more of an extension of medical school.

We worked 1:2 rotas; meaning we were on duty for over one-hundred hours a week. Admittedly, we did not work all the time, and could rest at night in bed if we were not busy. In the NHS the doctors were paid one-third of their hourly rate for hours in excess of forty. I do not mean one and a third! In the Royal Navy we received a relatively good salary, but as would be expected, no money for the extra hours. Forces' personnel are contracted 24/7, and although they take leave, it is a privilege, so there can be no such thing as overtime.

As I write this, the country's junior doctors have voted to go out on strike over their hours and conditions and, as you might expect, I have little sympathy with them.

These days, although the work is more intense, they are in the hospital for a maximum of 48 hours a week, are paid, relatively, considerably more and have much more dedicated time for teaching and training. Leaving any other issues aside, professionals should not strike under any circumstances. The fact is, that if they do, the work will fall to their seniors, who have already done their bit and endured long hours and difficult enough working conditions in the past.

I did both my 'house jobs' in the Royal Naval Hospitals in Plymouth and Gosport. I was very keen and arrived for the first six months as a surgical house officer in Plymouth two days before I was due to start. I slept in the Wardroom, which is the Royal Navy's term for the Officers' Mess.

At breakfast that first morning they were pleased to have me there a day early, because the previous house officer had already left. "You can start today," I was told.

Because I was now a full-time professional Royal Navy officer I couldn't say, "Actually, I was rather thinking of taking myself off for a look around Plymouth first."

It was a Tuesday, when each week, the Naval Hospital took in all the emergency surgical patients from the surrounding area, so it was going to be busy.

I was hard at work for most of that first 24 hours, and only got to meet my fellow house officers at breakfast the next morning. I was obviously supervised, but still had to do a lot of things on my own. The great thing for me was that by the following day a lot of my anxieties about my new life and work had melted away.

No bed for me now; it did not work like that. I would carry on doing my duties until six that evening.

And this was to be the lot of me and my colleagues for the next 12 months.

There were two general-surgery house officers, two orthopaedic and two medical; six of us in all.

We worked hard and played hard. Wardroom life was good. We all of us lived-in so there were always people around with whom to share a laugh. The Wardroom bar was always busy, and even when one was on-call and perhaps heading back to the Wardroom late in the evening, there would always be company. As already mentioned, in those days it was perfectly alright to have a couple of beers when working, before going to bed and hoping not to be called out, although one almost invariably was!

The night-life in Plymouth was good, and at that time Union Street - for years the place where sailors went for their wine, women and song - was still in full swing. Its bars were rough, as were the majority of its 'ladies', including those who charged for their services, but it was a lively place to be.

My boss for the first three months was a consultant general surgeon and urologist, Surgeon-Commander Wilkes, who had a reputation for giving his junior doctors a hard time, if they did anything wrong. In general, I got along fine with him. If I was ever in doubt I made sure I asked the long-established nursing staff what they thought he would want me to do. This was how things were done in the NHS as well in those days; a ward-sister knowing everything a newly qualified doctor needed to know, and teaching him the ropes as he went.

It is sad that this has not been the case for a very long time now, because the established sister, married to her ward, is a thing of the past. Even in the 1970s it was still quite usual for sisters to be spinsters, and if they married they left their jobs. So it was not uncommon for a senior ward-sister to have been on the ward for thirty years or more. The sister at Mary's who introduced my mother and father to each other was still there when I was a medical student. She still lived in the nurses' home.

I learnt early on in my medical career that having humility, knowing one's limitations and asking someone else for advice was the key to success. Some doctors are better than others, just like some mechanics, or plumbers are better than others. A less good doctor is not generally a problem if he understands his limitations. A poor doctor, who is arrogant and lacks insight with regard to his level of ability, is a potential disaster. All the bad doctors I have met, amongst other things, lacked insight.

Because we were so busy time passed quickly, and before we knew it Christmas had arrived. I was touched when Surgeon Commander Wilkes bought me a present, even though I had now moved on to orthopaedics.

Officer ranks in the Royal Navy start at Sub-Lieutenant, followed by Lieutenant, Lieutenant-Commander, Commander and Captain. After that one escalates to the heady realm of Commodores, Admirals, and Admiral-Of-The-Fleet, above which comes God.

A lieutenant-commander is equivalent to an army major, if you are more familiar with the latter. As a Royal Navy doctor the rank is preceded by the title 'surgeon', with a red stripe being worn between the gold ones on the uniform sleeve to denote this. Not yet an admiral, or even aspiring to be one, at this stage I was Surgeon-Lieutenant Swinhoe.

At Christmas I rushed to and from my fiancée's parents' house in Didcot between on-calls.

Yes - I had become engaged to Christine, a physiotherapist who I had met at Mary's. I mentioned her earlier - but more about that later.

In my final year at medical school I had lashed out and bought myself a four year old Hillman Imp motor car. I loved it, and spent a lot of time fitting extras such as a radio cassette player, spotlights, a small racy steering wheel, and of a more practical nature, an oil-pressure gauge, because the oil light kept coming on when the engine was idling.

I remember on one of my Didcot dashes I was happily jigging along to some music doing about 65mph (it couldn't maintain much faster!) on the motorway, pulling on the steering wheel as I did so, when suddenly it detached itself from the column and came off in my hands! I couldn't have tightened the bolt properly. Luckily I was quickly able to push it back on again before my life came to a sudden and tragic end.

Let me recount one medical story from my six months in Plymouth.

It was a Friday afternoon and I was on-call for the weekend, so would be working through until Monday evening. The registrar and I had completed a ward round with Surgeon-Commander Wilkes, during which it had been decided that one of the patients needed feeding via an intravenous line. For this he would require what is called a long line from the elbow; the end of which would then be positioned in a big vein in his chest. This was necessary because intravenous feed damages the small veins in the hand or arm. My registrar, who as well as being a bit lazy, also wanted to get away for his weekend off, told me to 'sort it out'. He was the same guy who had done my medical when I applied to join the Navy as a student, and he hadn't been very friendly or understanding then either.

"But I've never put one in before", I remonstrated.

Actually, I had not even seen one being put in, or come to that even seen one in its packet.

"The instructions are in the packet", I was told, and with that he left.

So - I went to the ward, found the patient and the required kit, as well as a helpful nurse, and sited the line. I tell this story because everything then happened so differently to how it would today. No doctor would ever be asked to do this without having performed several such procedures under supervision first, and if this had not happened he would be perfectly entitled to refuse to comply.

It may be something of a surprise to you to hear that I was prepared to do this. I was careful, I read the instructions, and I would have called for help if necessary. A lot of medicine is about common sense, and rather like lack of insight, a doctor who lacks common sense is far worse than a doctor with plenty of it taking on a procedure he has not done before. We all know that if we drive somewhere we learn the route quite quickly, but as a passenger it takes a lot longer. Learning a practical procedure in medicine is the same, and today there is too much over-supervision of trainees, to the point that the learning process is very slow. After all, isn't a good way to learn how to swim to be thrown in at the deep end!

There's a happy medium of course, but today the pendulum has swung too far.

Another issue today is that because doctors' hours have reduced so much, trainees are just not exposed to the volume of work needed to achieve enough experience in the time available. These days an operation may well be carried out by a consultant, who has done less than a quarter of the number of those operations that he or she would have done 30 years ago.

My last couple of months spent in Plymouth were very enjoyable and more relaxed.

My first orthopaedic boss was a nice guy, but was sent to sea in the New Year. My new consultant was a Surgeon-

Commander Bob Clark. He was very laid back and I enjoyed working for him.

My time in Plymouth ended as it had begun. The day before I was due to report to the Royal Naval Hospital, Haslar, in Gosport, I was told to leave early because they were short-staffed and needed me there to be on-call! So I headed off on my Suzuki GT 750 'kettle' motorbike as they were and still are known. I had bought this as a qualifying present for myself some eight months previously. My fiancée, Christine, was using the Hillman Imp. She had moved from London down to Plymouth a few months before and would follow me to Portsmouth shortly, to continue her physiotherapy career there.

I was very busy my first night in Haslar, but once I got over the initial butterflies it was good, as it had been in Plymouth, to be ahead of the game when the other house officers arrived. I was now doing medicine, working for a gastroenterologist called Surgeon-Commander Richard Hunt. He was something of a workaholic and again had a bit of a reputation for severity. However, I enjoyed working for him.

Throughout my life I have found that working for people with a reputation for having a temper has never been a problem for me, and I have rarely been the butt of their anger. I suspect this is because I have always worked hard and diligently, and I suspect these people's reputations have come from when they have had lazy chuffs working for them.

I enjoyed medicine more than surgery, and gave serious thought to becoming a hospital physician, even studying for the first part of the MRCP - the exam of the Royal College of Physicians, although I never took it. I now no longer found communicating with patients to be a major problem. Interestingly, out of work I was still shy with people I didn't know, especially in large groups, and I am sure I continued to use alcohol to counter this. At work the environment was structured, and one knew what was required, so I don't think it is unusual for shy people to find their work-environment easier to handle.

Looking back on my medical career reminds me of how much medicine has changed in the last 35 years.

Patients' expectations were not so high and thereby demanding in those earlier years; not yet whipped up by society and government telling everyone how important they are and how their care should be administered and conducted. At the same time, the environment in which clinical staff work has become so much more demanding also, not in terms of hours, but in many other ways. The camaraderie and laughs that we enjoyed together as junior doctors - an important part of making the job easier - has now disappeared.

Some may find jocularity difficult to understand in a medical environment, where patients are being cared for, but in stressful situations, being able to have a joke and a laugh with your mates is important, and the more relaxed atmosphere, thus created, helps medical staff do their job better. There is none, or very little of that jollity around today, when everyone is expected to be so serious. The lives of staff are also very different; more pressured, and instead of letting off a bit of steam in the doctors' Mess, which doesn't exist anymore anyway, everyone seems to go straight off home after work, There is much truth in the old films like *Doctor in the House* as far as the work place then is concerned, but obviously things are exaggerated in the films. Or perhaps *The House of God* by Samuel Shem is a better comparison, although the title is more suggestive of the way doctors behave today!

Patient care was different too. It was then very much the case that doctors did what they could for patients within the ward environment. I can remember putting 70-year-olds with heart failure to bed, giving them digoxin (a very old, but effective cardiac drug) and a diuretic and either they got better or they didn't. Now such patients' care would be escalated to high-dependency or intensive care, when in my day such resources were not so readily available. This further pressurises the modern medical environment.

We're all going to die of something.

I accept, that today it is reasonable to consider dying in the mid-70s a bit premature, but we are treating patients aggressively well into their late 80s and beyond. It seems to me that we save patients' lives from one illness, so they can die

153

a long and uncomfortable death from another, or become demented and spend their final days, which may be many, in a care home. I would much rather die a bit younger than end up living well beyond my 'sell by date' and suffering physically and probably mentally as well.

However, I have seen many a family wanting everything possible to be done to keep their 90-year-old grandma alive in an intensive care unit, which is hardly a pleasant place to be when you're 50, let alone at 90.

When they follow the family's wishes in these circumstances doctors are failing in their duty-of-care to the patient. In many cases it would be far better for the patient if they were made comfortable and then allowed to die.

A young person will leave a stay on an intensive care unit with many years of rehabilitation ahead of them before being restored to the physical and mental state they were in before their admission. An elderly person will never be the same again and will suffer for the remainder of their life.

Intensive care was invented during the 1950s polio epidemic to keep young people with respiratory impairment alive until their condition improved. Their long-term outlook was good if they survived the disease. Now intensive care is full of patients with chronic end-stage disease from which the kindest and more correct course of action would be to allow them to die.

Whilst doing my job at Haslar I felt unwell one morning.

In those days a doctor did not go off sick, because amongst other things they would drop their colleagues in it, who would have to do their work and on-calls for them, which might mean them working 24/7. So of course I went to work.

When I reached the ward, Sister gave me a funny look, and enquired: "What's that on your face." I looked in the mirror and saw that I had developed a red rash.

Rubella; then, called German measles. I had contracted it from a sailor who had been isolated from his shipmates in a cubicle on the ward.

Sister made me go to staff health and I was put off sick.

I felt guilty about this, because I didn't really even feel *that* unwell.

Nowadays even if a junior doctor has just a snuffly nose, they'll call in sick. They no longer have the same work ethic, and are also aware that their colleagues will not be made to bear the extra burden or on-calls for them, chores that will fall on the consultants' plates, who also had to do them as juniors! All in the name of progress, and the European Working Time Directive. A directive, which is ignored by the rest of Europe!

It was about this time that I changed my Hillman Imp for something a little classier.

A six-year-old Alfa Romeo GTV 2000cc.

I loved it to bits.

It had the famous Alfa straight-four double overhead cam engine and did 0-60mph in 8.9 seconds.

That was quick back then.

It was not red I am sorry to say, but did have a beautiful wooden steering wheel.

For the second three months at Haslar I worked for the cardiology consultant Surgeon-Captain Hazell. He was a real gentleman, and the registrar I worked with was a great laugh too. Looking back that was a very content spell in my medical career.

At this time there was a hotel, whose bar became an extension of the Wardroom; the Old Lodge Hotel in Alverstoke. It was very close to the hospital and I am sure it is still there. Unfortunately, the hospital isn't. Malcolm the owner was very liberal with closing time and Sylvia his wife produced great food in the restaurant.

If you had frequented it at that time, you would have found my friend Steve Beck sitting at the corner of the bar on many an evening. He too was a Navy doctor, who later, was to emigrate to South Africa after which we lost touch. He was in Andorra skiing with our group of friends, when, as you will read later, I was recalled to go to the South Atlantic.

Christine and I also went on a summer holiday with him to the Greek island of Ios. Andy (his first name was actually Jonathon) and Helen Anderson also came on that trip. We spent our time drinking at night and recovering on the beach during the day; not a very sophisticated holiday. It was rather like the sort of holiday 20 something year olds go on today! I am sure, (although somewhat doubting the likelihood), that Andy managed on the outward journey, to 'check-in' his hold luggage with his passport in the suitcase; obviously not possible in 2016. He successfully blagged his way through passport control with his Royal Navy identity card; fat chance today! Andy was a medical assistant in the Navy and Helen a Naval Nurse. Andy was a very funny Scottish guy and good friend, who left the Navy and joined the police force. Helen was a really lovely person, who I wish I could include in my WAGS chapter (to come later), but she was already going out with Andy, when I met her and I was engaged to Christine. So no go there! I last saw them in St Austell in 1989, at which time Andy gave me great tips for spotting unmarked police cars, which I use to this day.

Also in the bar at the Old Lodge, you would have met Ian Geraghty and Di Megginson, who were later married; they weren't even going out at this stage. Di was my favourite QARNNS (Queen Alexandra Royal Naval Nursing Service) sister in RNH Haslar. We were good friends. Di gave me a 'right telling off' in a letter she wrote to me when I left my second wife Jo in 1995. Quite right really, although I did not think so at the time; as a result we lost touch with each other.

Ian is a bit posh and is an MBE. The latter was awarded for being the doctor on a ship, which went to the aid of the local population, when a hurricane hit the Caribbean in the late 1970s. He later became the medical officer on the *Royal Yacht, Britannia*. He never invited me on her for a visit, but I cannot blame him in view of the rebellious nature I developed, particularly when at sea, which you will read about later. Such attitudes would not have gone down well on *The Yacht* and I don't think I would have gelled with his fellow officers!

Happy memories!

On 10th May 1980 I got married.

For the first time.

In all honesty, the day before the wedding, I couldn't help thinking it was a mistake, but it was all planned. It was a big church affair with a 'swords drawn' guard-of-honour formed by my Naval officer colleagues, followed by a large reception. I couldn't let everyone down could I? Especially my future father-in-law, with whom I had a great relationship and, of course Christine! It was foolish in retrospect, but more of that later.

The house year came to an end.

I remember with great relief handing in my pager to the switchboard, not ever considering the fact that I would have many more of them over the coming years, and would only finally see the back of them when I was aged 58.

One of the switchboard ladies was a particular friend to us all. She was a 40-plus widow who was always so nice and loved having a bit of suggestive dirty-talk with her young men whenever she had to wake us up with a call in the middle of the night. She was a good example of the kind of fun-people we had in and around medicine in those days. I do believe that in general society then was a better place to be, without the incessant pressure being brought to bear from all directions. There was a much calmer pace of life; one had time to "stand and stare" as the poem by *William Davies* goes.

8

Green Beret

AT THIS STAGE IN A NAVAL DOCTOR'S CAREER there were, and probably still are, four options: go to sea in a surface vessel; serve as a doctor on a shore base; volunteer to be a doctor in a Polaris (now Trident) nuclear submarine - or go to Lympstone and undergo the strenuous rigours of the Royal Marines' Commando Course; upon the successful completion of which one is able to serve with them and then with justifiable pride get to wear their coveted Green Beret.

Mine still hangs on a peg in my garage, to inspire me when I am doing a hard training session on my bicycle turbo-trainer. In case some of my readers do not know, a turbo-trainer is a static trainer to which a bicycle is attached, so that it can be ridden inside, whilst remaining stationary. It is somewhat like an exercise bike in a gym.

The Royal Marines are the Royal Navy's infantry, and historically they fired on enemy ships with their rifles when those wooden behemoths of sail were alongside each other during a battle. The Captain of Marines would have commanded landing parties made up of marines and sailors to carry out the King or Queen's business in 'foreign parts'.

The Marines went to sea, as part of the ship's company, in warships right through to the early 1980s. However, by then, their primary role was very much as land based Commandos.

During the Second World War the Commandos took volunteers from the Army and Royal Marines, as well as a few from the Navy, for their arduous training, but after the war the Royal Marines took over the role and became the Royal Marine Commandos. However, the roughie-toughie, bayonet-thrusting swashbucklers up front need to field their own equally rugged rear echelon support elements: their doctors, dentists, padres and 'schoolies' from the Royal Navy. As the name implies, a schoolie is a teacher. They also employ engineers, artillery and others skill-sets from the Army. Anyone who wishes to serve with the Royal Marines is required to pass the 'All Arms Commando Course', which encompasses the commando training section of Royal Marine training, successful completion of which entitles the extremely chuffed individual to wear the Green Beret.

In 1980, the Marines were short of doctors, so in early August that year several of us met up in Plymouth to engage in some fitness training before the course commenced.

With such long hours at work during the previous year, I had allowed my personal fitness to falter, having gone on only one or two runs in the whole year. I have never since been as unfit as I was that August.

The Commando Course is preceded by a three week *beat-up*, when a lot of more specific training is done to prepare the body for the onslaught to come. In the case of the Army, they used it to weed out a lot of the volunteers, since they always had more than they needed. We doctors joined a pre-course beat-up at Lympstone, the Royal Marine Training Centre. At this time, as new Navy doctors, we should have been at Dartmouth learning how to be proper Naval officers, but the need for Marine doctors meant us being able to forego that pleasure! We learned later, from those that did attend, that one subject of instruction was how to peel a grape correctly with a knife and fork!

Throughout my Naval career I never really got on with the pomp and ceremony of it all; nor with the snobbery of many of the officers. Had I gone to Dartmouth I expect there would have been some fireworks as a result of me rebelling about something or other. Avoiding Dartmouth delayed this by a few years, but it caught up with me later, when I served with the Navy at sea. I much preferred my time with the 'Bootnecks', as the Marines are known.

Our three week beat-up introduced us to various aspects of military life, including marching and weapon skills. The Army lads, who would join us on the course itself, would already have gained this knowledge from their basic Army training.

We did a lot of fitness training in those three weeks and broke-in our boots by running everywhere in them. We lived in the Officers' Mess and got to know each other. I became particularly friendly with Dave Griffiths, a Welsh doctor who reminded me of Rob Deery – quiet, with a dry sense of humour.

On a Friday afternoon we finally met up with the lads from the Army for the course induction. We did the traditional entry tests. We had to climb a thirty-foot rope with all our kit on, and then go for a mud-run in the river estuary. The kit for most of the Commando Training was 'belt order'. The belt had various pouches all the way round it into which had to be packed all the items needed to survive and fight in the field for a short time. Attached to the bottom, at the back, was a poncho which could be made into a rudimentary shelter. Additional to this load was our rifle. One of the artillery officers with us called Rod Jenkins, (I think I recall correctly), performed a classic scenario. He struggled to the top of the rope, from where we then had to yell out our name and number, at which point he'd run out of puff and power, let go, and came crashing back down to earth again. Fortunately, he was uninjured and turned out to be a real personality on the course and in the Mess.

There is a special technique to rope-climbing, which ensures that the legs are used rather than the weaker arms. Essentially, the rope is wound around one leg and trapped between the top of one foot and the bottom of the other. The legs are slid up the rope, the rope is re-gripped and the legs straightened again, thus propelling the climber upwards. I was lucky my PE teacher at Dulwich Prep was an ex-Royal Marine, Physical Training Instructor (PTI), so I had already mastered this technique as a child; a thirty-foot rope now presenting no problem to me at all.

The mud-run was performed in mud up to our thighs, in which everyone had to try to run, perform press-ups and other exercises and generally be screamed at, maligned and belittled. Then we had to go off and get all our kit clean again before a short weekend off and the start of the Commando Course proper, early on Monday morning.

There have been plenty of television programmes over the years about Commando training, so I won't belabour the detail. The rigorous demands put upon one build and build to the final test week. The penultimate week is the final exercise, which is designed to run the individual down to the point of exhaustion, so that they are tired when test week arrives. The tests consist of a nine-mile speed march, the Tarzan assault course - a high bit (the Tarzan part) and a low bit (the assault course part) being run as one. There then comes the six-mile endurance course in the woods and through lots of water and mud, and - finally - the real killer . . . the infamous, gut-busting 30-mile march with full kit across Dartmoor.

There is also a 12-mile march with a pack as well as 'belt order', but that is completed earlier in the course.

I found all the tests reasonably straight forward, except for the 30-miler which really did sort the men from the boys. Our group got lost in the fog, which meant we had to run a lot of it in order to finish within the prescribed seven-hour cut off time.

And at the end of all these concerted physical and mental ordeals we were formally presented with our Green Beret, which we'd already received beforehand in order to give us time to shrink and shape it into a suitably 'war-like', 'hard-man' style.

After the Commando Course we doctors caught up with the rest, who had been to Dartmouth, to do the New Entry Medical Officers' Course, designed to teach us about different aspects of medicine peculiar to the Navy, such as that required for diving and aviation incidents, as well as the medical administration side of things. It was all quite easy-going, and a fair amount of alcohol was consumed during those weeks. We all made a lot of new mates and acquaintances, who we would bump into every so often over the years that followed.

After that we all went off to join our respective ships, submarines and shore bases of various kinds.

I reported to Royal Marines, Poole, the home of a number of elements of the Royal Marines and Navy.

At the base were the Special Boat Squadron (SBS; the Navy's SAS) and the Landing Craft Company, who would put Marines ashore on the beach in a war. The Marines, who were to serve in a warship, received their pre-embarkation training at Poole. There was also the Transport Section (trained drivers) and 148 Battery, who were responsible for going ashore by various means in a war-setting and directing our RN guns onto enemy targets. They were a Royal Artillery unit, peculiar in that they had passed both the Parachute Regiment *and* Commando courses (real tough-nuts) thereby entitling them to wear both the cherry-red Para headgear and the RM's green berets.

I had my own medical centre to run, with about six staff: medics and nurses. The work was not onerous or busy and consisted mostly of dealing with the injuries and illnesses of fit young men - therefore I had time on my hands.

The Commanding Officer suggested that I should spend time with each of the elements of the base. As a result I went on a landing craft to the Channel Islands, where we had a few drinks and came back; I passed my HGV driving test, and I spent a lot of time playing rugby and going down town with the SBS guys. I also joined the local rugby club and played for their second team. I managed to wangle myself a place on a military parachute training course and passed-out following my eight jumps, which allowed me to wear parachute wings on my uniform, of which I was especially proud having been scared of heights ever since falling out of a tree at Dulwich Prep.

Let me tell you about two other events from my time at Poole.

A triathlon was organised for everyone to compete in - not swim, bike and run, but shoot, run and swim. I fluked the shooting and achieved a clean sheet and not being a bad runner or swimmer then went on to win the event, much to the disgust of a lot of very fit Marines! To add insult to their injury, my picture and a small piece about my victory then appeared in the *Globe and Laurel*, the Royal Marines' magazine.

The other episode, as they all too often did, involved alcohol. There was a function in the Officers' Mess for a load of dignitaries; I cannot remember why, but I was standing at the bar in my best uniform, its red stripes showing that I was a doctor, when someone behind me asked in an Australian accent:

"What do you do then? Can't be much work for you here?"

I was irritated by his implication, as I saw it, that I was either lazy, or superfluous, or both. I did not answer, but asked;

"What do *you* do?"

"I'm a diplomat", he said.

In fact he was the Australian High Commissioner or something equally important, while I was just a lowly lieutenant.

"Well," I retorted, "why don't you fuck off and be more diplomatic?"

Fortunately, both he and my Commanding Officer thought this was funny. I thought, and still do think, it was a pretty clever off-the-cuff remark - but it might very well have got me into a lot of trouble.

My year at Poole came to an end and it was time for pastures new.

Any doctor with the Royal Marines wants to serve with a Commando Unit, and I was going to 42 Commando, based at Bickleigh Barracks, near Plymouth, in Devon.

I arrived there just before Christmas.

It was the Marines' role to protect the northern flank of NATO, in case the Russians invaded through Finland. Therefore, every year they went off to train in the snow in Norway for three months, learning to ski and fight in this hostile environment. Their then incumbent medical officer, Ross Adley, stayed with me for that annual trip to Norway, which enabled me to carry out my Arctic Warfare Training.

We travelled there after Christmas, and the Headquarters element of the Unit was based in a camp near Narvik in the north, near the Arctic Circle. The different companies had bases elsewhere, each with a medical assistant, but the main medical support, which included me, was with the HQ. Usually two commando units travelled to Norway each year, but this time it was only one, so the medical officer from 45 Commando stayed with us to do his Arctic training - and he was my friend, Dave Griffiths. We all lived and slept in the Medical Centre (a 'sick bay' in Navy-speak) and Dave, Pete Hodgson (the dentist) and I shared a room.

The weather was strange that year; it did not get very cold, and a lot of time the temperature was around freezing or just above, which meant that skiing was difficult, and living in the field was wet and cold. It is much nicer for the temperature to be well below freezing so that the snow stays frozen and you as a result stay dry. We learnt to cross-country ski and survive in the snow during various periods of several days and nights spent out in the field. We had to live in improvised shelters and dig snow holes to sleep in. A doctor, a Naval cold weather expert sitting happily at home in his warm house in Britain, wanted us to do some research for him which involved peeing in bottles in the field and carrying it with us back to base. This made life a little more difficult. However, I enjoyed my Arctic Course, which was much more relaxed than the Commando Course had been. Once it finished I returned to my duties as the Unit Medical Officer, and took over from Ross Adley properly.

When the Navy or Marines are abroad they always hold an evening cocktail party for the local dignitaries, and others. This is, generally speaking, an excuse for a piss-up, not that an excuse for one was ever really needed.

HMS Invincible, the now scrapped aircraft carrier, was in Narvik as part of the overall deployment of British troops, so many of their officers were invited to the party. These included Prince Andrew, who was one of their helicopter pilots at the time. Prince Andrew had spent some time at Lympstone whilst training at Dartmouth, and had been looked after by an officer, Nick Matson, who was there with us in Norway, and was a friend of mine. He and I talked to the Prince and somehow during the conversation it was arranged that we should go skiing with him the following afternoon, which seemed like a fine idea at the time. By the end of the evening a lot of drink had been taken. My bed in the sick bay was about four-hundred metres away and uphill. It was also very icy, because of all the unfreezing and freezing of the snow there had been. In the early hours I left the Mess the worse for wear, still in my best uniform, and finding that I just could not stay upright resorted to crawling all the way back to my pad. I was probably lucky not to have died of hypothermia. I could just see the headline: **Drunken Naval doctor found dead in snow following . . ."**

And things were to go downhill from there.

The next day was Sunday and there was not a lot happening, so everyone gathered in the Mess for a few 'hairs of the dog'. I knew I was supposed to be going skiing, but Prince Andrew did not turn up at the allotted time; Royal prerogative I suppose, but it meant I assumed that our proposed skiing trip was off, so continued to enjoy the drinking session. To my horror, the Prince did then eventually appear and I felt obliged to join the skiing party, or, in my case, the falling over party. Prince Andrew was not impressed.

I was to meet Royalty close up on two other occasions whilst in the Forces, both when I was serving with the SAS in Hereford. The first time was when I sat next to the Duke of Kent at a lunch party. He must have thought a Navy doctor, amongst all these hard men very boring, because he didn't exchange a single word with me the whole time, despite my efforts at conversing with him. (Perhaps his nephew had already told him about me!)

The second time was when I was providing medical cover for Prince Charles, who was shooting on the ranges with the troops. There was again a lunch after the event, to which I was invited, but no one told me they had finished shooting, so I turned up late. I think Prince Charles made some comment about doctors and time keeping, which everyone thought was funny except me!

Back to Norway.

On another evening Dave Griffiths and I decided to go to the local hotel for a few drinks. Alcohol in Norway is expensive; even back then a bottle of whiskey would cost around £30! So to save some cash, I bought a bottle of gin from the Mess, retrieved a urinary catheter bag from the sick bay (a clean one!) and filled it with gin. I strapped the bag to my leg and threaded the tubing under my trousers and shirt to my wrist.

We were able to buy just tonic all night and by squeezing the bag squirt the spirit from my wrist into the glass. We were not very subtle about it and in the end were thrown out of the bar! Our rowdy behaviour could not possibly be the result of drinking tonic alone. However, I was proud that despite trying, the staff failed to find my secret stash of alcohol. Just as well perhaps, because taking alcohol off camp, which we were able to purchase duty free, was an offence. It was a bit of a walk back to base and Dave was a bit like I had been after the cocktail party, but at least he was not alone in the Arctic, with me for unsteady support!

The rest of the tour involved various exercises in the field; building up to the final week-long exercise, when all the companies practised military skills in the snow. 'M' company (more of them later) had to carry out a company attack downhill on skis, whilst carrying a lot of kit. I did not witness the event, but apparently it was like something out of a cartoon with marines straddling trees with one leg either side as they lost control. The Russians must have been quaking at the thought! In the field I was in charge of the medical care in the Regimental Aid Post. We had two tracked vehicles to get us about and were able to sleep in them with the engines running and the heater on; luxury! One of my medics was a great cook and could do wonders with military rations. We even had some 'medicinal' rum and brandy with us. The only hardship was having to leave the warmth for necessary personal hygiene and the making of yellow and brown snow.

It is perhaps indicative of the problems in my marriage to Christine that, having not seen each other for three months, on my return we went on a skiing holiday with several friends instead of spending time to ourselves. We were better together, when there were others around. So we headed to Andorra. Just before we left some 'scrap metal merchants' (as the news described them) landed on an island in the Antarctic; South Georgia. 42 Commando was to be what was known as the spearhead battalion after Easter, ready to move within forty-eight hours to a trouble spot. As we went on leave we joked that we would be off to the Antarctic! How right we were to be proved to be.

Our Andorra skiing holiday was going well, downhill skiing and relaxing after the rigours of cross-country in the Arctic. It was about day four that I was skiing down after a relaxing lunch and a mulled wine or two, and reached the ski-lift station.

"Anyone here know a Crispin Swinhoe", I heard someone say.

"I am that man", said I.

"You have to go back to England; the consulate has been in touch."

"Why's that?"

"No idea".

With that I headed back to the hotel to find out what the hell was going on. On arrival, before I rang the consulate someone told me the Argentinians had just invaded the Falkland Islands. It was April 1982. The consulate staff were totally unhelpful as far as my getting home was concerned, but the holiday representative found me a flight from Barcelona early the next morning. I booked a taxi to take me out of the mountains at about 5am. The others arrived down off the mountain and we embarked on a farewell drinking session. No fond farewells with Christine, or any romantic dinner for two. She stayed on skiing in Andorra as I went home with a hangover the next morning, and by the time she arrived home I had left for the Antarctic.

As far as going to war was concerned I was totally happy with the reasons. British Sovereign Territory had been invaded in an unprovoked attack, and we needed to get it back. However, successive governments had eroded our ability to fight a campaign away from Northern Europe.

We had no effective mobile air support. *HMS Ark Royal* the last fixed-wing aircraft carrier had been scrapped. Now, the *Invincible* class ships are seen as aircraft carriers, but they were not. Their role was anti-submarine warfare and they were designed to carry helicopters. Coincidentally, the Harrier Jump Jet had arrived at the same time as the carriers were being built, so a ramp had been added to the flight-deck so that two

Harriers could be carried, but they were intended for the ship and its escorts' defence only. Fortunately, for the Falklands War, this allowed extra Harriers to be put on *HMS Invincible,* and *HMS Hermes* had not yet been scrapped and could carry these aircraft as well. However, if the Argentinians had pursued the war differently we would have lost I am sure.

When I went to the first Gulf War in 1991, I felt very differently. Although I wanted to be there to experience another campaign, the war was not about Kuwait's sovereignty, but oil, greed and power.

The second Gulf War should never have happened, as it was driven by the egos of Blair and Bush. This has left the void we now see in the Middle East, which has allowed the rise of Islamic State. It is ironic that Blair was prepared to commit to a full-blown war in Iraq, and Corbyn currently (November 2015) is baulking at dropping a few bombs on terrorists in Syria. I find it very odd that core Labour voters seem able to vote for the likes of Tony Blair and at the same time will no doubt vote for Corbyn in the future. They are politically, and ideologically, poles apart.

Interestingly, they did not seem to fancy voting for Brown, when Blair resigned; not surprising I suppose, and a relief that even Labour voters are not all daft enough to vote for a Scot to run Great Britain, which Scotland does not seem to want to be a part of anymore anyway.

On the issue of Scottish independence, I would let the Scots have it and make sure they have to pay for everything they need out of their GDP; their own Army, Navy and Air Force for example. There would be no reason why Britain should defend an independent Scotland. I have the suspicion that the Scottish Nationalist Party (SNP) want to have their cake and eat it with regard to finances and other issues. Shortly, those wanting independence, who also want Scotland in the European Union (EU), will be voting to keep the UK, which they do not want to be part of, in the EU. Seems like democracy gone mad to me!

What would we do with the Union Jack if they left? I would favour a St George's Cross with a Welsh dragon in one quadrant.

I have a lot of time for the Welsh. They and the Cornish are of course the true Britons. We English are Saxons (Germans), Vikings (Danes) and Normans (French), with a little bit of British thrown in. Without the Scots there would also be a good excuse to do something about our boring National Anthem. It is so unfair that the Welsh and Scots have their own, whilst we English have to use the 'corporate' one!

As for Northern Ireland, I would simply give it to the Southern Irish to sort out. It is amazing that we consider it ridiculous that the Middle East is such a religious and political mess, but seem to forget that two branches of Christianity, in Protestants and Catholics, living on our doorstep still can't get along, even if they have stopped killing each other quite as much.

To be fair to the Irish, the mess is probably mainly the fault of the English lords, who invaded Ireland and, in the main, inhabited the north, and not the Catholics in the south. William of Orange is to blame I expect, but I admit my knowledge of that part of our history is not that good.

All I am saying is that surely a country as small as Ireland should be, and be able to be, united with understanding and reconciliation for the troubles of the past. However, contrary to that belief of mine, over the last 20 years worldwide we have seen more and more small countries seeking independence and being created. This is indicative of the strength of our desire to be independent both individually and nationally. At the same time the desire for power entices nations and individuals to seek to dominate others, which leads to the wars and chaos we see in our world. How sad it all is.

The huge inequality between those that have and those that have not is a huge driver in this. The wealthy, who include me tend to blame the poor. However, by not distributing their wealth, the well-off are in the main the guilty party I fear.

Now back to the Falklands War.

At Barcelona airport I bought a newspaper, and found that my 'O'-level Latin helped me decipher Catalan and learn a little more about what was going on. I am not sure the Spanish were very sympathetic to our cause with the sore of Gibraltar always present!

My parents picked me up at Heathrow and drove me down to Plymouth, which was already a hive of activity. Ross Adley had been recalled to 42 Commando as well, so we were able to support each other with the medical preparations. Like a lot of military events it turned out to be 'rush to wait', so there were quite a few final 'runs ashore' as a Navy piss-up is called. This saying, as one might guess, applies particularly to leaving a ship moored alongside for a night out in town.

After a few days, a little mystery arrived and I was called to a briefing for an explanation. 'M' Company had been selected to head an early move to retake South Georgia, the island some way from the Falklands, where the 'scrap metal merchants' had originally landed, and which was now under Argentine control. I would go as the doctor and Ross Adley would stay with the rest of the Unit. I was to take two medical assistants with me, Petty Officer 'Knocker' White and Leading Medical Assistant Dave Woodgate. Alan White was very experienced, and had previously served on the Falkland Islands, and Dave was the 'M' Company medic. They were both great guys and helped to calm my nerves at being responsible for the medical care of men in an opposed landing on a remote island in the South Atlantic.

I was 25-years-old, with less than two years under my belt as a doctor; one year in hospital and the rest looking after fit marines in peacetime. At this time, it was thought that we might be the only ones to see action and that the Argentinians might even give up the Falklands before the Task Force arrived. How wrong that proved to be!

'M' Company Group included various support elements, including us as medics, marines from recce troop and mortar troop, and others. We left in great secrecy from the barracks under the overall command of Major Guy Sheridan, the second-in-command of 42 Commando. Captain Chris Nunn was the officer commanding 'M' Company. We flew to Ascension Island, and from there boarded ships for the journey south.

The majority of 'M' Company went to a Royal Fleet Auxiliary ship carrying supplies and fuel - *RFA Tidespring*. The headquarters team, which included me, joined *HMS Antrim*, an old destroyer built at a time when this class of ship was designed to be a similar size to a Second World War Battle Cruiser. *HMS Plymouth*, a frigate, also sailed with us.

We kept ourselves busy on board, training and ensuring that all our personal and medical kit was complete. I was able to chat with Alistair Maclean, the ship's doctor, who I knew of old. We arrived near South Georgia. This is not intended to be an in-depth military account, so I will keep the details brief. We had been joined by 'D' Squadron SAS, who carried out a number of intelligence-gathering insertions onto the island, but which in the main, failed because of the appalling weather.

Guy Sheridan became very frustrated with their 'gung-ho' behaviour. He was an experienced cold-weather and mountain expert, and they failed to listen to his warnings that the weather would defeat their attempts. A particularly good example of this was when they put a section of men onto Fortuna Glacier, from which they had to be rescued, with the loss of two helicopters, but miraculously no men.

There was an Argentinian submarine in the area: the *Santa Fe*.

RFA Tidespring was full of fuel, poorly protected and a torpedo would have seen it explode into oblivion. It carried most of 'M' Company so the ship was ordered to leave the area. In retrospect, the Sante Fe was very old and in poor condition and probably posed a very limited threat.

Overnight the weather was atrocious. A true South Atlantic storm hit us. I went up to the bridge of *HMS Antrim* and found that when we were in the trough of a wave, the next wave towered 30-feet and more above us. It was truly amazing. The next day the weather calmed and a decision was made to land a force on South Georgia. Most of 'M' Company were north in *Tidespring* so a mix of marines from the headquarters staff, recce and the mortar troop were combined with the SAS to mount the attack. I went ashore with them, with 'Knocker' White; Dave Woodgate was on *Tidespring*. The *Santa Fe* was crippled by helicopters from *HMS Endurance*, the Navy's ship in the Antarctic. We flew ashore in Lynx helicopters at very low level. I was by the open door, and it felt as if my feet would touch the ground if I swung them out. It was uncomfortable and scary.

I flew in a lot of helicopters in my time in the Navy. In troop carriers, small helicopters like the Lynx, and the much larger Sea King from *HMS Invincible*. I flew at day and night, landed on pitching ships, was winched down onto submarine turrets, abseiled onto the side of mountains, and have also parachuted from them. Parachuting is good because you get out quick and don't have to land in the whirlybird!

Choppers are dangerous I believe, although I am sure statistics would prove me wrong.

Skilled motorsport celebrities have killed themselves flying them; notably Colin McRae from rallying and Steve Hislop from motorcycle racing. Generally, I would not fly in one voluntarily, although I must admit to having gone off on 'a jolly' in one in the first Gulf War, so that I could say I had been in Kuwait, Iraq and Saudi Arabia.

What is more, I flew with Navy and other British Forces pilots, who are the best in the world. I am saddened when I hear of people dying in helicopters whilst on holiday, because they have taken an ill-advised trip in one, as recently happened on the South Island of New Zealand.

Back in South Georgia, the Lynx hovered low over a piece of flat ground and we all jumped out. I was carrying my medical kit on my back and had a submachine gun, three full magazines and four grenades.

The Geneva Convention states that doctors may be armed to protect themselves and their patients, and I intended to comply with the Geneva Convention, with all necessary force!

We were on a plain with a small hill in front of us, which would lead to another plain. Had the Argentinians done what they should have and placed machine guns on the hilltop we would have been pinned down. We walked across the flatland and up the hill, from where we had a view of Grytviken, the old whaling station at the head of the bay, and the British Antarctic Survey (BAS) buildings on King Edward's Point, where the BAS team had lived until ousted by the invaders. White flags were flying from all the buildings. The Navy ships had bombarded them with their big guns before we landed and they had clearly had enough. I felt a mixture of relief, and disappointment that it was not going to get any more exciting.

The SAS were already half way round the bay towards King Edward's Point and would get there first. Guy Sheridan was having none of this and called in a helicopter. "Come on, Doc," he said, "jump in." So I did, and we flew across the bay, beating the SAS to it.

He and I and a few others took the surrender!

Just as well the Argentinians did not change their mind. I don't think my ammunition would have been enough. There was a casualty from the submarine, which had limped to South

Georgia and was moored alongside. He was under-resuscitated, so I sorted him out and had him evacuated to one of the ships. I found the BAS medical centre and bagged a room opposite, which I shared with 'Knocker' and Dave, when he arrived with the majority of 'M' Company, who were currently still at sea.

Later in our stay in my medical capacity, I treated a Bennett's fracture (a break in a bone at the base of the thumb) and played dentist once, pulling a tooth from the mouth of a Royal Marine officer. He had toothache and wanted rid of it! There is not much else of note to report!

That was my first war.

Very exciting at the start, but then we were left there to defend the island, and it was to be a long three months. We liberated a lot of Argentinian wine and I ran an officers' bar, which made enough profit to buy all the men a pewter tankard when we got home. We also liberated a lot of corned beef, which was a staple part of our diet. I have only recently started eating it again!

As I said earlier, this is not a war history, but let me relate a story which will lead me into something else.

Naval officers from *HMS Brilliant*, which had joined us, decided that the *Sante Fe*, the submarine, should be moved, because they considered her a hazard. After being attacked the submarine had limped to a berth alongside the jetty at King

Edward Point. They hatched a plan to use the boat's Argentinian crew to do the job, guarded by a number of marines. During the course of this process one of the Argentinian sailors reached for a lever that a marine had been led to believe would sink the vessel, so the marine shot him, several times. I was called and ran to the submarine, but the sailor was already dead.

This episode was unnecessary, very unfortunate for the sailor and his family, and for the marine. There was an inquiry and I was asked to carry out a post-mortem, which I had no skill at; neither did I require any!

He had been shot, he was dead; what else did they want?

In fact, I was helped by the medical officer from *HMS Brilliant,* who had completed some pathology training.

The enquiry (quite rightly) exonerated the marine. Mistakes happen in war and should be accepted, unless they are very far from what would be expected. Today we have the ridiculous situation where coroners in England investigate accidents in war and have gone as far as to blame commanding officers for what they have done.

What knowledge does a coroner have about war in a far off land? None, unless he just happens to be an ex-serviceman. As for sending soldiers to prison for something they may have done in the heat of battle, or shortly after, our government and legal system should be ashamed.

The role of coroners in Britain has increasingly far exceeded its original remit, which was simply to conclude regarding the nature and cause of death. Coroners now seem to have become judge and jury.

I have been in the coroner's court on three occasions.

The first time, in 1987, was when I was serving with the SAS. A soldier's wife had drowned in the camp swimming pool. I tried to resuscitate her for an hour, having been called from my home, which was nearby. I stated in court that the woman had received excellent care, because it would not be usual for a doctor to be nearby and have all the equipment required available. The coroner was complimentary and agreed. The second occasion was as an intensive care consultant, and although I had done nothing wrong, I did feel I could perhaps have done better, so I was quite nervous before the hearing. However, my care was considered to have been fine.

The third occasion followed the death in intensive care of a young man who had crashed his car. He had become very ill and I stood by his bed treating him in every way I could for 15 hours and after a short break returned to help my colleague, who was on call for the night. There was nothing we could do, and the young man died. I attended the coroner's court secure in the knowledge that I had done everything I could have for the young man. I found that the family had engaged a solicitor, and a so called 'expert witness', to criticise my care. I had a very uncomfortable time of it and left the court a changed man as far as my faith in justice was concerned.

One only has to turn on the television and watch the morning news programmes, to get the impression that it is always someone else's fault. In this case apparently mine, that the patient had been severely injured at the wheel of his car. I know he received from me the best care he could possibly have had, but it was still not good enough for his family.

In contrast there are two patients, who I cared for in intensive care, who my colleagues and I expected to die, who nearly 20 years on still greet me in Barnsley town centre, where I live and worked, and thank me. They help me to retain a modicum of faith in humankind, which I have to admit I do not have a great deal of.

Back to the war.

During my time on South Georgia I spent a lot of time with Chris Nunn, who was left to command his marines in the defence of the island, at the retaking of which the majority had not been present. We all felt we should have been sent to the Falklands to join the rest of 42 Commando there and another battalion should have taken over our duties on South Georgia. This was not to be, and Chris had a difficult time in many ways, not least keeping up the morale of his men. It was all made much more difficult for him by the death of his brother,

Richard Nunn, who was a Royal Marine officer as well as a helicopter pilot, and was shot and killed whilst flying to evacuate casualties from Goose Green on the Falkland Islands during the battle there. I tried to support Chris during our three months together, but in all honesty I think in many ways I was too young and inexperienced to do it well. We still intermittently keep in touch to this day and I have very fond memories of him and our time together.

We journeyed home on a Townsend Thoresen North Sea ferry; hardly a very auspicious end to our travels. The ferry was not very posh and in the severe storms we met, the crew did not seem to understand the merits of stowing things away properly to avoid damage. My main memory of that journey is reading *The Bourne Identity* by Robert Ludlum; a book which is far better than the film! We reached Ascension Island and from there flew the rest of the way home to our waiting families.

My then wife Christine had bought us a house while I was away, or very nearly. The paperwork needed signing and during the six weeks of post-operational leave I had, we moved in. It was a three-bedroom detached house in Dorset, which cost £30,000.

No one helped us buy it; there being no 'help to buy' schemes then available for young first-time buyers. I admit there was tax relief on mortgage payments, recently increased to £30,000 by Margaret Thatcher in her bid for us all to buy, but everyone got that, not just the young.

There is a lot of publicity these days about how hard it is to get on the property ladder. There are two issues here:

First, it is about priorities.

I suspect that these young people unable to find enough money for a deposit will be going on at least one holiday abroad a year, they will have a nearly-new car, and they will have a mobile phone amongst umpteen other luxuries. Some may be thinking that a mobile phone is not a luxury, in which case I would ask why we all apparently need to be instantly contactable and surf the web wherever we might be?

Many of these young people will have lived at home rent-free for a lot longer than we ever did in my day, which presents them with an ideal opportunity to save. I never lived at home as an adult, in fact not from the age of eleven, although I know that can't be considered normal!

The second point is - what's wrong with renting?

In many other countries this is the norm.

Buying a house is about choices, like everything else, and sacrifices will need to be made to do so. I do not think in the modern world this is understood or accepted; everyone wants everything on tap.

Another choice is whether or not to have children, which are expensive and may well make someone want a bigger house to accommodate them.

Children these days seem to be seen as a right, as demonstrated by IVF being paid for by the NHS. I have no idea why this should be the case, but that is another bag of worms and perhaps it is better I do not go there. Anyway, if one has children the consequences should be accepted; the state should not be expected to provide one with a bigger house, child allowance, more tax credit, free nursery places or anything else.

Finally, would someone please let me know why having children should entitle parents to positive discrimination regarding car parking spaces? In Barnsley, they are closer to the shops, wider, and available only if there is a child-seat in the car. I wonder how many people, who have no children drive around with a child-seat in the back!

My post-Falklands leave ended and it was back to Plymouth. Our house was in Wimborne, Dorset, so I lived in the Officers' Mess. The rest of 1982 passed without major events. We had a training camp in Thetford, in Norfolk, and I remember Channel 4 started whilst we were there. The first new channel since BBC2 - and how many do we have now?

Christmas then arrived, heralding another trip to Norway.

This year we were based further south, our Headquarters being at a place called Lom. The companies were spread around elsewhere. I spent some of my time with 'L' Company; the doctor who was replacing me was in Lom.

I was lying on my bunk early one evening, when someone came to find me to say I needed to go to Lom where there had been an accident. I headed off to find that an Arctic Survival Course had gone wrong and some 40 marines and attached personnel had been forced to stay overnight on top of a mountain in a storm. They had not had any bivvies (tents) with them, or sleeping bags, and had sheltered in snow holes. The following morning the storm still raged. Many of the guys were suffering from frostbite and becoming hypothermic, so they were forced to try to make their way down. They were now on their way back in buses, from the road they had reached. There would be a lot of cold-injuries to deal with.

We heated a lot of water in which to immerse frostbitten limbs, and waited. It is important to re-warm frostbite as quickly as possible. This can be very painful and strong analgesia may be required.

And so they arrived, many of them bearing significant injuries which meant that after our treatment they needed to return to the UK some days later for further care. Some lost the tips of their fingers and toes and most would suffer 'cold sensitivity' for the rest of their lives.

There was worse news; two of the men had died of hypothermia on the way down the mountain. One was a marine, who was lucky to have survived serious injuries in the

Falklands just a year before, which had caused his heart to stop for a short period. How unfortunate is that? There is nothing we can do about fate, but it is very cruel sometimes.

The other was my friend and colleague, Pete Hodgson, the dentist. Both bodies had been left up there on the mountain. There had been no point in risking slowing the descent of the others by moving dead bodies. They were picked up in helicopters, when the storm broke. My last memory of Peter is seeing his body in the back of a lorry, when he was returned to Lom. For a long time afterwards I had day and nightmares that he might not have been dead when they'd left him on the mountain. Severe hypothermic coma is very difficult to distinguish from death, especially in an Arctic storm. There is a saying that, when you resuscitate someone with hypothermia, 'they are not dead until they are warm and dead'.

A post-mortem was performed by the local medical authorities and I had nothing more to do with Peter after that. In retrospect, I am sure he was dead on the mountain, when left behind. Once Pete was in hypothermic coma he would have had a peaceful death.

On a final note, when he and I had both lived in the sick bay in Norway the previous year, I had watched him in the communal bathroom meticulously cleaning his teeth with one-way brush strokes as then recommended; to be expected from a dentist. I thought at the time, though that I was just not patient enough to do that, even if it would mean my teeth lasting until the age of 80. What a waste of time and effort that turned out to be for him. I know it would be nihilistic not to do things in case you die tomorrow and we cannot run our lives like that, but I could not help thinking that. As a result, at least once a month to this day, when I am cleaning my teeth, I think of Pete.

A doctor with a particular interest in cold-weather injury visited Lom, and openly criticised my management of the injured. It should be borne in mind that at the time I was troubled by the recent death of my friend and the pressures of dealing with so many frost-bitten marines, when I tell you that I explained to him in the Officers' Mess that if he ever tried to speak to me again, or even come close to me, I would kill him. Obviously I wouldn't have done, but fortunately our paths never crossed again after that.

The rest of my time in Norway was understandably not good. I spent hours doing long runs on an icy road around the fiord near Lom; exercise being something I often resort to when stressed.

I had already made friends with the local doctor and his wife, who were my age. For some reason, with another officer, I agreed to play bridge at their house. I hate bridge, am no good at it, and always get the bidding wrong. An indication of my fragile state at the time was that I completely lost my temper whilst playing with them, when someone criticised my bidding, and I stormed out of their house.

The next day the doctor's very pretty wife arrived at the sick bay with some flowers for me. Until Julie, my wife and I got together, this was the only time a woman had ever given me flowers. The doctor's wife invited me round for tea that afternoon, which included a tour of their house culminating with a not very subtle visit to the bedroom thrown in. I was the perfect gentleman and neatly sidestepped the lady's suggested implication. I am not sure why really!

A similar episode was to occur to me in Florida in 1989, when the wife of a US Navy officer indicated her boudoir, having already told me that her husband's return from sea had been delayed for a day - and *again* I behaved myself!

The Royal Navy now decided to play a blinder on me!

My time at 42 Commando was due to end with my return from Norway and I was going to start my general practice training at the Naval Hospital in Gosport. This would have given me some important time at home, having been away for nine of the last fifteen months.

There is no doubt I was not firing on all cylinders after my recent experiences. However, this did not stop the Navy from changing my next job to three-months at sea in the frigate, *HMS Phoebe*. It proved to be the final nail in the coffin for my already strained marriage.

It was a stupid, ill-thought out thing to do to me, but no doubt I was the easiest solution to fill the requirement. Doctors then expected, when they joined the Navy for five years, to do 12 to 24 months of what are known as general duties; ships, submarines or marines. Some did less than 12.

I had already done 30!

One may draw one's own conclusions, but I did not join *HMS Phoebe* in the best frame of mind, although I did have a good laugh most of the time whilst serving in her.

My final evening in Norway I invited the doctor and his wife to the Mess for a meal. When we said goodbye she kissed me passionately full on the lips in front of her husband, who I could hear tut-tutting in the background. Showing me the bedroom had not been the action of an innocent woman I would suggest!

9

WAGS

MY FIRST LOVE WAS DIANA RIGG AS EMMA PEEL IN *The Avengers*; Thames Television's spy-fi series that ran from 1961-69.

Needless to say it was an unrequited affair, not least because I was only 11 at the time, and she was in her late-twenties. I can remember watching the programme, whilst boarding at Brightlands in 1968.

My wife Julie says I have 'a thing' about quite a few actresses these days; Tamzin Outhwaite, Suranne Jones, Martine McCutcheon, Julianne Moore and Helen George to name but a few. I am not sure if there is any particular pattern there?

Whilst on the subject of actresses, why is it *Dame* Judi Dench, *Dame* Helen Mirren and indeed *Dame* Diana Rigg . . . and yet not *Dame* Julie Walters? In my opinion Julie Walters is a fantastic and versatile actress, better than the other three, so I guess it must be because she doesn't talk posh. Although great progress has been made towards the acceptance of regional dialects, in Britain today one's accent can still be something of an issue.

I admit to a certain hesitancy about writing this chapter. I have been married four times, so there is considerable scope for upsetting a few women before I do much else.

My eldest daughter, Fiona, was reading the start of this book a few days ago. She liked what she read and we briefly discussed this chapter. I voiced to her my fears about it, and she wisely suggested that I should just be honest, which I will endeavour to be, but which may not turn out to be to everyone's liking - honesty, a bit like beauty, being in the eye of the beholder. However, I can assure everyone that what I say will not always leave me in a good light. I am not naïve to the fact that for a bloke to have had four marriages, four children by two different wives, neither of whom he is now with, even in 2015, is a mite extreme! I have an idea as to why it all happened that way, which I shall be going into, and the mysteries of marriage, and the relationship between men and women - shortly.

I have already referred to my earlier romantic failures which took me as far as medical school and the age of eighteen. Early on at St. Mary's I realised that my *chatting-up* or even *chatting-to* women skills were woeful, and I still suffered from my terminal shyness in most circumstances, especially if I particularly liked a girl.

I spotted and was attracted to Jackie, who was in my year, but rarely had the opportunity to speak to her, and she met another bloke early in the first term, whose name was Ken. He was two years senior, looked cool (like a Bee Gee), wore what I thought were trendy hippy-type clothes, and drove a Triumph Vitesse two-litre convertible. What chance did *I* have? When I say hippy I mean he wore one of those seventies Afghan-style goat/sheepskin affairs made with the fleece on the inside and the soft suede-like leather on the outside, Jesus-sandals, and a sort of man-bag slung over his shoulder. He may, or may not have been cool, but at that time I would not have had the independence of mind to dress like that. Me? I was still the shy boy from public school. As for the car, if I was to buy myself a classic car today, it would have to be a two-litre Triumph Vitesse.

All that sounds rather jealous of me, which - OK - yes - I suppose I was!

I think it must have been Jackie's seeming untouchability that made me so obsessed with her, when in reality I knew little about her. She had attractive, but unusual looks and was friendly with everyone, which was the very antithesis of me.

I simply thought she was great.

We finally 'got it together' after the party thrown by my flatmates and me in Acton 18-months later. This was followed by that long, hot summer of 1976, when we took off on holiday together to Cornwall on my motorbike, camping using a borrowed tent. I remember visiting St. Ives and Newquay; otherwise my main recollections are listening, on the radio, to the Montreal Olympics and Nicki Lauda crashing at the Nurburgring; oh - and we burnt a hole in our borrowed tent! Jackie - who had already become the beneficiary of my virginity some time before - got herself sunburned, so the sun, sea and sand, did not stretch to sex, in the very compact two person accommodation!

On our return, Jackie went home and I found the flat in Finsbury Park, which we would shortly share with my friend Duncan.

Since I had failed some of my exams at the end of the summer term I was busy working for the re-sits. I was swotting in the library one day when, deliberately I am sure, well within my earshot, one of Ken's friends spoke to him, saying: "Are you still seeing Jackie this evening?"

I turned hot and cold all over, apoplectic and upset.

I went back to the flat, jumped on my motorbike and went roaring off to Bourne End where Jackie lived.

Ken was there.

There was a showdown, during which Jackie gave a very weak excuse for his presence, but to cut the story short I forgave her, Ken exited the picture, and we went on to live together during the next year.

I loved her.

What does *that* mean?

Different things to each of us and different things at different times and in different circumstances, I expect.

For me love has often been a needy process. Needing to be with that person; needing them to love me. Perhaps I wanted to fill a gap put there because of my upbringing, my lack of family life and separation from my parents. My father was never the loving type. He showed me very little affection and for a long time I was actually scared of him. Mum was loving when I was young, but once I had reached my teens became increasingly distant, both emotionally and geographically.

This was a gap I spent a long time trying to fill, more of which will be seen later.

Loving someone should not be about one's own needs, but about those of the one you love. Thus, love would be demonstrated. The ultimate form of this would be unconditional love. If you had this, and your partner left you for someone else because that is what they wanted to do, you would be pleased to see them happy, not miserable about your own loss. I know this is extreme, but it demonstrates the hypocrisy of love, which usually seems to revolve around the needs of the one doing the loving, not the person being loved.

For a man, the neediness of love is summarised by the truth and reality of the saying that, *'there is nothing worse than the wrath of a woman scorned';* i.e. beware the bunny-boiler!

Jackie and I enjoyed a good time living together for about six months, and then a strange thing happened.

We went to a school-friend's 21st birthday party in the Midlands, and Jackie would not let me out of her sight; nor would she mingle with any of my friends. We ended up spending the whole party sitting together in the corner. Shortly after this, she complained about the amount of time I was spending with my best mate, Duncan, so that - I'm afraid - soon afterwards - was the end . . . for Jackie and me.

I told her that our relationship was now over, which was administratively rather difficult in view of the fact that we were living together.

She moved out to live in Wilson House, and Kim Wagstaffe move in with Duncan and I.

I think that my finishing with Jackie must have been indicative of the fact that the reason I wanted a girlfriend was because one was 'supposed' to have a girlfriend, when in fact I preferred spending time with my male friends. I was not and never have been gay, although, of course, it would be fine if I was, but not for me . . . in the mid-seventies? The gay fraternity didn't have a very easy life of it in those days.

However, I did not waste much time trying to find a replacement. I was now a very active member of the rowing club at Mary's where there was a ladies' section, consisting in the main of medical and physiotherapy students. That's where I spotted Christine, who was one of them.

I was attracted to Chrissie, as she liked to be called, from the very beginning because she talked a lot about home, her family and her parents, which was not the usual conversational piece for my friends or me. It sounded nice to have such a close family.

And so we got together, but even at this stage it was mostly in a group, rather than us being alone together; either a group of rowers, or us and her family.

The first time I met her father, Roy, we gelled well and became great buddies. He was so unlike my own dad. He loved a few beers and a laugh, which was great for me. I enjoyed being with him, listening to his stories about life in the East End of London, from where he came. He was now living in Didcot, with his wife Dot, and they treated me like one of their own.

Christine and I were married on 10th May 1980, but in reality I think I was marrying the family life that I craved. Even when we were married, we were rarely out as a couple – it was always with a group.

Sadly, we drifted apart and then separated in the autumn of 1983, after I returned from my trip in *HMS Phoebe*. It was later construed that I'd been having an affair with one of Christine's friends, which was not true, but as a result I never saw Roy again, although I very much wanted to.

After our marriage was over, I got together with Jane, a physiotherapist friend of Christine's.

Jane was - and I am sure still is - a lovely, kind and honest person, who I regret I did not treat at all well, being an increasingly 'wild child', who became even wilder after my marriage came to an end.

A few months after I'd split up with Christine I went on a skiing holiday with Alastair Miller, a friend of mine. I drank too much, including in the middle of the day, which is probably how I came to fall out of a chair lift, although to this day I still think Alastair might have pushed me!

I tried to start a fight in a bar with some blokes from the Ski Club of Great Britain, who I thought were snooty – actually they were, but that didn't mean they deserved to be the recipients of my drunken abuse.

Alistair and I shared our chalet with some guys we had only met on the holiday. In the evening we played drinking games - not a good idea in my frame of mind. One night I decided we should play left-handed-only drinking - a bit unfair in view of the fact that one of the guys with us didn't have one, just a mechanical claw-prosthesis. "*You're* in trouble", I said to him insensitively.

This incident and the others, I relate simply to illustrate why I might have been perceived as being wild.

I had actually wanted to 'make a go of it' with Christine, because I believed we should, but she was not interested, and it was she that left me in the end. I suspect that experience subconsciously clouded my view regarding the sanctity of marriage and was partly responsible for what was to come in my married life in the future.

Whilst away serving in *Phoebe,* I knew things were not good with Christine, but had unilaterally decided that we should make it work, to the extent of having designs on starting a family. I cannot recall if any of this was verbalised, but clearly it came to nothing.

I have, a long time since, realised that in my mixed-up state I should never have become involved with Jane, but should have remained unattached and played out my ensuing rebellion alone.

Jane and I had been going out for a couple of months when, as part of my general practice medical training, I was sent to Hong Kong. This year-long trip should have been with Christine, and indeed was usually only available to married doctors, but the Navy let me go anyway.

Telling Jane to wait for me, I flew off.

So there I was, a red-blooded, unattached 27-year-old male unleashed in the Far East!

An accident waiting to happen.

Actually, I was a bit lonely and depressed in Hong Kong some of the time early on, but treated this affliction by going to as many parties as possible. I did also, however, do a lot of sport and fitness - one of the spells in my life when I was as fit as I possibly could be.

I played rugby initially for the Navy team and then one of the local rugby clubs; I ran, swam, played squash and used the gym, often three of these activities in one day. This kept me, if not on the straight and narrow, at least on a better course than I might have been.

Work-wise I was what would now be termed a GP registrar, but in reality, although training, I worked mostly alone. The practice looked after the sailors, soldiers and their families, as well as Chinese locally employed by the Navy, and their wives and children.

I enjoyed my work, which kept me under a degree of control, but I did have a very busy time socially, which usually involved - yep - a lot of drink. I was very far from being alone in this, there were a lot of young Naval officers in the Mess where I lived, not to mention the guys at the rugby club.

Shall we return now, to the WAGS.

The next young ladies cannot be classed as girlfriends, but warrant an honourable mention in any case.

There were five small Navy ships in Hong Kong, converted mine sweepers, used to patrol the local waters and catch illegal Chinese immigrants. However, every so often they had to undergo high-seas training in pairs, which involved a trip somewhere, a short stay; nothing too arduous - and then the return trip.

I wangled myself a berth aboard one of them, *HMS Wolverton* on her trip to Thailand with another ship. We were to visit Sattahip, near Pataya Beach, then (in)famous for being an American Forces' R&R (rest and recuperation) resort during the Vietnam War, with all the concomitant attractions that one would expect to find at such a location.

The trip down was good, and the bunch of officers in the ship I knew to be a fun lot. The Captain let me take watch on the bridge, which was brave of him, in return for which I ran a circuit-training session on the deck each day. We arrived in Sattahip and had a few cocktails with the consular representative, who visited the ships. He then offered a few of us a lift to Pattaya. Once in the car he asked us where in particular we wanted to go.

"Massage," we replied unanimously.

"Straight - or otherwise?" he asked with a grin.

As the doctor, and currently in a responsible condition, I said: "Straight".

He dropped us outside an establishment and in we all trooped. The massage was good, followed by an all-cleansing bath, but when the girl got into the bath with me I realised that there was no such thing as 'straight' in Pattaya; nevertheless, I declined her 'extras'.

This was in 1984, when HIV infection and AIDS had recently arrived and hit California in a big way, but before I continue with my story remember that at the time this was believed to be a disease contracted only by gay men.

Looking back now it is bizarre that even the medical world believed such a thing. Why should a disease spread by close bodily contact only affect gay men? There is no doubt that sense was clouded by the still prevalent sentiment that being homosexual was not 'normal' and HIV was seen as some kind of retribution, divine or otherwise. Anyway, as far as 'squeaky clean' was concerned, in 1984 Thailand, I wasn't gay therefore there was nothing for me to worry about.

From the massage we had a few (many) more beers, and then moved on to the official welcoming cocktail party. Once again, rather like in the Mess in Poole, I found myself performing in front of the senior diplomats. I remember standing on a table and making a speech; God knows what about, but not at all polite, I don't suppose.

A group of us left and by now any inhibitions I might have felt were completely lost as we entered another massage emporium where we found stacks of enticing young girls with numbers attached to their bodices, sitting behind a huge glass screen. We all selected a number, and chose to have a soapy body-to-body massage, from the girl attached to it. No prizes for guessing where that was going to lead!

Somehow I managed to return to the ship safely; in a *Tuk Tuk* I seem to recall.

The following night, for some reason that is not clear to me now, I went back to the same joint again, whilst still fairly sober, determined firstly to have a straight massage and secondly not to choose the same girl as the night before, whose looks were a bit of a vague memory. I succeeded in the first task, but failed in the second, proving perhaps that attraction is a somewhat fixed process! I guess this second visit must have been a typical kind of 'Swinhoe challenge' to myself to prove I *could* behave!

My stay in Thailand continued in a similar vein for several more days!

What I should call 'transgender people', but who were known then and still are when not being politically correct, as 'ladyboys', were thick on the ground in Pattaya. I was not caught-out during the time I spent there, making sure that I had a good look at all the girls' Adam's Apples before becoming intimate in any way - men's Adam's Apples (thyroid cartilages) being much more prominent than women's, and one part of their anatomy that ladyboys then didn't disguise. These days I think plastic surgery does the trick. So heterosexuals beware!

On our last night in Thailand, we were entertained in the Thai Navy Officers' Mess, where there was a band playing with a gorgeous looking singer who turned out to be - you've guessed it - a 'he'.

I am not proud of my behaviour in Thailand, but neither am I embarrassed by it. I was young, reckless and blowing off steam. By the time we left the place, if I was walking down the street a friendly face would quite frequently call out, "Hi doctor." I had obviously become quite well known there. My shipmates nicknamed me 'The Doctor of Pattaya'.

Our return journey was uneventful.

When I arrived back in Hong Kong, although I considered that HIV was not an issue, there were other infections that potentially were, so I started myself on a long course of erythromycin, an antibiotic that I worked out would kill all-comers: syphilis, gonorrhoea and chlamydia. I would have to take my chances with herpes.

It is interesting that the herpes virus has little airtime these days. I suppose it is seen as benign compared with HIV, so is not worth a mention. Back then it was the *incurable* one. The fact that incurable sexually transmitted diseases do not seem to curtail people's sexual activity in the slightest would seem to prove the power of the procreative instinct. Even in the days when the only, and ineffective, treatment for syphilis involved taking the poison arsenic, most people still seemed happy to go ahead anyway and run the risk of catching it! A game of Russian roulette if ever there was one.

A while after the ships returned I received a letter from the Hong Kong Blood Transfusion Service informing me that a married crew-member had donated blood that had tested positive for syphilis. I contacted the sailor and conveyed to him the news. He admitted to having indulged in some extra-marital sex; reluctantly agreeing, when I told him that he would have to tell his wife so that she could be tested. He did so, only for me then to receive another letter saying that the first had been a mistake and a second test had proved negative.

The poor guy.

Even though not of my making, I still felt quite bad about the situation.

Another patient-incident I experienced in Hong Kong had to do with a young woman who came to see me. She was the wife of a soldier, who had now returned to the UK. They had separated, but she had stayed on, and for some quirky administrative reason was still entitled to our care. She presented complaining of a lump in her breast. I examined her (with a chaperone present), found nothing untoward, and reassured her accordingly. Soon afterwards she returned with the same complaint, and the examination process was duly repeated. Then again - a third time. On the *fourth* occasion it dawned on me that it was me she wanted to see and be examined by! Actually, she was quite attractive, but I didn't fancy being struck off the General Medical Council Register for misconduct or malpractice at this stage in my career, so I made sure that another doctor saw her the next time. This time she 'accepted' his assurance that there was nothing wrong with her and that was the last we saw of her. Perhaps he wasn't as handsome as me!

I was propositioned by a patient on one other occasion in my medical career. I was conducting a gynaecology out-patient clinic as a senior house officer, with a consultant in the next door room who I could refer to for advice. An attractive woman came in. Her complaint was dyspareunia, which is pain when engaging in sexual intercourse and may have a physical cause, but is more often associated with emotional factors, either in or outside the relationship. I took a history, examined her, and not unexpectedly was able to find no physical cause for her distress. I explained this to her and started to explore other factors, which might have been the underlying cause of her problem. During the course of this conversation she asked me out, which I think might have been somewhat indicative that there were partner issues involved! Obviously, I declined her offer.

A few weeks after my return to Hong Kong from Thailand, Jane came out on a visit.

I had not been a good or faithful bloke.

We had a great time together, she was lovely, I showed her all the sights, we got to know each other much better and it was all good, so I was very sad when she left. Everyone who met her said how great she was, and how lucky I was. But that was not good enough for me!

In June I started a relationship with Jo.

Jo was an Army (Women's Royal Army Corps) officer, who worked in the Headquarters and lived in the same Mess as me. We had arrived in Hong Kong at much the same time and had been friendly for a while. She had been engaged to a guy back home, but by now they had split up.

A while after this, I returned to England for two weeks. Jane met me at the airport; sensing that something was wrong on the way to my parents' house she confronted me. Although I do not think I answered her question directly, she nevertheless picked-up on my discomfort and along with her 'woman's intuition' drove off in her car and out of my life.

Jo and I returned to England together in January 1985. She had left the Army and we moved into a flat I had bought in Southsea. I was now working at RNH Haslar again.

We were married on April Fools' Day 1986!

A small 'do' with just our parents and a couple of friends.

By then I was working as one of the doctors for the SAS in Hereford. Straight after our wedding I was placed on standby for anti-terrorist operations. Actually, I think I was on-call during the wedding!

Jo and I had just returned to our rented house in Hereford and were standing in the middle of a load of boxes of our belongings, when I was called out. Well at least it hadn't been any earlier!

I returned five days later with a suntan to find the boxes unpacked; Jo having tolerated my enforced absence very well.

If Jane had not (quite understandably) run out on me, who would I have ended up marrying? Jane and I had discussed that prospect. That question is unanswerable!

I am a firm believer that in life there are moments and decisions that fundamentally change its entire course. Being impulsive in what I do, I have only ever reflected upon them in retrospect, never at the time. I expect others are more considered and calculating about them, perhaps enjoying a smoother passage as a result!

Some such decisions for me, I am sure, were joining the Navy, leaving the Navy, and then taking a job in Sheffield rather than Southampton, as well as my final work move to Barnsley.

Oh, and I have failed to mention having an affair with the woman who was later to become my third wife - I get ahead of myself.

Jane was (perhaps I should put 'is', which doesn't seem quite right since I've not seen her for 31 years) an 'earth mother' type. She would have been happy, I believe, to have been a good old-fashioned mother and housewife. Sorry ladies, if that sounds sexist.

Jo chose to be a housewife for most of our marriage, and is a great mother. That is what she wanted to do and be, so she was successful at it, because she is a very determined lady, and if she puts her mind to a course she will follow it through to the best of her ability. However, underneath that she is also a career woman.

I failed to mention earlier that part of the reason I went out with her in the first place was that I saw her as a bit of a challenge. She had served in some difficult places in her time in the Army, having been rewarded with a *Mention in Dispatches* for her considerable efforts and courage. She could be quite intimidating as well!

Don't get me wrong I loved Jo, and we had a lot of fun in Hong Kong, and after, during our time together.

Would I have stayed with Jane if we had married? Who knows? I suspect not.

It is interesting that I think Jo and I drifted apart (of my doing, I am sure) when she decided she wanted to return to work - then only in a very limited capacity, but today she is CEO of her own company. Not long before we split up - which I shall come to, and was 99% my fault I hasten to add -

something happened, which irked me, in an out of proportion to the event, kind of way.

I was working in Sheffield as an anaesthetic senior registrar, frequently on call. We only had one car, which I always let Jo have whilst I either ran or cycled to work. However, if I was on-call, once I got home I needed the car in order to be able to return to work quickly if summoned. Not long after Jo had started part-time work I came home when on-call one day, to find her still out in the car. I was irritated by this, because I think I felt very let down that as the longstanding bread-winner my rare need to have the only car had been overlooked.

I do not relate this tale to excuse anything I later did, but because it is a small example of the sort of thing I see happening in friends' marriages now. It illustrates the stresses that family life in the modern world can generate, and is an issue that has escalated exponentially in the 20 years since the above experience happened to me.

I am old-fashioned. I look around at my younger friends who are married with children, where both partners are working, continually juggling their lives to meet all their family's needs, and I can't help thinking it was easier and better in the days when husbands went out to work, and wives stayed at home and looked after the house and children.

Many couples, who both work, would have enough money even without them both working if they didn't want so much in the way of material possessions, and I am sure their lives would be much more relaxed. A not insignificant amount of the loss of income would be mitigated by not needing to pay for childcare, a nanny and the rest. I do feel that we want it all ways these days. I do not look around me and see lots of happy people as a result of modern living, quite the opposite in fact. We have the need to liberate time in our busy lives by using lots of gadgets and other help, like cleaners, someone to do the ironing, someone to walk the dog, someone to deliver our shopping, (bought on-line), so that we have enough time in the day. We could have one partner stay at home and then have enough time to do it all ourselves. Radical I know!

On 12th March 1987, in the early evening, Jo gave birth to our daughter Fiona. She was delivered by forceps in a hurry and Jo could not sit down for a few weeks. I went back to work the next morning; no ten days of paternity leave for me in those days!

Actually, I cannot understand why a bloke would want to be at home with a new baby around and all the bother that he or she brings. However, to be fair they tend mostly to sleep, and are breast-fed, which the man cannot do, so it is quite a good time for some free holiday. It is later with teething, which seems to go on for months and months, followed by the terrible two's, and all that, when work appears to be a more attractive option. As one can tell I am not, and never have been, a 'natural' father. My four children are fantastic and were all great from about the age of seven onwards.

Whilst on the subject of small children, why do families go abroad with them?

All I remember of such holidays is following a toddler around a swimming pool to prevent him or her drowning, difficulties with meal times and food, and the continual fear of sunburn. Life would have been so much easier with a few days off at home in a safe, familiar environment, where one is not necessarily meant to be enjoying oneself anyway, so does not resent things going wrong so much, and one would have a spare couple of grand or more in the pocket, not being spent on the trip abroad!

Back then, to my children.

Alec was born 18-months later, in Plymouth, and with his arrival that was supposed to be it - my family complete.

Fiona and Alec have grown into great adults, mostly thanks to their mother I expect.

Having completed her English degree and a master's and then travelling the world for a bit, Fiona has worked for various charities for a number of years. She is completely unmaterialistic, which is a credit to her in this age of excess, and although she has inherited some of her dad's feisty edge, she is generally laid back about things. She is a socialist in the broadest sense of the word, and practises what she preaches in this area, unlike many. Her partner, Stephen, has recently gone out to Vietnam to teach English, and Fiona will be following him fairly soon. I am very proud of her easy-going, but adventurous attitude to life.

Alec followed his degree in engineering with extended travels around the world. However, now he is an officer in the Army. It was one of my proudest moments when he passed out of Sandhurst this year. He too seems to have avoided his dad's driven, obsessive, all-or-nothing attitude to life, which pleases me no end.

A fat lot of good it has done me! Oh, maybe it has helped a bit.

When Julie chided me a while ago for being like I am, telling me how hard it is for her living with me, I responded, saying: "Not half as hard as it is *being* me"!

This book isn't being read to listen to a parent droning on about how great his children are, especially when there are two more *and* my step-daughter to speak about yet.

So let's move on.

Jo and I enjoyed a good marriage in the main, until I 'cocked it up'. There were stresses and strains though, many of which were doubtless of my doing.

Early on in our marriage I was still in the Royal Navy and away a lot, leaving Jo with our two small children. After that I was working long hours as an anaesthetist, and when at home, studying for exams. When they were done, I discovered triathlon and went on to spend hours training and racing. Jo tolerated my excesses with mostly good humour. I am not going to suggest that she was perfect, but she was a good wife and mother, and I was selfish, I know now.

In 1995 I was on top of my game; firing on all cylinders! I had finished all my exams and I had become a very capable anaesthetic senior registrar - so good in fact that the consultants often managed to get me to do the cases they did not fancy.

One case in particular that I remember, was the first endovascular aortic aneurysm repair done in Sheffield. That is a repair of the biggest artery in the body using a synthetic tube fed into position from the groin under X-ray control. They sent me to the X-ray department where it was performed, to administer anaesthetic to the patient on my own - but it went wrong - not, I hasten to add, my anaesthetic. The patient bled profusely and I had to have him rushed up to theatre for a surgeon to try to sort things out.

Another patient I ended up anaesthetising was because no one else wanted to do it, since he was likely to die - which he did - but not until a while after I'd safely returned him to intensive care.

I felt good about my abilities at this time. I was also very physically fit and partaking in a lot of different races, both triathlon and running. I ran a marathon in 2 hours 54 minutes, which I celebrated by having a tattoo of a tiger's head on my back. This probably seems unremarkable now, with tattoos having become such a fashion item, but then for a thirty-eight year old doctor to have a tattoo was well ahead of the day!

All this, foolishly, was still not good enough for me, and I embarked upon an affair, which I hunted out; worse than that, I then fell in love with the woman concerned, and went on to leave Jo and my children.

Do I regret it now?

Well, I've been known to have described my action as having been reckless and stupid - but a lot of good stuff did come out of the episode. Julie and I are now married; I have two more lovely children, and have acquired Bethany - my step-daughter.

It was a circuitous and distressing route I took to get here, but without it I would not be in the happy place I am now. So - no, I do not have any regret as such. It was, however, one of those moments I discussed earlier that majorly altered the course of my life; another impulsive act that caused huge changes.

I met Alex at work.

I'd walked into an operating theatre one day, and there she was, as a new anaesthetic senior house officer. Twelve years younger than me, she immediately struck me as being attractive and interesting. Our affair started about six months later and went on for nearly three months before Jo found out about it.

I do not know how I managed to lead such a stressful existence for so long. I am sure Jo must have known what was going on for some while before the truth was out. It all unfolded at an anaesthetic department summer ball, which was bad, but was made worse by a couple of factors. Jo knew, but had guessed the wrong woman, so confronted a very surprised and affronted someone else entirely - when Alex wasn't even there! The day after that we were scheduled to be going off on a two week family holiday!

I spent the evening drinking too much, and next day awoke to an understandably frosty house. There must have been a conversation at this stage, which I cannot remember, about my intentions, and I must have told Jo that I intended leaving her and going to live with Alex.

Nevertheless, we still went on holiday together as planned, when - strangely - Jo became extremely functional about the whole affair, discussing how we were going to divide everything up between us, and other practical matters. Somewhat bizarrely, one afternoon we even had a few drinks and a friendly chat about all the things we had done together.

When we returned home, she said to me, "Are you sure you want to do this?" meaning moving out to live with Alex. I replied that - yes - that was my intention, although I do remember already thinking that perhaps it wasn't going to be such a good idea after all. I felt my 'boats were burnt', which in fact they didn't really have to be.

Alex and I already had one major background issue between us.

I had not found parenting easy, and as far as I was concerned my family was then complete. When Alex and I had one brief discussion about children, she said that of course she wanted to have them, whereas I just remained non-committal.

One might think how stupid I was; of course a 27-year-old woman is highly likely to want children from a marriage. My retort is yes that is true, but it is equally true that if a woman has a relationship with an older man who already has two children, perhaps she should be aware that he may not be quite so keen on the idea of siring even more. Neither stance is more or less valid than the other - although at this stage we were not actually planning to get married, and there was no certainty that the relationship would survive in any case.

I duly moved into her flat, and Alex and I started our life together.

Not long afterwards we rented a house.

I got to see plenty of Fiona and Alec, who came round every Tuesday after school and every other weekend. This arrangement continued until their mid-teens, when with their other commitments, arrangements needed to be more flexible.

Alex and I were married - on 7th November 1996.

The issue of us having children together, and my consistent resistance to the idea, became an ever-increasing bone of contention between us.

Before I discuss this further I must say that a desire, or otherwise, for having children is a completely separate issue to how you feel about them once they've come along. I love Heidi and Harry every bit as much as I love Fiona and Alec. I have not been a great dad in many ways to any of them, leaving the family home, as I did. Also, as I said earlier, I find children very difficult to deal with until they are old enough to have reasoned conversations with.

However, they are all very important to me and I desperately want them to have fulfilled and happy lives and to do the best that I can for them.

Alex kept insisting that she wanted several children, while I was only prepared to compromise on one, and we argued vociferously and most unpleasantly about it.

Another issue for me was that I was now a consultant, with far less out-of-hours work, whilst Alex was a registrar working a lot of on-calls, which meant her having to live at the hospital, so a lot of the childcare would fall on me. This had not been the case with Fiona and Alec, and I knew that regarding the childcare I had done when they were young, it would be a considerable understatement to say it had not come easily to me. Jo had said to me when I left, "You should definitely not have any more children." She knew, alright.

Heidi was born on 27th June 1998.

We had a boxer dog called Tommy and I spent long hours, when Alex was on-call, walking Tommy in the woods, with Heidi in her pushchair. She would fall asleep, allowing me some me-time when I returned home. I think it was around this time that my previously heavy social drinking became something of an alcohol problem. Once I had Heidi in bed on the frequent nights and whole weekends when I was alone with her, I would have more alcohol than I should have had. This spilled over into other times as well, and then even more of the time.

On the subject of pushchairs, why do they now need to look like a futuristic vehicle, cost a fortune, have pneumatic tyres and be called a 'travel system'? I see couples around town in Barnsley, who from their overall look clearly do not have much money, pushing their child in a chair that must have cost more than £300. Mind, they are smoking, eating chips, talking on their mobile phone and on occasion drinking from a can of beer, and if not that, then an energy drink; what strange priorities some people do have.

As for pneumatic tyres; why? I have seen mums stranded down the high street with a punctured pram. It's not as though the child is heavy, or perhaps I am living in the past on that one, when a slightly squashy tyre helps the chair up the curb. Alex and I did buy a three-wheel buggy for Heidi in New Zealand, before they were readily available in UK; however, that was so that I could run with her in it in the woods - not to go to Asda and show-it-off on shopping trips!

Time moved on and I thought (and hoped) that Heidi had fulfilled Alex's family needs.

She bought a horse, and at that stage it was agreed that there would be no more children, since the horse would take up quite enough of her time. Then she fell off and broke her pelvis, so for a time after that we became horseless, after it was sold.

In the spring of 2001 we went on holiday to Goa.

One evening when Heidi was playing in the toddler pool with us watching her, Alex said: "It's so sad she'll never have a sibling to play with." It was at that moment I knew the issue was never going to go away, so (impetuous as ever) I just looked at her, and said: "Right - we'll have another baby." In fact I cried a bit, knowing full-well that I wasn't at all sure how I would ever deal with another child, being aged nearly forty-five by then. I know celebrities (and others) have children much older than that, I suspect driven by their over-inflated 'egos'. I wonder how many nannies there are doing the real childcare?

If nothing else, I must at least be fertile.

Harry was born on 13th January 2002.

I like to think fertility is related to the quality of one's genes, because the better they are the more procreation would be a good thing from a natural selection point of view, but that argument is flawed when you consider the number of children produced by some very uninspiring people from completely the wrong end of the gene-pool! Of course natural selection in humans in the Western World is completely defunct, with a society that fosters all-comers and protects the strong and weak alike. I am not saying whether this is right or wrong, but it is a fact.

Soon after Harry was born we moved to a converted barn, with some land for Alex to continue her horse-dream. We needed two full-time consultant anaesthetists' salaries to fund the mortgage and everything else, so relaxed family time together was limited. I felt our lives had become very pressured.

I was in the trap that I now dislike so much, when I see it in others. However much people have, it never seems to be enough. They always want more.

Note the word 'want' and not 'need'; they don't need most of it at all.

Now that I am retired, Julie works part-time as a sister on intensive care and we have plenty of money for what we *need*. Don't get me wrong, I like and do have nice things, and we go on great holidays, but we observe sensible limits. When Julie and I got together, I could have worked all hours to pay for my divorces, as well as to buy a great big expensive house, going down the route of my colleagues, but we are very happy in our £150,000 three-bedroom semi.

What caused the collapse of my third marriage, to Alex?

First I would say that my description of our marriage is obviously my view, and I know I was a long way from being perfect in very many ways. In the end I just felt I could not cope with the life we were leading. To me it seemed like 'having our cake and eating it'. This, combined with the difficulties I had in parenting, plus my use of alcohol as an escape, was a recipe for failure.

When Alex was away at a horse event one day I remember looking at the children and clear-as-a-bell thinking, when you are older I am going to leave. Soon after, I thought if that's what's going to happen anyway, it may as well happen now, and I genuinely think that if I had stayed I would have tipped over the edge sooner rather than later. I said to a friend who visited one day, "Look at that view." Our house was on a hill in the country, and when the hill wasn't bathed in damp cloud had a fantastic view. "Well, do you know," I said, "I am so fed up with everything that even that glorious view does nothing for me."

I should add that I am sure that my excessive alcohol-intake did me no good at all, made me a poor husband and dad, and did not make me a very nice person to be with.

Heidi is now aged nearly 18 and deciding what she wants to do at university. She is keen to study something that is likely to lead to a financially secure career, and there's certainly nothing wrong with that. However, as with all my children, I just want her to be happy, and as I have said before, I know that being driven to aspire to material wealth is not necessarily the answer. Happiness has to come from within.

Heidi and Harry are like Fiona and Alec 'the apple of my eye'. I love them. Heidi is a very determined young lady, a very hard worker and a credit to herself. I know that whatever she does in life she is going to do to the utmost of her ability; who does that remind me of? I can't blame her for being like her father now, can I!

Like his older half-brother Alec, Harry is more laid back. He is 14 and loves his rugby. I very much enjoy going to watch him play and want him to do well at it. He is at the age where my rugby came unstuck, because of my loss of confidence to tackle the big boys. Harry has not inherited this problem! I am very proud of him.

When I did finally leave Alex, I moved into a rented house on my own where Heidi and Harry came to stay regularly. I became a better dad in many ways, doing more things with them and hunting out new activities for us to do together. However, Harry was then aged only three and I cannot deny that I found looking after two small children on my own very hard.

It was a couple of months after this that I started going out with Julie, whom I had known since 1991, when she was married and pregnant with Bethany. I was working as an anaesthetic registrar in Barnsley at that time, and she was, as now, a sister on the intensive care unit. By 2005 she was divorced and Bethany was aged twelve. We had always got on well at work and now we enjoyed time together away from it. I moved into her house in the September, when the lease was up on my rented property, and we were married on 14th April 2007.

Leaving my children out of the equation, Julie is the only person in my adult life I have loved more than myself. She is a wonderful wife, mother and step-mother: caring, understanding and kind. She tolerates my impulsive and obsessive all-or-nothing behaviour. This has included me training for up to thirty hours a week for Ironman and other long distance triathlons.

She has also been party to and accepted my excessive buying of bicycles, other human powered vehicles and motorbikes. She is my guide and moderator and keeps me more or less on the straight and narrow. I would never deliberately do anything to upset or harm Julie, and when I do say something or do something that does, I am devastated to the point that how bad I feel is more likely to cause an argument than my original action. This time, without a doubt it is 'until death us do part'.

228

Would this have been the case if we had been married 20 years before, and had all the stresses and strains of having a young family together, and all the issues that caused in my life? Who knows? I am just pleased that I now also have a lovely step-daughter: Bethany.

Bethany went to university in Chester to study Spanish and English. Chester is a lovely city and she has stayed there, working in a fudge shop, whilst she decides what she wants to do in the long-term.

At this point, perhaps I should write a disclaimer - the following:-

If any of the girlfriends or wives mentioned in this chapter bears any resemblance to the real persons imagined or otherwise,

that is purely coincidental and not intentional!

So what *is* my view on marriage?

It is an institution which I hear in at least 50% of cases now ends in divorce. I do not think that marriage is the problem *per se,* more that modern society is to blame. I would go further and say that marriage itself in 2015 is not the problem, the family as a whole is.

If a married couple so wish, they can each go off individually to do what they like, when they like, without it having any effect on the partner other than their absence. Once

229

children are brought into the equation that entire dynamic changes.

Many aspects of marriage were different in the past; men's and women's expectations of the institution not being the same.

It is true, but not necessarily fair, that generally speaking the man went out to work and the woman was a housewife and mother. In spare time the man did what he wanted and the wife and children either followed along or did something else.

From the day my mum married my dad to the day he died, she did just that. She cooked three meals a day, cleaned the house, looked after her children when we were there, and looked after his every need.

Now both parents usually work, competing for time off from the children, so they can have some 'me time'. Weekends are traded off one against another, and activities are squeezed into each person's spare time. Something else I see is that personal purchases are compared for cost and reciprocated.

I say all this because it is what I see my younger friends doing.

This must put an incredible strain on a marriage, which is already functioning within the ridiculous pressures that today's society imposes.

Not infrequently, and for understandable reasons, some partners cry out to themselves: "I simply cannot continue to do this anymore," - often, in a heterosexual marriage, the male.

230

The really stupid point is that he may well go off, have an affair, and start all over again with another woman. Now he has the stresses of another partner, a divorced former wife, children to take care off at a distance, and then perhaps some additional children as well. *Mea culpa.*

Another aspect of marriage that should be considered in relation to the past is that frequently circumstances meant it did not have to last as long.

Many young men went off to war and died; working conditions were poor, accidents happened and men died. Death in childbirth was not uncommon.

A woman would be at risk during her first labour from the possibility of having a pelvis that was too small to let the baby out, which would end in a horrible death from sepsis caused by the dead baby in situ. Or she would go on to have many pregnancies, increasing the risk of massive fatal post-birth bleeding - not to mention all the other causes of maternal death.

Both men and women died young from infectious disease and life expectancy, even for the relatively healthy, was much shorter. So many marriages did not have to survive as long.

We now hear of a significant increase in divorce amongst those in their fifties, sixties and seventies.

Marriage is fine.

However, beware the multitude of stresses put upon it. Whatever anyone says, men and woman are *not* the same -

either physically or mentally. We seem to have gone from the idea, quite rightly, that men and women should have equal rights, to the suggestion that they are the same: **rubbish**. In a successful marriage the husband and wife's expectations will be different. I am not saying return to the 1950s, but a little more of that would be a good thing!

10

All at Sea

ON BOTH OCCASIONS WHEN I WENT TO SEA I WAS
not very happy about it.

One might think; but he was a doctor in the Navy - what
else did he expect?

The circumstances of my appointment to *HMS Phoebe* in
1983 are already known, when having been away for nine
months out of fifteen I was due a shore-based appointment.
Instead I was sent to sea for three months.

When I was sent to *HMS Invincible* in 1989, I had
relatively recently been with the SAS for two years, during
which time I was away from home a lot. I had just completed a
year of my anaesthetic training - now my chosen medical
specialty - and wanted to be allowed to get on with it. In my
years in the Navy from 1980 to 1991, I did six out of 11 of
them in general duties, when most doctors would have done
much less than half of that in the same time scale.

So after having a short and none too good a holiday with
Christine first, I joined *HMS Phoebe* in April 1983. I enjoyed
the cruise around the Mediterranean that ensued, but I did not

gel with the average Navy officer, with whom I'd had little experience thus far.

My time in *HMS Antrim* on the way to South Georgia was short and I was with the marines, not a member of the ship's crew. The younger more junior officers on *Phoebe* were fine, a good bunch and we had fun, but the more senior officers were a dull, boring and snooty old lot.

The average middle-ranking Naval officer is not a particularly intelligent beast, and certainly no intellectual. This is because many of the bright junior officers leave to pursue a career elsewhere, and the clever ones who stay are rapidly promoted to the more senior ranks. However, I would say that even many of the latter are not that inspiring.

Royal Marine officers are different. They are not always particularly intelligent (some are very bright), but do possess a huge amount of common sense, imagination and *joie de vivre*.

This brings me to the difference between intelligence and intellect. Intelligence is the possession of knowledge, or perhaps the ability to learn and retain that knowledge. Intellect is using knowledge in a common-sense and imaginative way to change things constructively and successfully. As I have mentioned before, in relation to doctors the country's obsession with paper qualifications and academic ability means that many individuals, who are maybe not over-intelligent, but nevertheless have a well-developed intellect, are lost to society.

We left England and joined a group of NATO ships on an exercise in the Mediterranean. There was an Italian, a Turkish, and an American frigate - and us. It was a trip when I do not remember much about any exercises that we did, or about doing anything spectacular on the medical front.

I did manage to fall out with the Captain though.

He was not intellectual either, by the way.

One of the sailors had developed chicken pox. As is the way on a ship, he lived in a 'mess-deck' with about 12 other sailors. The Captain wanted me to isolate him in the sick bay. I said there was no point in doing that because the vast majority of sailors would be immune to chicken pox, having already had it as children. In addition, the most infectious time was before the spots appear, so if he was going to the sailor would probably have infected his shipmates already, and if he was placed in the sick bay then where would we be able to see our other patients? I won, and was vindicated, because no one else developed the disease.

This was not the only falling out I had with the Captain - of which more later.

I spent a lot of time annoying quite a few other officers by behaving like a Royal Marine and running round and round the upper deck to keep fit. It was 16 laps to a mile. The more they told me I was a stupid 'bootneck' the more I did it. I also wore my green beret at every opportunity, which I should not really have done because a Naval officer should only wear it when actually serving with the Marines.

The younger officers liked all this because I could get away with annoying the more senior ones, which of course they couldn't. Traditionally the doctor is supposed to show an interest in ship life and do things like go up onto the bridge to do a share of time there as what is called 'the second officer of the watch'.

Second officer is a misnomer for dog's-body, and a watch is a Navy period of time of four hours, except between 4pm and 8pm when the four hours is split into two 'watches'. I generally declined to go to the bridge, which did not please the Captain. Some really keen doctors would train to get their bridge 'watch-keeping' certificate, and then they could be in charge of their own 'watch'. This was a nuisance because it put the likes of me in an even worse light. As far as I was concerned my skill was medicine not 'watch-keeping'. I did not expect any of the other officers to come and help me out in the sick bay, so why . . .!

We called into several ports during our trip, including La Spezia in Italy, Palma in Mallorca, Monaco, Palermo in Sicily, Alexandria in Egypt - and Gibraltar. Once a ship is alongside in a port the crew gets time ashore to enjoy the sights. I made the most of my visits to all these places and each is remembered by me for different reasons.

In La Spezia a number of us caught the train to Florence in order to see that beautiful city. In the end we had too much red wine on the train and then rather than doing the galleries and museums sat in the square having some more. We had fun though.

Palma was a bit of a disaster really. I had a medical assistant who helped me on the ship and he decided he would take me on the 'run ashore' to end all 'runs ashore'. I was given such a good time that I became a nuisance and had to be put in a taxi and ferried back to the ship. On arriving back, I realised I had no money, so had to get the sailor at the top of the gangway to broadcast a message across the whole ship for someone to come to the deck and lend me some; an unavoidable little escapade that again did not go down well with the Captain, who stopped me going ashore on the first day in our next port - Alexandria.

I did better than another doctor called Colin Berry though, who on the same trip the following year actually missed the ship completely on her departure from Palma. This was a heinous crime. He had to cadge a lift on the American ship, which was still in port, and then be flown on by helicopter to rejoin his own; *big* trouble, that.

A sailor, whether he is an officer or a rating, is not allowed to return to his ship drunk. For the purposes of this definition being drunk is more or less being unable to walk up the gangway, so most of the time a sailor gets away with it even if several times over the legal driving limit.

I attained revenge for having been confined to ship on our first day at Alexandria. Before arrival in Egypt I gave talks to everyone about hygiene. Among other things I told them not to have salad, or ice in their drinks, because of dirty water, and the salad may well have been washed in water. These two pieces of advice were clearly aimed at the officers because the average sailor then was not going to eat salad or have ice in his drinks.

The first evening, accompanied by the Captain the officers went to the consulate for a reception. What did they eat and what did they have in their drinks? So - yes, the next morning they all had diarrhoea and came along begging me for treatment. "I'm afraid there isn't any," I told them (rather gleefully, I confess). "All you can do is let it run its course and stream out of you in its own good time!"

Later in our visit there was an organised trip to Cairo to see the sights there. There was not enough room on the bus for myself and three mates, so we took our own taxi and driver. We filled his boot with beer, and set off. Our driver was a real character who enjoyed taking us all over Cairo, and to places that I am sure were not on the official itinerary. We had a fantastic fun day. By the time we started heading back to Alexandria it was dark, and for some bizarre reason our driver drove up the wrong side of the dual carriageway with his lights off. He said he wanted to save the battery, but this did not explain being on the incorrect side of the road. We all just shut our eyes and went to sleep!

Palermo was only notable for us going to a restaurant and having one of the very few meals-out I have ever had in my life that was truly disgusting; almost inedible. It was made up of hot food, which was cold, and cold food that was soaked in olive oil, and I do not know what else.

On to the delights of Monaco we then sailed.

Unfortunately, we arrived there the week after the Grand-Prix had just taken place. I am sure that was planned. However, we were still well entertained. We had entry to the famous swimming pool on the circuit, enjoyed evenings out with the local wealthy, and took a day trip to Cannes. The highlight in many ways was that we were entertained by a very generous ex-sailor on his private boat; a converted Navy minesweeper. After leaving the Navy he had made his fortune in linoleum! He was incredibly generous and entertained nearly all the sailors on different days during our stay there.

The final stop of the trip was a ten-day ship's maintenance period in Gibraltar. Christine flew out and stayed with me whilst I was there. It was not too good a time really, because she was already suggesting that our marriage was over.

Going to *HMS Invincible* in February 1989 turned out to be the beginning of the end of my Naval career. I had completely grown out of the institutionalisation from which I had suffered ever since boarding school, and it had since become replaced by a rebellious nature and a firm belief that regardless who the individual might be, respect was not an automatically imbued right, but something which needed to be earned.

In many areas within the Forces, a doctor was able to get away with a degree of such scepticism. It might even be seen as a useful quality, but not in a Navy ship, which could be a pretty humourless place if the truth be known. Certainly not in *Her Majesty's Ship, Invincible!*

When I boarded *Invincible* she was in Portland, training her personnel for the high seas and any possible situation that might present. The Portland staff inspected every aspect of the ship and her performance, in a very 'jobsworth' way.

By this time I had served with the Marines for nearly three years, including a war and two arctic winters, and had been a doctor for the SAS for two years, deployed on real missions, and so playing sailors and being supervised by staff with limited credentials didn't go down well with me.

An early report from the medical inspection team - not doctors, but medical assistants - said I was not taking things seriously enough. Substitute for that the fact that I questioned their knowledge and suggested that their way of wanting things to be done might not necessarily be the best - and that might have been a more accurate observation.

I was now a Surgeon-Lieutenant-Commander. With a good confidential personal report from the Captain of a sea-going ship my chances of promotion to Surgeon-Commander would have been significantly enhanced, but after less than a month in *Invincible* any chance of that was clearly dead in the water. Thankfully though, I found two soul-mates in the ship; Al Cronin and Pete Dawson. They were also both commando-trained and had a similar view to me regarding the ways of the Navy. We were also all keen fitness freaks; Al even having a gym he had set up in one of the areas of the ship. There was also a Concept rowing machine, an exercise bike, and a large flight deck to run round. I reverted to my 'at-sea' mode and trained two or three times a day, often with Al and Pete.

There were two of us doctors on *Invincible*; the other a surgeon. The idea was from days gone by when the Navy had proper aircraft carriers, with the incumbent greater potential for serious injuries to occur. It allowed the doctors to carry out operations on casualties and sick sailors at sea if needs be, rather than having to divert the ship. However, now that ships had helicopters - *Invincible* had quite a few which could swiftly evacuate sick sailors - the concept was out-dated. During the whole of my year on board I administered just two anaesthetics.

I mention the other doctor because he was nothing like me; he took everything very seriously and dropped me in the mire on several occasions. He was also senior to me in rank, and therefore my immediate boss, which meant even more nails in my promotion coffin, and my entire career in the Navy.

It was early on in my time in the ship that I had one of my most memorable helicopter excursions.

I had to escort a sick sailor from a Polaris submarine. These submarines and their Trident successors carry a doctor to reduce the risk of the submarine having to surface to evacuate casualties. It is hoped that the doctor will be able to manage most eventualities, because surfacing compromises the position of the boat, thereby allowing the Russians and others to know where our nuclear deterrent is located.

On this occasion evacuation was required, which involved me being winched down in high seas onto the conning-tower of the submarine! When the signal had first come in requesting help, by the look on his face I could tell that my senior medical colleague had no desire to do the job himself. I don't blame him you already know what I think of flying in helicopters.

Clearly, I survived to tell the tale and I suppose I should be pleased to be able to add 15-minutes spent on a Polaris submarine to my list of life experiences. It was somewhat annoying that the ailing sailor did not really look that ill at all, but not as annoying as it would have been for the Captain of the submarine!

Later in the year came the trips away, mainly four months around the east coast of the USA. We left Portsmouth and our first port visit thereafter was Wilmington, North Carolina. Of course between each visit there were a lot of Navy-type exercises, but leaving those aside, I had a great time.

Pete Dawson was the ship's liaison officer, which involved him sorting everything out for the visit.

When a ship is alongside in a foreign port, there are always hordes of locals who come forward to offer hospitality to her crew. The ship always holds a cocktail party hosted by the officers on the first night to entertain local dignitaries. This and a lot of other activities need overseeing by the liaison officer, both before the ship arrives and during her visit. The LO needs to keep the Captain informed about what is going on, so Pete left the ship a few days early by helicopter in order to make these advance preparations. By the time we arrived he had hired himself an open-top Mustang at the Navy's expense, so at least we had our wheels sorted for the visit.

During the cocktail party another officer and I were chatting up a couple of the local women. The best way to describe them would be 'Thelma and Louise'. Speaking with a great southern drawl they invited us out for lunch the next day, which we accepted, and were picked up in a massive open-top Cadillac and taken to a restaurant where they also insisted on paying the bill! They (or their husbands at least) were obviously wealthy. It was hilarious, having them show us and our English accents off like a couple of pets. After lunch they took us shopping for new handbags and dresses; not for us - for them - all of which was completely innocent and great fun.

Then it was back to sea again, before our next visit - Fort Lauderdale, in Florida.

Whenever we were in port, Pete, Al and I would search out a local gym in which to be able to work-out; usually managing to wangle ourselves complimentary passes for the length of our visit. In Fort Lauderdale we were so pleased about the gym we'd found that we were late for the cocktail party and got quite a bit of hassle for it from one of the senior officers, but once the dust had settled, the rest of that stay was spent mostly in the gym or on the beach.

For the next visit - San Juan, in Puerto Rico - I was the liaison officer. Accordingly, I duly went ashore a few days early.

One of my main tasks was to ensure that the ship's allocated berth was deep enough. Could I find this information, despite many visits to port authorities? No - I could not! So in the end I gave up.

The morning the ship was due to arrive I was nervous and up early. I went for a run and fell over and then was unable to stop the grazes on my knee bleeding through my trousers. It was a bit fraught. I stood by the berth watching *Invincible* arrive, my ear acutely attuned to any sound of scraping, which would have been the undoubted prelude to my subsequent court martial, because there couldn't possibly be any crime worse than being the cause of the Royal Navy's premier vessel running aground!

Thank God though, my luck held.

I found that liaison job a big hassle, with stuff to do all the time and a Captain pestering me for information, so although it was not often that I looked forward to going to sea, I was pleased when it was over and the time came for us to leave Puerto Rico.

Next we stayed alongside in Jacksonville, Florida, for six weeks at Christmas.

The crew could either bring their family out for two weeks, or go home for two, arranged so that at least half the sailors were on board at any one time to look after the ship and do the required maintenance - our reason for the long stay.

I chose to go home.

However, I *was* in Florida for Christmas. And it snowed! Some of us had met a young lady at an on-board party before then, who'd invited four of us out to her parents' house for Christmas, so we were well looked after.

Later I went with her and some of the other officers to Walt Disney World Resort in Orlando for a few days, this time staying at her parents' *other* house! That is the only visit to Disney, Florida, I have made ... and it was without children!

Early in our visit, I had been to the gym and was jogging back to the ship when a woman shouted out to me. Pete and I had chatted-up a couple of US Navy wives at the recent cocktail party, whose husbands were away. "Come for a coffee," she cried. This would be the second time a woman got to show me her bedroom while her husband was away, when my response to the veiled implication was to remain impeccably faithful to my wife!

Our next two stops were Norfolk, Virginia - and Barbados. In Norfolk, Pete, Al and I were invited to dinner at a local family's house. Our host was an ex-US Navy officer who was a very bright man it seemed. He was cagey about what he now did, but it felt like he was interested in recruiting us for the CIA!

Whilst in Norfolk, Al and I hired a car and visited Washington DC together. It is a beautiful and interesting city, and we had a great time seeing its sights.

In Barbados, Pete and I cycled round the island, an event which was to rekindle my passion for cycling and bicycles.

On our return home it was time for me to leave the ship.

I went along to receive my final report from the Captain, which was not good: He described me as being 'a poisonous influence' in the Wardroom and followed by saying I should not go to sea again. Pretty much career limiting for a Naval doctor!

The Captain of a ship is only occasionally allowed into the Wardroom, by invitation, so someone had clearly been reporting to him my cynical remarks about the Navy and the ship.

When I left the ship, it occurred to me to query to myself why the Captain would not have confronted me earlier about what I'd been saying if he didn't approve? I would then have had a chance to modify my behaviour, but I guess, I am not sure I would have! Only one further factor was now needed for me to realise that it was time for me to leave the Navy.

I now returned to anaesthesia, first at the *RNH Haslar*, and then on secondment to the NHS in Southampton. The latter was incredibly busy and challenging. I dealt with many difficult patients on my own and learnt a huge amount. I decided that if anaesthesia was what I wanted to do, then the NHS was the place for me and was where I should be able to reach my full potential.

And so now, I duly resigned from the Navy.

I do not know what it is like nowadays, but in those days the Navy took it very personally when you suggested that you felt you would be better suited elsewhere. I was summoned to see a surgeon commodore, (in fact it was my boss of old; then Surgeon Commander Wilkes), who told me how stupid I was being. However, despite the financial loss of an immediate pension if I had continued serving for just a few years more, I knew I was making the right decision.

My personal reasons apart, the writing was on the wall for everyone because the Forces' Medical Services were soon to be reduced dramatically. In just a short space of time all the

Forces hospitals would be closed and become mere wings of NHS hospitals.

Interestingly, many of those Navy doctors who looked down their noses at me when I left were also packing up and leaving themselves, less than a year after I had done.

While I was in Southampton was when the First Gulf War had been brewing, and I had itchy feet to be out there amongst it. After I'd resigned, the Navy doctor responsible for deciding who went where telephoned me and said, "Swinhoe - you have resigned, so as a punishment we are sending you out to The Gulf."

Whether his remark was an attempt at humour I don't know, but it typified the attitude of many doctors who joined but then moaned about it if and when things began to become a bit tough. Why should going to the Gulf be considered a punishment? Idiot! The Gulf was just the place I wanted to be.

The Royal Army Medical Corps had already shrunk significantly, and was struggling to find enough medical support for the conflict. They were putting together an extra field hospital from elements of the Territorial Army (TA) and Reservists. They were a motley bunch. The Navy agreed to send the Commando Medical Support to bolster the hospital, and I was to be part of this element.

A great chance for me to wear my green beret one last time before leaving the Navy.

Our group met up in Plymouth after Christmas 1990 for training, a lot of which involved chemical warfare defence, since everyone was convinced that Saddam Hussein had chemical weapons he would use. We were also given numerous vaccines, since biological warfare was another possibility. Amongst others, I was inoculated against anthrax.

We had multiple final nights out in Plymouth before flying to Saudi Arabia. The night the war started found us camped in tents in Riyadh. Air raids on Iraq began and I remember when listening to Forces Radio the disc jockey announcing, "For the population of Baghdad," before then going on to play Phil Collins's *Something in the Air Tonight*.

Soon we moved to our tented hospital in northern Saudi Arabia.

I made two great friends in the Gulf - Mike Stewart, an Army surgeon, being one of them. He and I were a surgical team together. We were both desperate to get nearer the front line and volunteered to move forward once the land war started, but nothing came of that. So instead we did about 20 operations in the hospital, mostly on pathetic looking Iraqi prisoners of war. They were conscripts who had been left in the forward trenches, whilst the more elite Iraqi troops had run for Baghdad and relative safety.

The rest of the time Mike and I went for runs out in the desert and did other physical stuff with Rod Dunn, our other mate. The three of us annoyed everyone as much as we could, and once the cold, wet and unpleasant weather improved - sunbathed.

There were some real oddballs in the hospital, from all sorts of backgrounds, which is why Mike, Rod and I couldn't help 'taking the mick' a lot. They were an uninspiring bunch and the three of us did not tolerate fools well!

I had first met Rod in Norway in 1982, when he was doing an attachment to the Royal Marines as a medical student. That year we went on a downhill skiing trip to Sweden. As NATO troops we shouldn't have been there, so I had to deal with any injuries without involving the Swedes for fear of causing a diplomatic upset. So then Rod only went and broke his leg of course. I wrapped it in a big bandage and slapped him on a train back to Norway on his own, being prevented from accompanying him in case there were any other casualties; or, more like, I wanted to finish my ski trip!

Rod later lost the end of some of his fingers from frostbite on the top of Annapurna and after that did Special Boat Service selection, which by then was combined with SAS selection. He should have passed, but came unstuck when he was caught getting food from a farmhouse whilst on the combat survival phase, which was a completely taboo thing to do. He is now a plastic surgeon in Salisbury.

At the end of The Gulf War, we threw a little celebration, which included some sketches by some of the personnel. Rod gave a mock horse-race commentary, using various people's names, which caused a bit of an in-drawing of breath when he said: "And we are at the last and Captain X has cleared it in the lead, which is a little surprising since he has no spine". The officer referred to was quite an important member of staff, or so *he* thought, anyway.

Before being sent to the First Gulf War, some of the Reservists tried to avoid call-up with the excuse that they had signed-up to fight the Russians in Europe, not Saddam Hussein in the desert - as if come-the-event the former undertaking would have been any easier! This was ridiculous, of course; they had taken the Queen's Shilling and thus accepted the commitment to go wherever she sent them.

After the conflict a disproportionate number of TA and Reservists appeared in the media claiming to have Post Traumatic Stress Disorder (PTSD), and to be suffering from the effects of the tablets we took to combat the consequences of exposure to chemical weapons, and the vaccines given to protect us from biological weapons - the whole questionable issue being referred to as Gulf War Syndrome.

PTSD is a genuine and terrible condition from which many really do suffer, so it was a shame to see its integrity damaged by those hoping to get a fast buck out of it.

This is also true of other conditions 'used by shirkers' too of course. Many people suffer from true Chronic Fatigue Syndrome (ME), but as a condition – the diagnosis of which relies entirely on the patients' history – it is open to massive abuse.

There is a physical condition called fibromyalgia, the symptoms of which are essentially 'pain all over', but there are no concrete tests to diagnose it. I am sure many are genuinely suffering, but many are not, and by claiming they have it manage to live off the welfare state for many years.

I will admit though that the NAPS tablets prescribed to mitigate the effects of some gases did make me feel odd and stopped my normal 'morning glory' male erection - not that I needed one out there - so after it became clear that the threat was minimal, I stopped taking them.

I would not want anyone to think that what I have written about some of those who served in the Gulf in 1991 means that I have anything other than huge respect for our Armed Forces. Today, our Army, Navy and Air Force have seen year-on-year escalation in their commitment, concurrently mirrored by continual cuts in their budget. A lot of the fat will have been weeded out, but now there are not enough frontline servicemen for the tasks the politicians want them to undertake.

We all want to sleep safe in our beds at night, but want it all ways. Low taxes so that we can continue to lead our lives of excess, and enough servicemen and a big enough NHS to keep us all safe and healthy.

The general public ought to realise we can't have everything we want, and accept choices need to be made. But they will not, and nor will the politicians raise taxes to pay for what is required, because it would be political suicide. So we will carry on along the same route until something really gives and everything falls apart. I have fantastic regard for the modern soldier, sailor and airman and would gladly pay more tax if I thought it would go to defending our realm. I would not want the same money ploughed into the NHS though, for reasons that will become clear later.

I returned from the Gulf and finished my Navy career at RNH Haslar.

I had a fantastic time in the Navy and would not want my cynicism to make anyone think otherwise. I did 'see the world' as they say, and was lucky to have been able to do so at government expense, but I would defend myself by saying that the Navy also had a very good time out of me. What I did find was that I was happier working with the Marines, and during time I spent with the Army, than I was with the 'Real Navy' aboard ship at sea. I really did find the average Navy officer to be extremely pompous, dull and lacking in intellect.

11

22nd Special Air Service Regiment

BEFORE PROCEEDING FURTHER LET, ME TELL YOU that an SAS soldier - known as a *trooper* - is not some kind of superhuman, ninja-like action hero as portrayed in films and often suggested in factual programmes as well. They do not have the abilities of a Jason Statham and his contrived activities in *Transporter*; such people do not and cannot exist, in real life. But an SAS trooper is totally committed, determined, strong and extremely able physically, and will demonstrate considerable endurance, particularly in adverse conditions.

In 1985 I volunteered to be seconded to the SAS as one of their medical officers. In many ways, I am not sure why, because my experience with this undoubtedly elite band of brothers in and around South Georgia in 1982, had not been a particularly good one. I considered them to have been foolhardy in their reconnaissance attempts prior to the landing.

They would not listen to valid advice from others, and they ignored the risks from the weather.

However, I saw the chance to work with them as an exciting prospect, and certainly it was another personal goal to be achieved. I had a very interesting time during my two years attachment with 'those who dare, win' - and met some great people, but I also met some difficult individuals.

The SAS were based at Stirling Lines in Hereford. I say were because I believe the camp has now moved to a new location, although still in the vicinity. The base was named after their WWII founder, David Stirling.

I was preceded at my Hereford posting by another Navy doctor who was a very different kind of person to me. He was a 'networker' with the 'gift of the gab', two qualities (I suppose they are?) I have never possessed. I think he integrated himself into the role better than I did. He, I believe, as a result of his personality, was treated as an interesting, but outlying addition to the Regiment. In contrast, I wanted to be an active and integrated member of the team, like I'd been with the Marines - but this proved impossible for me to achieve.

The attached ranks with the Marines do the Commando Course, which if they pass entitles them to wear the Green Beret and become part of the Royal Marines' family. Those seconded to the SAS to provide the supernumerary skills they require, are not expected to attempt their extremely rigorous selection process, and because of this are very much treated as 'attached outsiders' during their tour.

It is fair to say that the SAS would probably be unable to find sufficient people to fill their skill-shortages, who were tough enough to endure and pass their selection process, but since that is not possible, to then, in my experience, dismissively treat them as second-class citizens does not seem right.

Royal Signals personnel attached to the SAS do their own separate selection course, which does not entitle them to wear the badge.

With the SAS, it is their famous winged-dagger cap-badge which denotes successful completion of selection, not their sandy coloured beret. After a period of probation with them, attached personnel are issued with the sand-beret to wear, but only displaying their own regiment's cap badge, which in my case was the Royal Navy's wreathed crown-and-anchor.

Because the commanding officer didn't like me to wear my green one, they gave me my sand-beret early. They wouldn't have minded if I'd worn my navy-blue one, but there seemed to be something about the Royal Marine green that got up the SAS's noses!

There is the scene set.

Then, there were two medical officers with the SAS, and performed in conjunction with my RAMC colleague my work covered a variety of areas.

I looked after the everyday medical needs of the personnel in the camp, including those eager and exhausted aspirants in the process of undertaking the SAS selection course.

We were on standby in case of serious injuries in the close-quarter battle range, where in hostage-rescue training live ammunition is used, as a result of which there'd been a death there just the previous year.

I went on exercises abroad to provide medical support, as well as on operations at-home-and-abroad.

One of the doctors was always on-call for anti-terrorist operations, which included being in attendance on any exercises carried out in conjunction with the police, and these took place fairly frequently.

I also supervised and supported the training of SAS medics. Their theoretical knowledge was taught in camp, before the troopers were sent on attachment to hospitals around the country. Every SAS trooper within a section has at least two specialist skills, one option of which is being a trained medic.

The two years I spent with them took me all over the world and to all sorts of places, where I saw a lot and learnt a lot about all sorts of new things, and about other people, as well as about myself. I did re-witness some of the attitudes I had seen

257

in the South Atlantic, but the vast majority of the time I saw a very professional bunch of soldiers working incredibly effectively in a variety of extreme environments.

What now follows is just some of all that.

Soon after I arrived in Hereford I needed to re-qualify as a military parachutist. This would mean that I would be able to jump if required, and receive a 'princely sum', in the region of £1.50 a day extra in my pay! *Parachute pay* is only paid if a serviceman is in a role in an operational unit. I had not parachuted since I finished the course five years before. I did not want to admit to this, in case it meant repeating the course. So I simply asked the parachute jump instructor (PJI) for a date when I could do some qualifying jumps. The night before I was sure something awful would happen to me, since I could not remember many, or indeed any, of the drills, including how to check and fit my parachute. All I could recall was that you jumped out and usually had a painful landing! The possibility of death crossed my mind!

In the event I went with a group of SAS guys to Weston-on-Green in Oxfordshire and did four jumps; two from a gas-filled balloon (there is a metal cage suspended below to jump from) and two from the tailgate of a Chinook helicopter. The landings were not even as painful as I suspected they would be from my memories of old.

There is nothing glamorous about military parachuting. The jump is from 600 to 800 feet, and the parachute is opened by a line fixed to the aircraft, or balloon. There is just enough time to check the chute has opened properly (and pull the reserve if necessary) and then, looking down, the ground will be rushing up towards you. Landing should include a controlled roll to limit the impact, but it is simply a relief to land in any fashion, with limbs intact! A balloon jump is worst, since it means standing on the edge and simply stepping off; very 'cold-blooded'. Leaving an aircraft is easier, because you are following the guy in front and hesitation will more than likely result in a push from the person behind!

So I qualified for my extra pay and I was never required to parachute again. So that day of strife earnt me about £1000 in my two years in Hereford!

I went with 'B' Squadron on an exercise to a country in southern Africa, the name of which was secret, although I am not sure whether it is still covered by the Official Secrets Act. The South Africans produced a press accusation that we were training the local army. We weren't.

Most of the Squadron was based in a small town out in the bushlands.

The SAS is divided into squadrons the size of a regular Army battalion, and the squadrons then into troops. Each squadron has an air troop, a boat troop, a mobility troop and a mountain troop.

An air troop specialises in parachuting, a boat troop in the water, a mobility troop in beefed-up land vehicles, and a mountain troop - obvious. Our air troop was not based with the rest of us, but at an airfield in the capital.

I spent some time up in the hills with Mountain Troop. During this time one of our troopers fell and I was helicoptered up onto a cliff to try to save him. He was actually already dead, and I nearly ended up the same way when the local pilot struggled to keep the helicopter in position as I abseiled down and landed very close to the edge.

I also made a local tribesman happy by draining a large amount of fluid from a gargantuan cyst around his testes, which then unfortunately returned, as they will tend to unless removed by proper surgery.

One week was also spent with Boat Troop out on a massive river where we saw a lot of wildlife at close quarters, particularly hippos, crocodiles and snakes. One hippo came far too close, and took a large bite out of the back of one of our inflatable boats, leaving me unsurprised to learn that hippos are the cause of more human deaths than any other animal in Africa.

We slept in hammocks by the river, which considering the number of crocodiles about seems a little crazy, but at least we were off the ground!

Regarding snakes, I went to an amateur snake demonstration whilst I was in the base camp, performed by a local soldier. He seemed to enjoy baiting them and then letting them loose. I was dressed in shorts and flip-flops and had to stand perfectly still whilst a cobra crawled between my feet. Still, I was luckier than the guy whose leg it chose to crawl up! The second time I watched the demo I stood up on a water bowser!

Another anxious moment occurred when we used a local aircraft to transport us back to base. The pilot was looking more and more nervous as we piled all our kit and ourselves into the small plane. The runway was short and on mud and grass. We rumbled down it slowly, and painfully gaining speed; significantly overloaded. I am not kidding you, when I say I saw the red flag that marked the end of the runway out of the back of the plane with us definitely still not in the air. Fortunately, shortly after we lifted off!

Swinhoe had escaped death again!

I had a lot of trouble with the water in camp. It was pumped straight from the river to a water tower. Bilharzia, a water-borne disease caused by a nasty worm which invades various parts of the body, was (and always is) rife in the area. The worm burrows in through the skin, so washing as well as drinking-water needs to be sterilised. Drinking-water was easy; I could fill the bowser and add chlorine, but I could never persuade the locals to leave the water-pump off and only fill the tower when it was empty, so that I could sterilise the water after refilling the tank. In the end I gave up and just crossed my fingers. In all honesty though, one would be most unlucky to catch the disease in the shower - unlike swimming in the river bathed in water.

On the final exercise I was given one of Mobility Troop's 'Desert Rats'-style Land Rovers to bomb around in, with one of the signallers, and it was great fun driving it through the African bushland.

The whole trip was terrific and I enjoyed myself very much with 'B' Squadron, being marred only somewhat, because I was unable to get on a safari and see more of the wildlife. It had all been planned for our last few days, but there was an incident and the Squadron's Officer Commanding (OC) stopped all trips away. I think there was some history; on a previous tour there had been some trouble and he'd been put on a 'last warning' to keep his guys in order. The OC was a good bloke, so I am sure he had his reasons.

Whilst in camp I had an impromptu stag night, which for some reason that now escapes me involved drinking a lot of Pimms.

If anyone can work hard and play hard those SAS guys certainly could, and I became friends with a couple of hard men who'd 'been round the block a few times'. I wish I could still remember their names.

One was the Squadron's Quartermaster-Sergeant, and the other a sergeant with the signallers who were with us. The former taught me some basic, mean, self-defence moves to use if ever I was in a tight spot. I have remembered them to this day, always knowing that if the need arose I would have no compunction in using them.

The signals sergeant was a great old-fashioned salt-of-the-earth soldier who looked like a character straight out of *Zulu*. Unfortunately, he had, or was developing, a problem with alcohol. On our return he decided to leave the Army, and although I hope not, I rather suspect that in all probability he would have met a sticky end from the booze.

I ended up asleep in a dustbin at the end of the night, with my bum in it, and my body and legs meeting in the full pike position. To the OC's surprise I dared to continue the action with these guys again next morning when we headed off to a local safari lodge to continue the celebration. I am not sure how I survived it actually!

It was on my return to UK from that trip that Jo and I were married, when as referred to previously I was then called out on an operation immediately afterwards and she stayed at home unpacking boxes in our new house while I went off to the Mediterranean.

Intelligence had been received that a senior terrorist, or freedom-fighter depending on one's point-of-view, was going to fly across the area. The plan was for the RAF to force down his plane, which the SAS would assault, if the bad guy didn't give himself up peacefully.

We were on the airfield making plans for this operation, when one of the 'powers-that-be' dreamed up an additional brilliant idea.

They thought it could be beneficial to take the opportunity to acquire extra information about the inside of the plane and its passengers after it had landed. It was decided they would request that the doctor (me!) should be allowed on to the plane to ensure that everyone was alright and not in need of any medical assistance. I would have a good look round, and then be allowed to leave; as if! It was more likely by far that I would either be kidnapped or shot, a foreshortened second marriage being my most likely outcome.

I was not impressed, but would have had no choice in the matter had my services been thus required. Thankfully the whole affair turned into nothing more than a wild goose chase, and after a few days in the sun we returned to England and I'd nicely managed to top-up the suntan I'd recently acquired for myself in Africa.

Ironically, not long after that I went on an anti-terrorist exercise with one of the squadrons and the Metropolitan police, at a railway station. During the course of this exercise there was a need, as part of the scenario, for the doctor to go aboard the high-jacked train. After the mock-terrorists had become very angry with me and accused me of spying, they decided they would 'hang me' on the platform. They took me off the train and stood me on a stool with a noose around my neck, the rope hanging over a metal beam. It was at this stage that the lads - quite rightly, too, in my view - initiated their assault. This brought the exercise to a close, much to the police's annoyance, not I suspect because they loved hanging (pun!) around on railway stations at weekends, but because it cut short the length of their overtime payments!

On another occasion during my time in Hereford, I was sent to administer medical attention to some foreign soldiers undergoing secretive SAS training, on location somewhere in Kent. My brief was to go to London - specifically Pimlico tube station - and there meet a member of the secret services. He would be dressed in a pin-stripe suit and be carrying a copy of *The Economist* tucked under his left arm.

As always, I arrived early.

As a Royal Marine corporal told me on my Commando Course; "in order to be on time it is necessary to be five minutes early. Therefore, if you are not five minutes early you are late!" I have stuck to this sage advice ever since and sorely wish everyone else would do the same!

I went and stood outside the station.

A black car drew into the kerbside and parked on a double yellow line.

A man got out of the passenger-seat dressed in a pin-stripe suit.

The man closed the door, walked a few steps, stopped and turned back.

He re-opened the door, reached in, and - hey-presto - re-emerged having retrieved a copy of *The Economist*, which was promptly then tucked under his left arm; all very covert, I'm sure!

We duly met, exchanged cursory pleasantries, and headed off to our venue.

This little tale demonstrates the lack of truth there must be in the fact that when we think of the secret services we understandably conjure up images of 'Bond films', or 'Spooks'. In the same way that SAS troopers are perceived as being indestructible ninjas; real life just ain't like that!

I am sure there are some very impressive field agents, but the majority of personnel are simply human beings with a set of skills that make them suitable for such employment. I have always maintained that no job is particularly difficult and with suitable training many of us could do most of them.

However, certain occupations do carry a reputation well beyond reality.

In medicine, neuro-surgeons and cardiac surgeons are seen as having a reputation one step removed from God, but please let me assure you that they are no more skilful at what they do than many others, who pursue seemingly less glamorous specialties. Doctors choose which branch of medicine they wish to practise, and having entered it the vast majority will complete the required training and become consultants. So none of the specialties can be that difficult - can they?

This must be true in light of the huge limitations in the medical school selection process, which has been discussed already.

My next trip away was to New Zealand.

We flew the 12,000 miles out there and 12,000 back again in a C140 Hercules transport aircraft; a great RAF workhorse with four lovely turbo-prop engines that give one such a reassuring sense of power and safety, especially knowing that in an emergency it has the capability of flying on just one of those engines - but a Hercules is not the most comfortable form of transport.

The journey took us five days on the way out, and six coming back. It was great really; we were in the air during the day, and then in the late afternoon landed somewhere for a hotel stopover and a party!

We stopped at Bahrain, Colombo, Singapore and Perth, before landing in Auckland on the way out, and had an extra stop-over in Cyprus on our way back. And there's no trouble with luggage weights on a Hercules transport aircraft!

Julie and I have just booked our holiday in Spain for next year, and on our Easy Jet flights a mere 20kgs of luggage cost an extra £40 each! We all know that the more weight there is on board, the more fuel is consumed, therefore the more it costs the airline for the plane to reach its destination. However, how come Julie and I are required to pay for 20kgs of luggage when we will be at least 20kgs lighter than many of our fellow passengers? Neither do we take the mick by carrying with us the allowable free 10kgs in a cabin-bag, which looks like a suitcase and in reality, is. In the past, quite rightly, the bag allowed in the cabin was simply for things that might be needed on the flight. Not anymore!

Like most things, the solution is obvious. I would have no objection to having my weight checked at the airport (they check everything else!), and we should then be charged per kilo, which would include our body weight. Perhaps there should be some kind of handicap system for those who are naturally bigger, as opposed to fatter, and I don't mean body-builders on steroids! I refer to the Steve Redgrave's of this world.

Whilst on the subject of holidays there has been a prolonged debate going on about the site of the new runway at Gatwick, or Heathrow, or even somewhere else. Like anything considered undesirable but necessary, no one wants it on their own doorstep.

To me, if it goes to an existing airport site, local residents should only have the right to complain if they meet both the following criteria:-

First - that they lived there before an airport was built, which is unlikely. If someone buys a house near an airport they have already accepted its existence. There will be noise and pollution; the advantage is that presumably the purchase-price will have reflected this by being cheaper than the norm. There are always choices.

The second criterion is that the person does not use commercial aircraft. If they do they are part of the problem (our need for more planes and runways) and have no right to complain. One cannot have it all ways, but such is human nature that many of us think that we should.

I loved New Zealand, and as a result of that trip nearly emigrated there in 1993. In fact, I received a telephone call in the middle of the night more or less offering me a job, but it was in a very remote location and understandably Jo wasn't keen.

When I first started out in anaesthetics the plan was for me to be a GP/anaesthetist somewhere remote. There were a lot of jobs around like that back then, and New Zealand would have been a good choice. Several doctors would work as general practitioners, with each of them also having a specialist skill to use in the small local hospital. One would be an anaesthetist, another a surgeon; there would be an obstetrician too, and perhaps a paediatric specialist. This plan, in fact came to me from my trip to Africa with 'B' squadron, where near our base there had been such a hospital. However, I lost sight of that intention somewhere along the line.

For much of my stay in New Zealand the PJI and I swanned around the South Island organising and preparing drop-zones and medical cover for the parachute insertion of SAS troops. We were not very busy work-wise, so there was a lot of time for us to explore the beauty of the place. I returned to the North Island in 1998 for a holiday, and had a good tour round there on that occasion. It was just as beautiful as the South. So I would thoroughly recommend a NZ visit to anyone, with a pretty sound knowledge of the place to justify that recommendation.

My final tour with the SAS was to be some more time spent in a sub-zero Norwegian winter.

I loved going back there and doing some more time in the field on skis. I did go through Lom again whilst I was there, and - yes - it did cross my mind to pay a courtesy call to the doctor's wife, but I felt pretty sure that she would have moved on by then; not with her husband necessarily!

On my return to Hereford my eldest daughter Fiona was born, so my story has now reached 12th March 1987 again.

I enjoyed my time with the SAS, but it is a great shame and sad to me that I was not able to integrate more, or be accepted into their inner circle.

Whilst serving with them I grew a beard, which unlike his Army or RAF counterparts a Navy officer is quite entitled to do. Despite the fact that for reasons of disguise some troopers grew their hair long and looked like hippies when working in the anti-terrorist team, the Commanding Officer told me my beard had to go. So why was my perfectly legal non-conformity unacceptable? I never did find out.

I did meet a lot of really lovely guys, who treated me with considerable respect. I have always said that respect is not a right but needs to be earned, and I don't think that I consciously did anything that should have brought my commitment to them into question, hence my puzzlement that quite a few of them chose to be so cold and distant.

Whilst we were in New Zealand there was a story that I'd passed a remark to one of them that implied he might have been malingering. It was not true and was simply a misinterpretation of what I had said. I was with 'G' Squadron at the time, comprised in the main of soldiers from Guards' regiments, and not renowned as being the friendliest of squadrons.

Let me tell a story that is engrained in Royal Marine folklore. It is probably apocryphal, but still fun. There was once a Royal Marine officer, who spent a brief period with a Guards' Regiment. Quaint custom; but if a Guards' officer does not wish to be spoken to at breakfast, he wears his hat. Such a guy was sitting at table munching his Wheaty-Bangs one morning when the Royal Marine came and sat next to him; soon after doing so, asking; "Would you mind passing me the marmalade please?" To which there was no response.

"Would you please pass the marmalade,' he asked again.

Again - no response.

"PLEASE WON'T YOU PASS THE MARMALADE?"

The Guards' officer slowly raised one eyebrow, and said: "Do you not know that when a Guards' officer wears his hat at breakfast it means he does not wish to be spoken to?"

Whereupon the Royal Marine exasperatedly flung back his chair, quickly stood up, raised his right leg and smashed it straight down into the Guards officer's cornflakes, sending shards of broken china, splashed milk and crunched-up cereal flying everywhere.

"Is that so? And do you know that when a Royal Marine plants his steel-shod boot in your cornflakes it means PASS THE FUCKING MARMALADE!"

Jo, Fiona and I left Hereford in July 1987 and set up a new home in Plymouth, where I started my anaesthetic career at the Naval Hospital, where I had not worked since 1980. We had a very enjoyable year there, which was busy for me both at work and on the social front. I was learning my new anaesthetic skills, as well as studying for the first two parts of the required specialist exams. At the same time, Jo and I made new friends and had a great time with them. I remember always running to and from work, being on-call frequently and a lot parties.

Steve Squires was a senior registrar in anaesthetics, who became my mentor at work. Steve is one of those people, who can walk into a room, say something and upset everybody without realising it! We had very similar outlooks on life. He, and his tolerant wife Penny, were a significant part of our circle of friends.

I remember Steve setting off the fire alarm in the hospital Wardroom at the end of one raucous evening. This was clearly taboo, particularly since we had been warned-off doing it by Steve Merrill, another anaesthetist, who was the Mess President. The Mess President is a senior officer, who is responsible for the smooth running of the Wardroom. The prank had been done on several occasions before and the fire brigade were fed up with the false alarms; not to mention the cost of their services. Steve Merrill was a good guy and 'got us off the hook'; I had been implicated in the outrage as well!

Me, your honour? No!

We frequently had dinner parties with our friends during our year in Plymouth. After too much alcohol, late in the evening, we would often play silly games. 'Twister' was popular and resulted in a lot of laughs.

Andy and Rosie Burgess, another great couple, were often contorted on the 'Twister' mat. Andy was a junior anaesthetist at the same stage of training as me; a fun guy to work, and to share a lot of laughs with. His wife Rosie was great fun too. She had to take considerable 'stick' for being a staunch Labour supporter, probably made worse, because this was the less than successful Kinnock era! She even went to the Labour conference that year. I have no idea where it was held. It wasn't the one where Kinnock fell over on the beach, but it still gave us plenty of ammunition to taunt her with!

My first year in anaesthetics put the writing on the wall for my leaving the Navy; cemented later by my trip to sea in *Invincible* and what ensued. I have very fond memories of that year in Plymouth. It is a shame, that rather like those I mentioned from the Old Lodge in Alverstoke, I have lost touch with the friends I made. It is just not possible in life to stay close to the many people with whom you have shared a bond. However, I do know that if we met again we would still enjoy each other's company and the years would fall away.

I have noticed when I have met people again after a long while that, although they have aged, mannerisms always seem unchanged. This is evidence perhaps of the strong influence of our early years on the person that we become.

12

The Grimy North

I HAVE LIVED IN YORKSHIRE FOR NEARLY 25 YEARS now - Barnsley itself for over ten and I love it - and am proud to be here, so I hope my fellow northerners will excuse this chapter's title.

I was born and bred a southerner, and lived in London or just south of it - apart from Denstone College and my two years in Hereford - until I was 35-years-old.

When I returned from the First Gulf War in 1991, I needed to find myself a job in the NHS as an anaesthetic trainee.

I had heard that the training programme being run in Sheffield was good, so I sent my CV to Ian Barker, who was in charge of the training there. As it happened he had a soft spot for service doctors, and sent a positive reply telling me that an advert for jobs would be out soon. The day came, I duly applied and was eventually informed that I had an interview.

Before the interview date I rang someone in Sheffield and asked what I should do about visiting beforehand. Whoever it was I spoke to said I should visit all the local hospitals that I would possibly go to as part of my training.

"Which are they?" I asked.

"Barnsley, Chesterfield, Doncaster and Rotherham", the lady replied

Well; I put down the telephone wondering just what on earth I was doing! Chesterfield was a place with a crooked spire, which my flatmate in London, Kim Wagstaffe had been very rude about, and he'd been brought up there. Barnsley was - to me at any rate - mines and the miners' strike, about which I held a very southern view at the time. Doncaster was a station the train went through to get to my grandma's place in Sunderland, and Rotherham I had no idea about at all.

To me - they were all just part of 'the grimy north'.

I went for the interview, was given one of the jobs on offer, and left the Navy on 26th October 1991.

Jo, Fiona, Alec and I moved to Sheffield, and I immediately got stuck into civilian life. It took me a while to get used to the disorganised nature of the NHS though.

In fact, it took me a very long time, and I only finally stopped 'bashing my head against a brick wall' in about 2008!

I do not want to use the whole of the rest of this book to explain all the NHS's shortcomings, so what I will do is make an effort to explain the difficulties and problems now, and then give it up once and for all. Now that I am retired the organisation's administrative and managerial failures do not have to bother me anymore.

There are three areas I should like to cover.

- The care that the NHS provides *vis-à-vis* what it *should* provide, or perhaps it would be better to say what the country can afford for it to provide
- The management structure of the NHS
- The NHS's failings and political meddling that goes on.

The NHS was set up in 1948 to ensure that whatever a citizen's means, they would be able to receive care, but in particular - and this is important - care for acute and emergency conditions.

I am not saying that elective care was not provided for also, but it was not the primary issue and the scope of such care was much more limited and less expensive back then. Joint-replacements did not exist, and cataract surgery was rudimentary and therefore only undertaken when one's vision had become very poor indeed; to name but two examples. I have been heard to say; *"if all the joint replacement and cataract surgery that is done today is really necessary, then all the old people when I was young would have been walking around with a strong white stick!"*

Minimally invasive (keyhole) surgery had not been invented. Therefore, because they were far more likely to lead to complications many procedures were only carried out as a last resort. Today we jump in with expensive treatments because we *can*, when they are not necessarily needed. The patient's condition might well improve without, or the offending body part might happily co-exist with the individual until they die of something un-related.

I will use gall-stones to illustrate my final point.

If one goes to the doctor complaining about abdominal discomfort, the individual may be referred for an ultrasound. This may reveal gall-stones as being the possible cause of discomfort. However, gall-stones are very common, and although they are there, they may well not be the cause of the discomfort at all. We all sometimes get indigestion. However, because a laparoscopic removal of the gall-bladder is relatively minor, out those stones will come - at a cost to the NHS. Back in the days when the only way to remove such stones was to have a rather nasty operation, a hospital the size of Barnsley would perform the op about twice a week, whereas today there will more likely be 10 laparoscopic procedures a week. Stones may be more prevalent now because of the terrible lifestyles we lead today, but that is not the main reason for all the excess surgery.

All the joint-replacements, cataract surgery, gall-bladder surgery, and the whole gamut of ops performed cost a lot of money to provide, and all are well outside the original ethos of the NHS, which was to ensure that the acutely ill did not suffer for lack of money.

The provision of all this care is unsustainable without significant increases in taxes. Governments will not raise taxes because they will not get voted back in if they do, and the general public want it all ways - their luxury lifestyle and a free NHS that provides everything immediately.

And, as medical science progresses, this situation will worsen.

We hear about poor care on our hospital wards, and although I am not saying for a minute that the doctors and nurses are not at times culpable, a major issue is lack of staff and overcrowded wards.

Staff are expensive, and numbers cannot be increased without more money, so resulting poor care must inevitably only become more frequent. What is even sadder is that because of the drive to keep down waiting times for elective care, this is often where the focus lies. The acutely ill are the Cinderellas, more likely to receive sub-standard treatment.

The sensible solution is that *emergency* care, including cancer care, should be free to all, while *elective* care should be provided through health insurance.

We hear much about how it would be so terrible if healthcare was not free, and yet families happily spend a fortune on unnecessary luxury goods, but then baulk at the idea that some of their disposable income, in many cases these days of a considerable size, should be spent on their precious health.

The low-paid and unemployed would, of course continue to receive all their care from the state.

The alternative resolution would be a ring-fenced tax, all of which would go to the cost of healthcare. This would need to increase year-on-year to cover the ever-escalating costs. The advantage, with a system like this, is that the population would see how much the NHS is costing them, and no doubt complain!

It is unfortunate that so much of that money would, as now, come to be dissipated on the ever-burgeoning costs of the constantly increasing number of NHS managers, who keep appearing, most of whom have little if any function other than that of administering the unnecessary and massive bureaucracy that they themselves - with the help of the politicians - have generated. A self-fulfilling situation if ever there was one . . .

. . . which brings me nicely on to that topic proper; managers and management in the NHS.

I want to make it clear that, although they are paid managers' salaries, 95% of them are not managers. They are administrators, and generally pretty poor ones at that, I might add.

In 1991, when I first went to work in Barnsley Hospital, we had a general manager in charge, a deputy, a manager for each area of the hospital - and a matron, while all the other departments; -'personnel' (oops should call it human resources) for example, were small. The doctors were employed by the health authority and had efficient, very capable, longstanding secretaries. Between them they did a lot of the management themselves, and the whole thing worked fine.

I want to mention that the anaesthetic department in Barnsley has always had secretaries in this mould. Actually, they are more like personal assistants to all the anaesthetists and the department as a whole. Sharon Robinson was there in 1991, when I was in Barnsley as a registrar, and still works there now. Back then her colleague was Mary Hampshire, who subsequently retired and Tracey Deakin took her place. Now Julie Alexander has joined them. They do a fantastic job for everyone, so by improving the lives of many. They are under-valued and under-rewarded by the mediocre managers, who supposedly supervise them, but are in fact their administrative inferiors!

An example, of their fantastic commitment to their co-workers, and others is that they have supported me in three fund raising events held in the foyer of the hospital. They collected money in buckets, ran tombola tables and raffles and generally ran round after me!

One was a mock long distance triathlon, which I did prior to competing in Ironman France. I completed the swim on a Vasa swimming ergometer that I have; the cycle on my turbo-trainer and then I ran a marathon by doing laps of the hospital. This was in aid of Sport Relief.

On the other occasions we collected for anaesthetic equipment for the hospital. With the participation of a number of my fellow anaesthetists, as a team we completed a virtual Land's End to John O'Groats cycle on turbo-trainers over the course of five days. Later that year (2014) I rowed the Channel and back on my Water Rower (a rowing ergometer).

Yes, in the past, waiting lists were long, but guess what Tony Blair and Gordon Brown did by shortening those waiting times so much?

The following:-

The main reason that patients go for private care is to be seen more quickly and to have their operation carried out promptly, so the Blair/Brown reduction in waiting times then attracted patients to the NHS, who would otherwise, either have paid for their care or used their health insurance, which with the reduction in waiting times many people then went on to cancel.

It may be said that we should not have to wait at all, but the natural history of many conditions is that they will improve of their own accord, so allowing a certain amount of time for that to occur is good, both for the patient and for the economy.

Nowadays the managerial structure in Barnsley looks more like this:-

. . . there is a CEO, a Director of Operations and a Finance Director; a Director of Personnel, a Chief Nurse and a Deputy

Chief Nurse; a Director of Estates and a Medical Director - and then every area of the hospital has a Clinical Director, a Manager, a Deputy Manager and umpteen administrators and secretaries.

Not too long ago there were 11 matrons.

Now when the hierarchy record the role of matrons, they refer to it as being clinical, thereby enabling them to improve the apparent clinical-to-administrative staff ratio. Their work is not clinical, it is administrative. In addition to which every ward has its own Lead Nurse, who does very little if any actual clinical work. Another administrator is born!

With the ever-increasing overload of computer and paper-work that all these 'managers' have been generating, for many years now, the sisters and staff nurses have also been spending more and more time (far, *far* too much time) 'pen pushing' rather than delivering care. Most ward-patient care now is provided by Health Care Assistants, all earning close to, or little more than, the minimum wage. They are the least skilled clinically, but have to take ever increasing responsibility; they do, in the main, a fantastic job in difficult circumstances.

NHS managers will tell anyone who asks, that their main interest is patient care and safety.

Trust hospitals now have at least, to break-even financially, and preferably to show a surplus from their budget each year. If they do not, the CEO will be in trouble and could lose his or her job, as could any of the other directors - then only to be replaced by others, of course. Therefore, their prime concern, and the concern of the managers who work for and below them, is to save money; not patient care or safety, which is left to the doctors and nurses to achieve, and to achieve in very sub-optimal conditions.

Every time we get a new government, the following happens:-

First - they move 'the deck chairs' around, which, always generates even *more* managers and even *more* bureaucracy.

At the same time, they artificially raise the public's expectations, thereby placing our already almost terminally hard-pressed doctors and nurses under even *more* pressure to improve patient care within an ever *more* difficult and stressful environment.

It is the government which creates bodies like NICE (National Institute for Health & Care Excellence) and others, who dictate to everyone *how things should be done* without taking any notice of, or responsibility whatsoever for, the fact that there is not *possibly* enough resource to do it that way.

The government concurrently appoints 'Czars' as they are called, who are given various high-falutin' titles authorising them to dictate how those things that should be done, should be done. Very often these gentry are from a big city, and in addition to any of their many other failings, they haven't got a clue how things are in the real world, in a general hospital, in Yorkshire, or anywhere else for that matter.

It is ironic that they should be called Czars.

In Russia, early in the 20th century, their Czars were arrogant, greedy and stupid, and hadn't a clue what was actually going on in *their* country either. One can only hope that the modern Czars go the same way as their namesakes, although I suppose execution might be considered a tad extreme!

That's it!

I don't want to sully my book further spouting anymore about the failings of the NHS, but now let me tell you, the reader, a little about my career and my life whilst serving that august (not) organisation.

I started working for the NHS in Sheffield, at the Northern General Hospital, which then was considered to be the smaller, friendlier hospital. It has since become a sprawling mess of additional buildings, very unfriendly and huge. In most other countries the site would have been flattened long ago and a lovely new hospital built in its place, but - well . . .

I was only there until just before Christmas 1991, when I then moved to Barnsley Hospital, which I found to be a refreshing surprise. The staff there, were friendly and welcoming; the nurses were from a bygone age; an age when they enjoyed helping doctors . . . *and* they wore old-fashioned, striped, starched blue and white nurses' uniforms with white hats; they looked like and were the real thing! Pure joy.

Chauvinist of me? Perhaps by today's lights, but the atmosphere there was wonderful. Apologies to all the male nurses, who clearly did not wear the same uniforms, but also were good guys!

I spent a lot of time working in the intensive care unit, single-handedly operated by an anaesthetist called Dave Lee, a brilliant, clever and old-fashioned physician in the very best sense of the word, who taught me a huge amount, but at the same time let me get on with things by myself. When the time came eventually for me to leave, he took me and my then wife Jo out for a 'thank you' meal.

When I completed my training, it was Dave Lee, combined with the atmosphere in Barnsley that were the main reasons I returned there, where I was then to remain as a consultant for 19 years. Sadly, it was through the course of that time when everything to do with the NHS progressively began to decline.

Speaking about old-fashioned clinicians, they relied upon the symptoms the patient said they had, and their own examination as a major part of the process used in arriving at their diagnosis, whereas clinicians nowadays rely heavily on sophisticated investigative protocols, foregoing conducting any detailed personal patient history or examination. I do accept that this latter-day approach does often facilitate arriving at the diagnosis quickly and easily, but I would submit that in the process the medical practitioner's art is being lost, and with it much of the satisfaction.

In Hong Kong many years ago a lady came to see me complaining of tummy ache. She had been to see several other doctors with the same problem, but without receiving a satisfactory diagnosis. When I took her history she told me that the pain mainly came on following the consumption of fatty food, and that after any such painful episode her faeces were pale. This was a classic history of gall-stones, so I told her so and referred her to a surgeon, for which she was delighted and returned later to thank me. In this case, by the way, the history demonstrates that the stones were the cause of the pain and not an incidental finding. They *did* need removing by the surgeon. I was proud of myself. Today, an ultrasound investigation would achieve the same result, but it would be far less satisfying for the doctor I believe. Or maybe I am just old-fashioned?

It was whilst in Barnsley that I took the final part of my anaesthetic exams. I had worked very hard for it, but because of silly errors on my part I failed. My excuse is that I was up all night working on intensive care only a day before the written papers were taken. I was devastated by this, and went through quite a shaky period when I even considered giving the whole thing up, which was when I was offered the post in New Zealand I referred to earlier. This was after I had subsequently passed the exam in Ireland, which then was an allowed option. I also applied for a job with a drug company during this disillusioned phase and reached the final interview stage, competing with only one other applicant for the post.

These are two more examples of major crossroads in my life. How different my course might have been.

Passing the exam in Ireland was a great weekend away. Jo came with me. The written exams were on the Friday and my oral and clinical tests on the Tuesday, so it was completed very quickly, whereas back in England there was about a four-week gap between the two parts. A lot of Guinness was drunk and I nearly missed my flight back on the Wednesday, Jo having returned home before me already.

This was in the November of 1992, and without doing any more study I then passed the exam in England as well, in February 1993. I now needed to secure for myself a new job in order to progress.

I spent a year as a research registrar working in the University, and then in 1994 got an appointment as a senior registrar, again in Sheffield. From there on it took just another two years before I became a consultant in Barnsley.

By now I loved Yorkshire, and there was absolutely nothing that would have taken me back south again. Had I stayed in Hampshire, when I left the Navy, perhaps I would never have discovered the joys of the North.

My decision to be a consultant in Barnsley was not because I did not have offers in Sheffield, but because I wanted to try to make a difference in a smaller organisation, which did at that time need improvements in its services. The Anaesthetic Department in particular was very run down and I was lucky to be able to be instrumental in sorting it out and attracting a lot of good people to it.

Small district hospitals do struggle with recruitment of quality doctors, particularly when they are in a place perceived as unglamorous as Barnsley. Back then there were more consultant vacancies than anaesthetists to fill them, so candidates were able to pick and choose where they went. It is easier today, because the speciality is fielding a surplus of trained anaesthetists.

As the years went by, with the help of my colleagues I was able to change many aspects of the care in the hospital. This book is not a story of the changes at Barnsley Hospital though, so I will not become boring and bogged down with relating them; however, there was also a lot of frustration as the atmosphere within both the hospital and the NHS changed, making it more and more difficult to achieve what one knew was best for the patients.

During my time, I was a Clinical Director for about six years, and the hospital's acting Medical Director for a year, and found it immensely frustrating that the non-clinical managers always seemed to prioritise different issues to mine. So by 2008 I had had enough, and I must confess with a considerable degree of relief, gave up my last managerial role.

After that, besides still being a busy anaesthetist, I concentrated on training nurses to be 'advanced practitioners', i.e. to take on roles that are traditionally those of doctors, but which very many nurses are perfectly capable of performing.

Nursing *per se* has not progressed or moved on over the years as it should have done, because of the old-fashioned and parochial attitudes of the nursing hierarchy.

Unfortunately, this was particularly a problem in Barnsley, which frustrated many of my attempts to move nurses and nursing forwards.

I retired from medical practice in April 2015, and as I write it is now Christmas of that same year.

In many ways it is a shame that I don't seem to miss the hospital to which I committed my entire consultant career. This is perhaps partly because from my years at medical school onwards, I was always a reluctant doctor, as a result of which I do not particularly miss patient care. As mentioned before, I was definitely one of those medics who, although I did the job to a very high standard, it was only because I took pride in my work (and so it had to be of the best), not because I was on any mission to help my fellow man.

Before ending this chapter I should like to mention a few words about the miners' strikes, because I live in Barnsley and as I said at the beginning of the chapter, in the past I had a very southern view about this issue.

What *is* a southerner's view, one may ask?

I would say that they would say it was all about the power of the Unions and greed of the miners.

There is truth in the former, but not much in the latter.

In the 1970s, when the miners went on strike in the era of the Heath government, there was little in the way of coal reserves at the power stations. As a result, there were power cuts and the country went into shutdown, which was not good for an ailing economy, so the miners received a significant pay rise, in order to get them back to work.

However, anyone who thinks the miners were not worth more money and better working conditions at this stage would be wrong. If you do not agree with me, may I suggest a trip to Poland, or somewhere, and a few days working at the coalface, in order to see how hard it is!

In 1984 there was plenty of coal at the power stations; a fact I am sure that Maggie Thatcher made sure of before she started her battle with the communists - and there is the point.

Whether or not the miners should have had more money at that time was not the point. The Unions and their communist leaders needed sorting out, and Maggie chose to use the mines to do it. The miners were hijacked by this conflict.

There was also already an agenda in place to close many of the pits and I am sure the strike hastened their demise. I cannot condone this, whatever the reason. It destroyed communities and the families within them.

We are told that foreign coal was becoming cheaper and therefore our mines were uneconomic. Surely, it would have been better to have subsidised the mines and kept people employed, rather than pay them benefits to do nothing. It seems to me this could have been cost-neutral, and even if it wasn't, its adoption would have prevented the human destruction that closing the mines caused - which brings me to another point. I have a feeling that government subsidy of industry is illegal in the European Union.

We are to have a referendum regarding our future membership of the EU. The population at large does not have the knowledge to decide whether we should stay or leave Europe. Any information they are fed will be biased by both the 'yes' and the 'no' campaign to their own ends.

Our fate should be decided by a group of intelligent, knowledgeable people with no vested interest, which of course would be impossible to find.

So, if there is one reason to leave, it is reflected by what I said above about subsidies and our right to govern our own country. Why fight a war 70 years ago to keep our sovereignty intact, in order to willingly lose it to the Germans and the rest now? We might as well have let them come straight in here in 1940!

However, despite that, maybe it is my generation and those older than me who are more likely to share this view. Perhaps for our children's sakes we would be better off in a united Europe, with negotiated changes to European regulations for our country. With the fragmentation of so many countries into smaller states over recent years that may be the best formula.

I guess it is about maintaining as much of our sovereignty and individuality as we can, inside a strong Europe. Countries should be allowed to maintain their own identity and peculiarities. However, I am not sure that this will be possible.

Ultimately I think it is either stay in and lose control over our borders, immigration and right to determine our own laws, or leave, and put up with a short and probably medium-term fall in our wealth as a result of loss of trade.

I will, I am sure, live in Barnsley for the rest of my life.

Our house is only 600-yards from the hospital, where Julie works in intensive care, as she has for 30 years. So even in retirement I am nearby, and we do not intend to move when Julie herself retires in two years time. She has lived here all her life and I have now lived here longer than I have anywhere else.

I love the grimy north, and it is not grimy.

There is beautiful, rugged countryside only a 15-minute bike ride from my house!

13

Cars, Motorbikes & Bicycles

THE INTERNAL COMBUSTION ENGINE IS A SUPERB invention. However, it is a huge shame that because mass public transport systems have not progressed as they should have done, it has become a scourge. It should no longer be used to power our principal form of transport - the car - on ridiculously crowded roads that are littered with roadworks and speed cameras.

Our main form of transport should be the futuristic forms of monorail, and other transport systems powered by the fuels of the future, as foreseen in the comics I used to read as a child, thereby leaving the internal combustion engine to propel cars and motorbikes along lightly-travelled roads for the entertainment solely of us 'petrol-heads'.

Many years ago on BBC's *Tomorrow's World* they featured a railway wagon that had both carriage and lorry wheels that could be lowered; the idea being that freight could be carried for the majority of the journey to a depot by rail, when upon arrival the carriages' road wheels could then be lowered and the wagons then towed by trucks, without having to transfer the load. What a great way to reduce road traffic! Like many such splendid ideas seen on that programme (which ran for nearly 40 years, from 1965-2003) it must have got lost somewhere along the line.

As mentioned earlier, my first motorised vehicle was a Yamaha 125cc motorbike, but as soon as I'd passed my test I upgraded to a 1972 orange and black 350cc Yamaha YR5, which I couldn't afford, which made its purchase even more exciting. It was not the fastest or most beautiful of creatures, but it was all mine and absolutely *great* for me.

When I was chatting recently with my friend Steve Bamford, he remarked how we used to love our possessions so much in those days. I agreed, and think that must have been because they were so much more hard come by. Today it all has to do with who's got 'the biggest', or 'the fastest', or the 'most expensive' - excess and greed raising their ugly heads again.

I loved that bike so much that I have just bought another one; a 40-year-old 1970 American import version, in candy-purple and white. I go out to the garage just to look at it and that alone makes me grin, to say nothing of the thrill I get hearing the rattle of its two-stroke exhausts, when it is fired-up!

I cannot really remember why I sold that first version. I think I decided I just wanted a commuter vehicle to use from Finsbury Park to medical school at Mary's, for which I acquired a Honda ST70cc 'monkey bike' that was perfect for the job. I went everywhere on it, enjoying it enormously, and only ever experiencing two problems:

I was outside cleaning the little monkey one day and unthinkingly left its keys in the ignition when nipping back upstairs to fetch some fresh water, and when I came down again - yep - the keys were gone.

Two nights later, the bike was nicked.

It was found by the police a few days later, thankfully undamaged, which I am sure would not happen today.

On another occasion, I was riding home when I was cut up by a car full of young lads. I imagine I might inadvertently have flicked them a V-sign or something, but anyway, for some reason or other they followed me home and tried to beat me up. Fortunately, I kept my helmet on and did my best to 'nut' them. In those days fights could have a satisfactory outcome just by everyone backing off and calming down, which is what happened then. Today, though, I would probably have been kicked to within an inch of my life, stabbed, or even shot!

When I became a Navy Medical Cadet and first started earning, I treated myself to a Yamaha RD400. This item was the absolute 'bee's knees', the hooligan bike of the day which would touch 100mph, and under acceleration its front wheel would come up at the 'drop of a hat'; another favourite in my life.

I do not want to turn this into a boring list, so in summary that bike was exchanged for my first car, the previously mentioned Hillman Imp.

When I then became qualified, I told you my present to myself was a water-cooled two-stroke Suzuki GT750. It was ballistic in a straight line, not so good in corners, and returned less than 30 miles to the gallon!

Speed kills is the slogan we hear so much today.

No, it doesn't; generally speaking, it is stupidity that kills.

Of course, the faster you are going if you have a crash, the greater the damage; it is not the speed that causes the crash though, but the behaviour of the driver or rider.

If I were to travel through a busy built-up area doing 60mph at 10.00am, or at anytime come to that, then I would be a moron endangering other people's lives.

If I were to overtake on a blind bend and crash into an on-coming vehicle, it would be my overtaking on the blind bend that was to blame. However, if I also happened to have been riding in excess of the speed limit, then my speed would be accredited with being the cause of the crash, which wouldn't have been the case.

If I was riding my motorbike at 90mph on a dry Lincolnshire road on a Sunday morning at 6am, I would be 'progressing at a speed which the road conditions allowed' - to speak Highway Code-wise. If then I was to make a mistake, fall off, crash and kill myself that would be my business: At least I would have died doing what I loved, and as a bonus not ended up in a nursing home aged 90, demented and costing the tax-payer loads of money.

Speed is becoming more and more vilified. Like the next man, I hate it when I see people driving foolishly and endangering others, but there are plenty who drive slowly and also manage to do that quite effectively.

Why do people who drive too slowly for the prevailing road conditions buy cars that have the capability to accelerate and achieve speeds that their owners would never entertain engaging?

Why do we have speed cameras all over the place, but allow manufacturers to build cars that will exceed the national speed limit by three times?

We have the technology to control cars and prevent them from exceeding the limit - a chip and a satellite could do that - so if we are so obsessed with the *Speed Kills* campaign, why hasn't such a constraining system yet been implemented? It must be some bizarre interpretation of what could be considered an infringement of human rights perhaps, but also, more importantly, to do with the backhanders and other perks those politicians receive from car manufacturers.

It is not illegal to accelerate quickly to the speed limit is it?

Then why do the same people who have these cars, whose engine is capable of reaching 30mph in about four seconds, not do that when they are able to?

This is typified at traffic lights.

Theoretically, if all the drivers in a traffic-light queue can see the lights, then when they turn green everyone could start to move at the same time. One never sees revving Formula 1 cars waiting for the car in front to move off first, before following suit. I know this is unlikely to occur, but the slow reaction time of each driver, combined with their slow acceleration, means that only about 50% of cars that could cross the green light, do so. This is not to do with any impatience on my part, merely an observation regarding traffic flow.

Back to my vehicles.

After the GT750, my final motorbike before I then had a long break without, was another Yamaha; an XS750cc four-stroke with shaft drive. I used it to commute between Poole, where we then had our house, and Gosport. It was not a very exciting machine, so I sold it just before going to Hong Kong and giving up motorbikes completely for 13 years.

My cars -

My cars went through a bit of a strange phase after I'd sold the Alfa Romeo, which I've mentioned before. Next I bought a lime-green Mini 1000cc. I'd gone to the garage to get a 1275GT version, but that had already been sold, so it was purely on a whim that I bought the other. I did not use the car much anyway at that time, since I commuted on the XS750, but I thought Christine would like it - which she didn't!

After that there was an eight-year-old Mk11 Cortina, which Christine managed to write-off for us just before we separated. It was replaced by an old Rover P6 2200sc I bought from someone in the Navy. It is strange to think that both our Cortina and Rover run-arounds would now be considered classic cars!

After my year in Hong Kong I decided that I should have a faster and flashier vehicle, so I test drove a Peugeot 205GTi - the hot-hatch of its day. I also considered an Opel Manta GTE, either of which I could have bought new, but instead I ended up buying a second-hand BMW 323i. I loved that car, but in many ways I still wish that I'd bought the Peugeot. I only drove the BMW for about 18-months before the arrival of dogs and children (in that order) dictated the successive acquisition of more practical vehicles.

Then from 2009 I bought two top-of-the-range Alfa Romeos, one after the other; first a Mito, and then a Giullietta. I liked each of them very much, but in some ways they were not as much fun as the £800 GTV I'd had in 1980.

I feel this further illustrates the point that part of the joy of 'acquisition and possession' is in having to work hard and save, and the awareness that what you now have was difficult to get; whereas - these days . . .? All too easy.

I now drive a Renault Scenic 1.5dci that accelerates quickly enough and drives fast enough for our modern day roads.

A fast, flash and expensive car these days is little more than a status symbol; perhaps something that makes their proud and gloating owners smile contentedly when parked outside on their drives, but I don't think most people who own these really expensive cars actually have the ability to drive them as they should be driven - even if our roads were empty.

Motorbikes are a different kettle-of-fish. A motorbike can still be ridden in a 'fun' way. I have owned a series of them since I returned to motor-biking in 1998.

I have had sports bikes, tourers, muscle bikes, and shared a Kawasaki with a friend: Tim Moll. We bought that bike between us, specifically for use on a racetrack. We rode it at Catalunya in Spain. We also did a lot of 'track-days' at many English circuits together too. Unlike my school years in athletics, I was never anywhere near the fastest on the track, but still I had great fun and there were no police lurking about the place to spoil it.

Tim and I have also done a lot of motorcycling trips abroad together to watch motorcycle racing. They were all great fun and each one is remembered for different reasons; usually something that nearly, or did go wrong! Getting lost in Antwerp for what seemed like hours and me riding on the wrong side of a road, nearly head-on into a tractor are examples. Not being able to find fuel on a Sunday morning and running on fumes, as well as losing Tim as he disappeared off in the wrong direction also spring to mind. There were no mobile phones to locate each other with, back then!

On a different occasion, I went to a small circuit in the South of France called Nogaro, for several days on track, with my friends Steve Bamford and Garry Sylvester; Barnsley lads. We rode down to Portsmouth to catch the ferry; arriving early. We had a few beers before we boarded and then a lot more on-board. Somehow we found our cabin. The next thing we knew and heard was an announcement over the loudspeaker at 6am. "Would the three motorcyclists collect their bikes and leave the ferry immediately!" We dressed, rushed to the vehicle deck, which was deserted, and left. It was raining and dark, our visors steamed up, Steve skidded on some diesel and we were lucky not to crash in the dockyard; long before reaching a track! We then rode more than 500 miles south, through France, stopping only once for refreshment and then instead of rehydrating with water, we drank black espresso. We, particularly Steve, were in a bad way when we reached Nogaro, but in all honesty we were lucky all to be still alive!

When I first started doing 'track-days', they were pretty raw and basic. Riders would turn up on all sorts of bikes, ride round the circuit all day, and then ride home again. Then, like most pastimes that start out as just fun, things steadily became more and more serious, with specific race-bikes being brought in vans, along with generators to provide electricity for tyre warmers and all manner of other such sophisticated items of kit. That's when the whole thing started to lose its appeal for me; taking things to such extremes seeming to be the modern way. I prefer things to be kept simple, and that's what makes them more fun for me. Know the acronym KISS? *Keep-It-Simple - Stupid.*

The story of my motorcycling exploits would not be complete without mentioning Neil and Ann, a lovely British couple who live in the Ardennes in Belgium. They run a bed and breakfast in their house there, primarily for motorcyclists, but also cyclists and others. Their place is like 'home from home'. I have visited twice with Julie and, on other occasions with friends. I have been there to watch motorcycling, do a 'track-day' round the Formula 1 circuit at Spa, and to ride the Nurburgring, which is not far away. In 2015 Julie and I visited so I could cycle my vintage *Eddy Merckx* bicycle at the 'Sean Kelly Classic' cycle event in Belgium. What more could one want?

If you, the reader are a motor-biker, cyclist, or are interested in the 'Battle of the Bulge', the famous tank battle of WWII, have a look at *www.aeaventures.com.*

I now run a BMW road bike - a R1200R. I never thought I would, because they have always seemed rather steadfast and boring, in fact there are those who would say that BMW might stand for *Boring Middle-Aged Wanker*. Maybe it has something to do with my age, but I love it, and so does Julie, who rides pillion. (Shades of Emma Peel in her black leathers? That's a thought!) The machine is easily quick and sleek enough, comfortable, and looks great. It does everything I want it for.

Whilst getting bikes, cars and the open road off my chest, let me just mention a few other issues.

One: pedestrians are faring worse and worse.

I have referred to this issue before, but feel it to be worth repeating.

I walk along pavements a lot with Charlie.

Charlie?

Our Dalmatian - remember?

When doing so I encounter all sorts of obstructions, not least of all - cars, which seem able to park on the pavement with impunity. Indeed, in Barnsley there are streets where the council has posted signs actually instructing drivers to please park on *half* the pavement!

We rightly worry about carbon emissions, global warming and cancer in the case of diesel fuel, and yet pedestrians, who are much cleaner, are treated like second-class citizens.

Few drivers these days seem to have read the Highway Code, because generally speaking they certainly don't treat pedestrians with very much kindness or respect, viewing them simply as annoying obstacles to be by-passed as quickly as possible.

Not many people know that it is an offence for a car to splash a pedestrian on the pavement. I know this because I have been soaked myself on many an occasion.

In Barnsley, the Pelican Crossings' sensors that determine how close a car is before the lights change to red, are set so high that the lights don't turn red unless there is no car in sight. Clearly, if there is no car in sight I can cross anyway, and do not need the lights to change to give me permission to do so. Again - the car is king. I derive my revenge though when the traffic is commanded to stop *after* I have crossed by the now-changed light!

Roundabouts.

Roundabouts were invented to aid traffic flow.

For a number of reasons roundabouts do not work anymore, clearly demonstrated by the fact that they have now installed traffic lights on many of them. The reason these lights are now needed is because everyone drives round them so fast that cars cannot safely filter on - one place where it might be really beneficial to have speed cameras, but there are none – set, I would suggest at about 15mph, depending upon the size of the roundabout.

I remember the days when traffic had to give way from the left, so cars entering the roundabout had right of way. That would cause fun now. As for mini-roundabouts - well, *they* aren't even worth discussing, other than to say that just *one* of them is bad enough, but then presumably for a laugh, 'they' follow up the frolicsome folly by installing two or three in close proximity to each other.

I love bicycles.

Velocipedes are a brilliant invention; efficient, non-polluting, keep their user fit and take up far less storage space than a car or motorbike.

When I am on my bicycle it is like being in a different world.

I lose myself entirely in the physical activity, the motion of the pedals, the beat of my heart, and the acceleration of my breathing. As well as all this, cycling is when I am granted the time to 'contemplate the conundrums of life'. It makes me feel truly alive, and grateful to be so. My mind can feel free to wander, particularly if I am out early in the morning and the roads are less busy. I love that time of day, out on one of my bicycles watching the sunrise and feeling at one with the universe.

Why, then, in this country, are cyclists treated so badly by both other road users and the government alike.

Boris Johnson, I know, has done his bit - but the facilities available for cyclists are to say the least rudimentary. Most cycle lanes are an afterthought, not wide enough, and - quite frankly - dangerous.

However, leaving this aside, it is a fact that many road users think that we should not be there cycling along beside (in competition with) them at all, as demonstrated by their apparent desire to kill us whenever the opportunity presents. Again, few will have read the Highway Code, so amongst other things, therefore, do not understand that two-abreast is fine, although having said that, the vast majority of aware cyclists will go single-file to allow cars to pass them when the need arises.

I have friends who have said that as a cyclist, who pays no road tax, I have no 'rights', in response to which I retort that I do pay road tax, on my car and on my motorbike. If I am out riding on my bicycle my car is not polluting the atmosphere, I am causing less wear on the road surface and taking up less space, whilst keeping myself fit and saving the NHS money in so doing - to mention just a *few* of the benefits of my being a cyclist. Imagine how much quieter our roads would be during the rush hour if everyone who lived less than ten miles from their place of work were to cycle there? A perfectly reasonable expectation *if* the cycle path network was increased and made safer, and employers would provide cycle parks and shower facilities for their staff.

On Boxing Day, I was out in the park walking Charlie when I saw a small boy and girl enjoying their Christmas presents. The little lad was on some kind of motorised board thing, and his sister on an electric scooter, so it looked like my dream was dead in the water.

Then, the following day, on 27th December 2015 I was out on a bike ride when I saw a family out for their Sunday walk. Their son-and-heir was powering along on his shiny new orange bicycle - he was the 'engine' - while his little sister was pushing a dolls pram; so despite a woman in an unnecessarily large Audi, having tried to run me off the road earlier, my faith in humanity and the future of mankind was partly restored.

I have related earlier about my first bike, which I spent hours and hours riding round the block in London, and the fact that my old school friend, whose parents used to put the milk bottle on the table and my parents considered 'common', Peter Edwards, was given a racing bicycle with derailleur gears, which I coveted. It was probably because it would be such a long time before I had one of my own, that I own so many bikes today.

In 1969, about five years after Peter had been given his, I'd asked for a new (racing) bicycle again. With us both having moved house, my friendship with Peter had lapsed, but I still craved having a bike like his.

My birthday duly arrived and with it a new bicycle, which was awaiting me in the garage. Imagine my disappointment, then, when upon excitedly flinging open the door I discovered that Dad had bought and done up for me, some old second-hand bike, certainly not with superior, low-slung derailleurs, but with Sturmy Archer hub-gears, straight bars, (not drop-handled) and resembling the sort of thing an old man would ride.

To this day I do not know why?

We were not poor: I am sure my parents could have afforded a racer - even a second-hand racer would have been fine.

A few years later my sister was to take that bike back to school with her, never rode it, and left it to rust in the bike sheds and I didn't care at all! Perhaps it sounds spoilt of me, but I just wanted a proper bike. Sometime later, our grandma bought my sister an expensive coat for a present and, in lieu gave me £50 . . . *with which I bought myself a Carlton Ten -* <u>my very own RACER</u> - *at <u>last!</u>* – this, despite my parents having tried to persuade me not to spend my whole £50 on one. They *must* have been early covert bicycle-haters, rather like the road-users of today, although today people are not so covert about it.

My adult passion for bicycles had started in 1989 with Pete Dawson, the commando-trained soul-mate I'd met and trained with on board *HMS Invincible*.

Soon after I'd left *Invincible* I had a Peugeot bicycle built for me with Reynolds 531 tubing, which was good, not the best, but good. When I left the Navy a while later, I spent £1,200 of my £6,500 resettlement allowance on a top model, the frame of which was made of Columbus SLX tubing by Daccordi, in Italy. I now had the Peugeot to train on and the Daccordi for racing triathlon.

I still have both these bikes, which have each been refurbished and new components fitted. They are lovely!

Cyclists today are obsessed with weight; therefore they buy carbon frames, but steel is always best. It is stiff like carbon and rides with a great feel. What do a few ounces matter? All my bikes now are of steel construction. Steel has so much more character to it than the average mass-produced carbon frame that's usually been churned out from a mould in Taiwan!

I *did* have two carbon-framed bikes, one of which was stolen; the other was very nice indeed, expensive, and not produced in the Far East - but I sold it when I stopped racing triathlon.

I have two Eddy Merckx bicycles; Eddy being the greatest cyclist ever to have lived, although Bernard Hinault, Jacques Anquetil, and Fausto Coppi come close.

I have a fantastic local bicycle shop called *Race Scene*. They sell beautiful Italian frames, and I have recently bought a new bicycle from them. It has a stainless steel frame by Casati and is a retirement present to myself to compliment the

Daccordi I bought 25 years before! This time it cost a little more at £4500.

The guys at *Race Scene*, Richard, Freddie and Mick, are great blokes and supply me with my every cycling need; Julie would say 'want'. I want the stuff, but don't really need it! Richard owns the shop and is always welcoming (not surprising considering the amount I have spent!), Freddie knows everything there is to know about bicycles and cycling and Mick is a first rate bike builder and mechanic. Check it out at *www.racescene.co.uk*.

I cannot leave this chapter without mentioning a word or two about the television programme *Top Gear*, which I regularly used to watch until it became repetitive and overly contrived and it seemed they were struggling to find new material. When the Team Clarkson left I thought that perhaps a breath of fresh air might revive the programme, and there was much excited speculation about who would take over.

I have nothing against Chris Evans, the new boy, but surely he has enough television and radio time already? I felt him to be rather an uninspired choice. It is, however, indicative of something I have noticed about celebrities on the BBC, and to a lesser extent the other channels. They seem to have their 'favourites', who then become over-exposed for a few months, or in many cases years, before presumably there's a massive falling out, or with a now over-inflated idea of their worth, the 'star' demands too much money. Then the cycle recommences, with a fresh group of celebrity favourites.

Currently, Matt Baker is at the top of his form and enjoying massive exposure. He seems like a great guy, but this past year he has been appearing everywhere; principal anchor on *The One Show, Countryfile,* a show about sea life off the coast of California, and he has become *Mister Gymnastics.* Helen Skelton, who I like and admire; the one time presenter of *Blue Peter* and relief presenter on *Countryfile* went through a phase like this, as have many others. Variety is supposed to be the spice of life, but clearly not on television!

14

Sports

I AM LUCKY TO HAVE BEEN ABLE TO PARTICIPATE IN a lot of different sports in my life.

One of the great advantages of being given the privilege of a private school education; actually probably the only advantage of private school, is that sport is a big part of life there.

I feel sorry for kids these days, when the state schools they attend do so little sport that they scarcely have any chance at all. If they want to try something out on their own initiative they need to join an external club, and if they then discover they don't enjoy that particular sport, they have to go and join another club, then another and another, until they find what it is they are looking for - but usually it's all too difficult and life's too short, so many don't bother.

The idea of a holistic education, which includes sport and activity, seems to have been lost. It is ironic, really, in the face of an education system that has abandoned the three 'R's, the history of our country - and more, so that children can be taught about all sorts of other pointless stuff instead - that sport is not included. Although I suppose I should be grateful, because that must mean some educationalist somewhere considers sport *not* to be pointless, otherwise clearly it *would* have been included.

I have already told the tale of my on-off relationship with rugby, but I have never been a football fan, although I used to watch Crystal Palace regularly when my dad was their doctor, and I played football at school until I was ten-years-old - but now I despise the game.

With the ridiculous salaries paid to under-fit and, in the main, under-skilled sportsmen, who show no respect for the referee, continuously swear at everyone, pretend to be injured when tackled, hug and kiss each other like hysterical schoolgirls when one of them scores a goal, as well as inciting the crowd with their antics, diving to the ground, when not even fouled, football today has come to epitomise the last word in all things bad. What appalling role models footballers are to the millions of children, who worship them.

If the hierarchy had the will to do so, their game could be 'cleaned up' within six months. All that would be required would be to introduce a ten-minute visit to a 'sin-bin', and a sending-off for the second misdemeanour for all the offences I have mentioned, and teams of about two would end up playing each other after about half-an-hour of the match! The clubs would then *have* to sort themselves out.

However, one only has to go to watch a kids' football match and witness and hear the behaviour of their parents to realise there is little chance left for the game. They yell and scream coarsely at their children and the referee alike in an aggressive and unkind fashion. At these matches, one also realises why British players are generally so poor, when talent and flare is stifled at such an early age by negative play; to win is all. I will not waste any more time on football, except to mention that the recent exposure of FIFA's corruption would seem to say it all!

At University I rowed in an eight for several years. We were far from the best, but it was fun and a very sociable pastime that helped to keep me fit. I also ran and circuit and weight-trained. This pattern of activity continued throughout many of my years in the Forces. However, towards the end of the eighties I discovered triathlon.

Not that many years ago I would have needed to explain what triathlon is, but not so today. Back then, though, it was still only a fringe sport, which was nice because the commercial side did not exist, there were a lot of local events over all sorts of distances, and it was a fun sport to be in.

Now, as with supposed progress in other sports, there is increasing professionalism, more money, an officious governing body, centralised control and generally a forsaking of the amateur do it for fun element.

Recently I did a triathlon level-one coaching course with a view to getting involved in it that way. However, the main focus of the course was on ridiculous and obvious health and safety requirements, not coaching skills at all, the latter about which I have plenty of knowledge anyway, so I have not, and now will not, pursue it further. So I cannot pass on the experience I have gained during 15 or so years in triathlon, because I am not indemnified without possessing an officially recognised qualification, which needs to be at level-two to be of any use. So although I passed level-one, it was £300 wasted. We live and learn, although in my case perhaps sometimes I don't!

I competed at triathlon for quite a while in my mid to late thirties, not brilliantly, but I was always in and round the top 25%; my best finish being fourth place. Then I met Alex, and stopped as I moved-on into what I now call my wilderness years.

In 2008, when I gave up drinking, I decided I wanted to get myself *really* fit; that's not to suggest that I'd become a couch potato in the meantime, I hadn't, but I needed a new goal, so thought a short distance triathlon might be a good start. I entered one in the September, for which I bought a new bike. I loved it, and the bug hit again. However, aged 52 I was a bit older now and injury a bit more of a problem, so I missed a couple of events in early 2009, because of a pulled muscle, or three.

Not being one to proceed in a logical manner, I thought 'Push on, Swinhoe', and entered myself for Ironman France, scheduled for June 2010. This event consisted of a 2.4 mile swim, in this case in the sea; a 118 mile cycle-race, in this case in the Maritime Alps; and a 26-mile marathon, in this case along the heat of Nice seafront promenade. I started training in September 2009, averaged about 20 hours a week, and one memorable week peaked at over 30. I was still working full time as a hospital consultant, so spare time was limited. Julie was brilliant and tolerated my, as usual, obsessive approach to the commitment.

I apply a motto of mine to many things in life: *"If some is good, more must be better"*. Obviously not always true, but that is of no concern to me!

I had a T-shirt made, which I still have, which displays on the front; *"Training is life. Anything before and after is just waiting"*. For the enlightened amongst you, you will know that this is a quote of one of my heroes Steve McQueen, as Michael Delaney, in the film Le Mans. The word *racing* has been changed to *training*!

While I was training for Nice we bought ourselves a tandem, so that Julie and I could cycle together. There is quite an art to riding a tandem properly. Once on the saddle the person at the back, called the stoker, does not put their feet down at all. In fact they wouldn't be able to reach the ground with them if they tried.

When you see tandems on television, often in comedies, both the rider, called the pilot, and the stoker can put their feet down whilst seated – which is much safer and easier I suppose.

The other tandem myth is that the stoker can sit and do nothing. They, in fact, cannot independently freewheel, so whilst their feet are on the pedals they must spin them. They can adjust their effort and not do much work, but Julie always worked hard.

The pilot has to tell the stoker what he is doing, like for example when he changes gear or, in particular, wants to freewheel.

We had some good rides and the concept did work; I would come home really tired, usually having done a couple of hours training on my own before us going out. However, Julie was not particularly keen on two of the things I used to do.

Once I am on any bicycle I hate stopping, so will try to judge it so that I can keep moving at junctions and traffic lights. I think Julie found this a bit unnerving at times, and it needed lots of communication around freewheeling, which I would forget to do. Also, if we were going up a hill, working hard in a low gear, as soon as pedalling became easier upon reaching the top, I would select a higher gear, so as to keep the work up. It made it harder work, was good for my training, but hard for Julie. We sold the tandem a few years later because once we had Charlie to walk a couple of times a day there was just not enough time.

I made all the arrangements for the event in Nice, including booking an apartment there for two weeks so that I could acclimatise before the event, and stay on there with the family for a week afterwards. I'd had a very expensive bicycle made and did not fancy leaving it to the whims of airline baggage handlers, so I drove myself down to the South of France. Julie, Fiona, Alec and Bethany arrived by plane on the day before the race was scheduled to take place.

Everything went well.

The swim was fine, apart from my goggles steaming up so that I swam blind for half of it. The cycle felt good and despite all the long hills, the longest climb being about 10 miles, I arrived at the start of the marathon in reasonable shape.

It was four laps up and down Nice sea front.

The first two laps went fine, but come the third I started to feel a little strange. Fortunately, I guessed correctly that I was short of salt and a few Ritz crackers from the aid stations sorted out that little setback, despite my choking on the crumbs.

The only other two issues were weeing, and the other business; the relief of both for which I became desperate!

The weeing part was easy; there were showers set up for us to run through to help keep us cool, so whilst dripping wet no one could notice 'a little extra'. The other meant a stop-off at a by now unbelievably disgusting Portaloo; needs must though.

At the end of the event I put most of my kit straight in the dustbin!

I finished the whole thing in 11 hours: 17 minutes, which 'though I say it myself', wasn't half bad for a 53-year-old. The family enjoyed watching the spectacle, and we had a great week together afterwards in Nice, Monaco and all around. Nice is one of the nicest cities I have visited, and although well above our price bracket I told Julie for a while that we should retire there!

The long distance triathlon bug is a dangerous one to get. After a day of physical pain . . . just a few days later . . . much to Julie's chagrin, I was contemplating the next one.

On my return I had a souvenir Ironman logo tattooed on my right shoulder to celebrate and a little later entered Ironman France for 2011; this time wanting to complete in under 11 hours.

For the first couple of months of 2011 I kept becoming injured, so things did not look good and that resulted in me pulling out of the race. However, by spring I was injury-free again, and so entered Challenge Henley instead.

Ironman and Challenge are both franchises, each of them running long-distance races of the same distance, so my under-11 hours goal was still on. Things were looking good, but then because of a recurrent calf strain I was unable to run for six weeks before the race in September.

On the day, the swim went fine, despite my kicking-off from 100-yards behind everyone else, having become confused about where the start line was.

The cycle race was hard and hilly, but I did it faster than I had in Nice, although towards the end of it I was tiring a lot.

The same as in France, the run was four laps. For the first two of these I was well on the pace, but then I just faded and my legs wouldn't work properly! At the end of the third lap I stopped-by where the family were watching from and said, "I might be a while with this one," as I started on the final lap. It was very painful and hard, but I kept going and ended up finishing in 11 hours 17 minutes again - a time that had clearly been decreed to be my best for a long distance triathlon!

Julie, Fiona and Alec came to watch Challenge Henley as they had watched in Nice the year before. This time Fiona brought her, now long term, partner Stephen, but at that stage we had not met. As a result, one of his first memories of me is my rushing from the table in a pub after the race to vomit as a result of exhaustion and dehydration.

This scenario is not unfamiliar to me!

In Hong Kong I spent several hours in a cold bath in the officers mess after a rugby sevens tournament fighting off nausea and vomiting caused by heat stroke.

However, my best effort followed a marathon in 2012. I had competed in Sunderland and not taken enough fluid on board, underestimating the heat and my efforts. I started the drive home (my friend Pete, who I had run with said I looked dodgy before I left). I started to feel ill in the car, and spent the journey having to stop the car at frequent intervals to vomit at the roadside. What is more I was on my own, so had to drive.

I reached home and got in a cold bath and tried to keep some fluid down in vain. So I drove up to Barnsley Hospital and walked onto the intensive care unit, where Julie was working and asked her to call the junior anaesthetist, so he could insert a cannula in a vein in my arm and administer a saline infusion. He kindly did so and we took a couple of bags of fluid home to give me overnight!

For ages after that there were bags of intravenous saline and intravenous cannulae in the top of one of our wardrobes! Julie was not impressed understandably, fearing for my health. I was pleased it proved I could push myself to the point of exhaustion! I did the marathon in 3 hours 20 minutes at the age of 55. The following year I returned. This time Julie came and I completed it in 3 hours 10 minutes and did not need a post-race saline infusion!

For the 2012 triathlon season I concentrated on shorter races and was the winner of my age group on numerous occasions.

Then for 2013 I decided I wanted to try to qualify for the Ironman World Championships, which are always held in Hawaii. Qualification for which entails coming first or second in one's age group at another Ironman event - which I chose to be Ironman Wales.

For the last few years I had been using an internet coach from 'Team Dillon' to help keep me on track with my training. This is run by Michelle Dillon, an Olympic triathlete. My first year with them Craig Twigg, who'd won several prestige long-distance triathlons, coached me very well for 2010s Ironman France. In 2011 I'd coached myself, but then in 2012 Annie Emmerson, a World Champion duathlete (run/bike/run, but no swim), but who is also a great triathlete looked after me, in what was probably my best year in triathlon. The coaches from 'Team Dillon' would set all my training and keep in touch with me by telephone and e-mail.

For 2013 I asked Michelle herself to take me on, and all went brilliantly. I ran the previously mentioned marathon in 3 hours 10 minutes in the April, and then trained hard after that for eight weeks prior to a holiday Julie and I had booked for June. Whilst on a run the day before we left, my right hip hurt and didn't feel good at all. I thought a stress fracture might have been caused from my intensive training regimen.

After our holiday, during which I rested it as much as possible by only swimming, I arranged an MRI scan for myself, the results of which showed that I had developed significant arthritis in both hips. It was strange that I'd had little or no warning about the onset of this condition and that the pain started so suddenly. I was referred to various

323

specialists, because as it turned out I had abnormally shaped hips; presumably from birth. However, the considered opinion was that the damage had already been done and that any surgery might well make things worse. The left hip has since become worse than my right, which is now much less sore.

Nevertheless, I completed the swim and cycle at Ironman Wales, dropping out before the marathon. I raced one duathlon in 2014, after which both hips hurt a lot for quite a while, so I then 'retired' and now I swim and still enter cycle events, but no longer run.

I did the 'Eroica' in Bakewell in 2015; a cycle sportive in which one is only allowed to ride bikes manufactured before 1987. I have two such bikes, which fit the bill, and will be there again in 2016. It is a lovely event, lasting for a whole weekend and with all manner of things going on for both the riders and their families. 'Eroica' started in Italy, and there are now similar events taking place across the world.

I shall be doing the Ironman 2.4 mile sea swim and 118 mile cycle in Wales in 2016, at what is called the Long Course Weekend, but my running days really are definitely over. Unsurprisingly after the rigours they've endured, my hips hurt a lot, but I will still be hanging on for as long as I can before letting any orthopaedic surgeon anywhere near them, although eventually I suppose I shall have to succumb to receiving a new pair. All of this only goes to show that one never knows what lies around the corner - so it is important to 'live it' for today. I count my blessings that (thus far) my health setback has been nothing more serious, or terminal.

I watched the BBC's *Sports Personality of the Year* a week or so ago, and - my word - hasn't that programme gone downhill as it's become more and more 'glitzy' and the public have been given the vote? Although I didn't always agree with their choice, at least the sports writers, who used to choose the winners had a concept of the merits of different sporting achievements.

Sports personalities?

First let me say that although I have not been a tennis fan since the days of Björn Borg and John McEnroe in the 1970s, I do recognise that Andy Murray is a great sportsman. However, in 2015 he did not win a Grand Slam; the Davis Cup Team rightly won the team event and that should have been it.

Kevin Sinfield is a fantastic, loyal, Leeds rugby-league player, who should have won a lifetime achievement award, but that honour went to A. P. McCoy, another fantastic sportsman. However, I found it odd and unnecessary that because the show was held in Belfast it seemed that the BBC believed the whole evening had to be about Northern Ireland. My views about that part of the world I have already mentioned.

I saw the number of votes published in *The Times*: Murray received about 270,000 and Sinfield 250,000; Jessica Ennis -

who was third and the first person who could have justifiably been in first spot received only seventy-odd thousand. Most of the rest were nowhere, including the fantastic athlete Mo Farah and the young swimming star Adam Peaty. The voting simply highlighted the demographics of the voters - nothing more. I shall not be watching next year.

What fun the show used to be, when they had scenes like Redgrave and Pinsent battling it out on Concept rowing machines. Voting demographics were also demonstrated in the *Strictly Come Dancing* 2015 final, when the voters must have been frustrated middle-aged women looking for a toy boy! A young male popstar won and he was not the best dancer on the night and that is not my opinion, but that of the professional judges. Why have a competition in which the best person does not win?

From the point of view of watching sport these days, my main interests are cycling and motorcycling. I do watch some rugby, but am usually disappointed by England's lack of flair and the modern defensive game. Professional triathlon is ruined by allowing drafting on the bike leg, turning it into a running race preceded by a bit of swimming and cycling.

The English language lacks enough words to describe sports and games. Some games are sports, but not all of them are.

In order to explain, let me say that snooker, darts and golf are games, like tiddlywinks is a game, but they are not sports. Rugby is a game, which is a sport. Sport needs to include a significant level of physical effort as well as skill. A game where another person carries the 'bats' (clubs) for you cannot be a sport in my view, and whoever was it decided to describe fishing as a sport, when stating that it is the "most popular sport in this country"? Catching fish? It's not even a game. Perhaps the English language is deficient two words, although I suppose 'pastime' might do to describe fishing. Having said that, I also want to say, that being a fisherman in a trawler is an incredibly tough job performed by real 'hard men'. Anyway, my point is that the likes of snooker, darts and golf need a new collective noun.

However, I am not saying that darts and snooker players and golfers are not skilful, but so too are chess players, and as far as I am aware we do not call that a sport. On the subject of the aforementioned games, it seems they are now just about the only ones the BBC can afford to buy the rights to and televise. Looks like a darts player's name will be engraved on the *Sports Personality of the Year* trophy before long! Or has one won already, and I have understandably erased it from my mind?

My favourite sport, cycling, has epitomised the problem of drug usage in sport. I do not defend it, but wish briefly to explain the issues as I see them.

Winning gives prestige, but more than that these days - untold wealth.

Cycling has always been a paid sport, and therefore the earnings from it have always been an incentive to win at all costs to ensure being able to earn a decent 'living'. I say 'living' because past rewards were little more than that, and even today, particularly bearing in mind the toughness of the sport, the rewards are well down the scale.

So before the advent of erythropoietin (EPO) cyclists used alcohol, amphetamines, cocaine and caffeine for their boosts. In all honesty I doubt the benefit was that great and certainly not sustained from race to race.

Tommy Simson died from a cocktail of these, plus dehydration, on Mont Ventoux in 1967.

The modern day problem exploded with the arrival of EPO, which increases the volume of red blood cells in the user's blood. Its use was effectively condoned by the UCI, cycling's governing body. At the time EPO could not be tested for, so they set a haematocrit below which a cyclist could compete.

A haematocrit is the percentage of the blood that is made up of red cells when it is 'spun down' in a centrifuge. Red cells are the oxygen-carrying element. The more red cells there are the more oxygen can be delivered to the muscles, and so the more power and endurance an athlete has. The haematocrit level was set at 50% or below, and although this would represent the upper limit of 'normal' for you or me, we would be highly unlikely to be at that level, unless we had stayed at altitude for a long period.

So the cycling teams which used EPO kept their cyclist 'legal'. They also used to dilute their cyclists' blood with intravenous saline drips, prior to testing, thereby endeavouring to reduce the haematocrit.

It is a huge shame that a great sport has become so tarnished, but hopefully in the long run the ensuing scandals will ensure that the sport will become clean in the future. As for the disqualified winners, all they did was cheat better than anyone else, because so many of the cyclists and teams were guilty.

With or without drug assistance, what professional cyclists do on a daily basis during the grand tours is almost superhuman. However, I think that in all sports any drug misdemeanour should result in a total life ban; after all they all know full well that they are cheating by using them. Avoiding such a ban is simple; don't use a banned substance! However, I am sure from a legal perspective this would be unachievable. A human rights lawyer would no doubt have something to say about such a law.

It's New Year's Eve tomorrow.

This will be followed by the January overcrowding at gyms and swimming pools around the country as the well-intentioned weight-loss resolutions kick in.

For me this is an annoying time of year in the swimming pool, when the lanes are overcrowded by swimmers who have no insight into their ability, or may I say lack thereof.

When a lane says 'fast', that should mean fast, which would also mean generally no breast stroke, unless you are a Duncan Goodhew or Adam Peaty. It certainly does not mean a woman slowly swimming up and down in the wrong lane, not wanting to get her hair wet and giving you dirty looks when your front crawl splashes her. There is a nice wide slow lane for that. I exaggerate a bit, but not much. Fortunately, they will all have given up by March. That is not surprising, not least because of all the aerobic sports, swimming is the least likely to aid weight loss, especially when one is no good at it.

As for gyms - that is all madness too.

Modern day men and women drive perhaps 20 minutes to the gym, they then change and spend some time in the gym itself, often doing ineffective exercises on the various pieces of equipment. They return to the changing-room and spend some more time there before driving home, or perhaps to work, for say another 20 minutes or more.

Many of these people are at the gym to aid their weight loss. The process I have described takes about two hours. Instead, what they could do is leave the house and simply walk for two hours; even walk to work. That would burn far more calories, not pollute the atmosphere, and they would save themselves a shed-load of money in membership fees.

There are no short cuts to fitness and weight-loss, and a simple aerobic exercise is the best way to achieve both; walk, run or cycle outside in the fresh air. Do not go to a gym, or sit on a vibrating plate thinking the fat will wobble off, or employ a personal trainer, most of whom seem to think the only use of aerobic exercise is as a 10-minute warm-up. Instead, buy a dog with the money saved, who will give an added incentive to be out in the fresh air. If someone, who is underweight requires additional weight, in the form of muscle, then weight-train at the gym, but otherwise **don't bother**!

Whilst on the subject of weight loss, a few words here about serial dieting. If one wants to be thinner, eat less all the time. Don't put on weight, then diet to lose it, which is the bizarre ritual that rules the lives of a huge number of people.

It is really a very simple formula; if a person consumes more calories than they use, they will put on weight.

The problem is that the majority of us have no idea how few calories we need.

For a middle-aged woman, that will be about 1,500 a day, plus any extra that are burnt doing exercise. A one-hour run at a decent pace will use about 600 calories, so a 40-year-old woman running (not jogging) for an hour a day, and maybe if she is lucky burning another 100 doing her daily work and chores, will need no more than 2,200 calories - and only 1,600 of them without the run. A man can afford about 200 calories more, and if he has a physically demanding job, may be able to add another 100 or so to those.

Crash-dieting leads to the loss of muscle mass as well as fat; muscle burns more calories than fat. So each time a dieter achieves a target weight, muscle has been lost, and when the weight is put back on again it is fat and not muscle that will be gained, unless the person deliberately exercises to build strength. So with each diet the metabolic rate will fall, weight is put back on quicker than before, and will be harder to lose. There is no good news as far as dieting is concerned, and the best way is not to need to diet in the first place. Eat well and eat less all the time.

Obesity is now very widespread and costs society a fortune in terms of the health issues it causes.

What used to be called maturity onset diabetes (now called Type II) was a result of the pancreas, the organ that produces insulin, the hormone that controls blood sugar, wearing out and therefore not producing enough of the hormone.

Now a great deal of this kind of diabetes is caused because the person eats so much that the normal pancreas simply cannot cope; frightening, but true!

Maturity onset diabetes was often controlled by a low calorie diet alone; otherwise it required oral medication.

Before I retired, grossly overweight patients used to tell me they were on a diet for their diabetes. They sat in front of me barely fitting in the chair as they spouted these words! What kind of diet they were on, I have no idea. Not one that resulted in weight loss, that's for sure.

Many very overweight patients with diabetes nowadays have to use injections of the hormone insulin to control their blood sugar, when losing weight would solve the problem, for many of them, completely!

Insulin was manufactured for use in the 1920s, so before then these people would have rapidly died from over-eating. The things we now accept and take for granted!

There were no such life-saving opportunities available for our grandparents!

I think that is the end of my chapter on sport, and my quick foray into the mad world of dieting. The word itself is a misnomer; I should say 'following a calorie controlled diet', but that's a bit of a mouthful if you excuse the pun.

15

Religion

QUITE A FEW PEOPLE HAVE TOLD ME NOT TO WRITE this chapter. I think they feel I will offend and have some kind of 'contract' taken out against me.

However, I am not going to write from a given perspective, and my criticism is generic.

There are four root causes of all evil; alcohol, the internal combustion engine, mobile phones (and the associated social media) - and religion.

I have already covered alcohol.

The internal combustion engine is evil because of the way it continues to be used, not for what it should have been.

The mobile phone and social media I shall refrain from wasting much time on. My pet hate is when I see young women with a small child talking on their phone, listening to music via it with earphones, or texting, ignoring their child. I am shocked that anyone thinks that is appropriate. Something else I have seen are parents with their child in a pushchair nearly pushing him or her under a vehicle at a crossing, because they are so preoccupied with their phone.

I can thoroughly recommend a film called *Disconnect* (by LD Entertainment) which very successfully demonstrates the horrors of social media, the internet and the like.

Religion is evil not because of what it is, but because of what it develops; namely the ego, and what is, and has historically, been done in its name.

I have covered the role religion plays in the development of oversized 'egos'. It is these 'egos' which leads zealots to practise all sorts of evil in the name of their chosen religion.

I was intrigued by the Archbishop of Canterbury's sermon this year (2015), in which he described Islamic State as being the new Herod. This led me to think how conveniently he had failed to make the same comparison to the Crusades. As I understand it, during the Crusades Christians went forth to butcher Muslims in the name of Christ. They had to horseback-ride and walk many a long and arduous mile for the privilege of doing so. It seems to me that religious persecution is a pretty much well-established and formularised process.

Henry VIII did us all a huge favour when he separated us from the influence of Rome, albeit he did it to his own ends.

However, as mentioned previously, this did not prevent Catholics and Protestants butchering each other on our own doorstep quite recently in Ireland. Why do human beings behave like this? The reason is, like in all wars, conflicting 'egos' are coming to blows.

Incidentally, why are our newsreaders required to precede reference to Islamic State with 'so called' all the time? This is done, presumably, to observe the fact that it is not an internationally recognised country, but I am sure the creators of that 'so called' state don't care what we call it. I find it unnecessary and so annoying.

It is different, but somewhat like the media speaking of the Second World War and referring to the Nazis and not Germans. Have I missed something? Weren't the Nazis Germans? We British are not afforded the same delicacy when the atrocities we inflicted in the name of Empire are described. We don't hear "it was the Victorians not us Brits"!

In about 2008, when I gave up alcohol and re-started my healthy lifestyle by returning to triathlon, I also started to read a lot about Buddhism. I think this came about because I decided that meditation would be good for me and calm my 'shed-like brain'.

I was also very uptight about my work environment and the stupidity that was daily surrounding me there. I had just finished my final foray into the world of NHS management, with the intent of changing things for the better, but had realised it to be a hopeless cause. I needed to learn to follow the essence of that delightful nun's prayer. *Grant me the serenity to accept the things I cannot change, the courage to change the things I can and the wisdom to know the difference.* I came to see meditation as being a possible way forward for me, and later would learn that Buddhism as a whole was a much greater teacher.

Buddhism does not indulge the ego; in fact quite the opposite. I think I should say here that I believe neither does Hinduism, but that is not a religion I know much about.

Buddhism teaches us that we are all no more important than anyone else on this planet, including all the animals and plants. We are simply a constituent part of the whole world; a collection of matter, which has formed into 'us'.

Thoughts are thoughts; no more and no less.

They are not a being, but the effect of our life experiences. I know I am repeating myself, but I make no excuse because this would be fundamental to a better world if we all realised it.

A problem with the peaceful nature of Buddhism is that if you practise it you risk becoming a punch-bag, if everyone else around you isn't of the same mind.

Buddhism does not mean you cannot have thoughts. There can still be clever people: inventors, philosophers, scientists and the like. It is not nihilistic, but thoughts are just thoughts.

We all suffer because of these same thoughts.

We look into the past with, maybe, varying degrees of regret, but what good is that? What is done cannot be changed. We worry about the future, and yet most of the things we worry about will never happen, and if they do we couldn't have prevented or changed them anyway. Buddhism says live in the present moment. Enjoy today, it is the here and now and it is real.

Another excellent lesson taught in Buddhism is that should someone say, or do something that you consider unkind, or unjust, or untrue, every time you think about it you are then reinforcing that person's victory over you. That is exactly what we do, isn't it? Someone says something to us once and our minds repeat it over and over again, increasing our anger and hurt.

This is not a book about Buddhism so I will leave it there, but I do recommend its beliefs to everyone.

I do not fear death because I know I am not an entity. I was nothing before I was born, I am no more than a collection of thoughts now, and I will be nothing when I am gone. I might fear the process of dying, but not death. The latter is pain-free.

Some may be thinking; in that case, what does he have to say about the Buddhist belief of reincarnation?

I explain it as follows.

As I said in the introduction, we are no more than a collection of carbon, hydrogen and oxygen. These atoms will still be there after we are gone and will be incorporated into other matter, living or otherwise. Some of my carbon may end up in a worm, eaten by a bird, which migrates to Africa and is then eaten by a hyena, which is killed and eaten by a lion; so some of me will be a lion. Alternatively, the worm may live a

338

long and happy life, in which case I will have become a worm for a while!

I have mentioned that the process of dying may be painful. How ironic then that the NHS spends a fortune prolonging the lives of very elderly people, but hospice care to relieve the pain and suffering of the dying is primarily funded by charity.

Those strange priorities raising their head again.

16

Retirement & Beyond

I STARTED WORKING AS A DOCTOR ON 31ST JULY 1979 and retired on 12th April 2015. More than 35 years spent being something that I really should not have been, and toiling at a profession I didn't really like.

More fool me!

In mitigation it is hard to give up a secure living, especially when responsibilities come along like marriage, children and mortgages, but that should not stop us. We spend a lot of time at work, so it will always take up a major portion of our lives. Therefore, if it is at all possible we should definitely be doing something we enjoy.

For me, my first 12 years spent in the Royal Navy were great fun. I didn't do that much medicine, and what I did do was in a great environment, surrounded by some great people. I was exposed to all sorts of experiences, of which, to this day I am proud.

When I first left the Forces, I was busy training to be an anaesthetist and achieving the goal of becoming a consultant. That was a challenge and gave my life in medicine a purpose.

However, once I'd become a consultant I can't say that the job gave me all that much pleasure, and it certainly didn't make me feel particularly rewarded.

Working in the NHS was soul-destroying, and became increasingly so as the years went by. It really does not look good for the future. My opinion of this major portion of my life is, I am sure, the reason that the nearly 20 years I spent as an anaesthetist in Barnsley takes up such a small portion of this book.

Since retiring I have not missed work at all, other than perhaps some of the interaction that went on there. However, I have kept in touch with the three genuine friends I made; Jim Finnerty, Pete Claydon and Tim Wenham. I cycle and swim with Tim and Pete regularly, and Jim's and my own similarly held views on the ridiculous state of the world we live in, are discussed often; enjoying great laughs, exchanging our view in the most irreverent of ways.

Am I sad that such a great chunk of my life meant so little to me?

No - I am not; not least because I know that neither did the NHS care for me very much, either. That is not a moan - just a statement of fact, that whoever you are and whatever you contribute, to a large number of employers, particularly public sector organisations, you are just another employee. *He that does his best just goes the way of all the rest.* In fact, it is worse than that, because often it seems that these days 'failure' is actively rewarded.

There is little truth in the saying; "cream always rises to the top"; one look at politics tells us that!

So what now lies ahead?

For a start: huge optimism for this new chapter in my life.

I loved being a student and it feels like I am now a student again; a slightly arthritic and older one to be sure, but I feel like one nonetheless; a *mature* student, perhaps, but why not?

When I was at university my grant cheque, and later my Navy pay, went into my bank account each month enabling me to do more or less what I wanted to; as you know I wasn't a diligent student! Now the money comes in the form of a pension, and with that I can do what I like as well.

How good is that?

Perhaps we should turn life around and be given our pension from the age of 20 to 40, have fun, and then repay it by working from 40 until we die? Realistically I'm not too sure that would work because we would be too busy bringing up our children to have enough free time to enjoy the first part.

Mind, there is no reason why we should not all start our families at forty.

In April, Julie and I will be off to the Far East, to Thailand (no body-to-body massage this time!) - Cambodia and Vietnam as my early 60th birthday present. I have always wanted to go to 'French Indo-China' as it was. I am sure we will do plenty of trips in retirement; South America, the Rockies, Northern Italy and a return to Norway and the Caribbean, spring to mind; all of which feature on my bucket list.

The timing of my death is a tricky one.

I don't want to end my life as a demented, infirm and smelly old man. On the other hand, if I was to die tomorrow it would be a shame, because of all the things I still want to do.

However, if I was dead I wouldn't know what I'd missed, so it wouldn't matter. As someone once said; "you're a long time dead, you know," to which the reply should be, "yes and I was a long time being born, but it didn't really bother me."

Some things have to be left to chance I suppose.

However, I do think that voluntary euthanasia is a perfectly reasonable idea.

On that subject, how unfair it is that people who have a terminal illness and want to die are not allowed help to do so.

If I wanted to end it all tomorrow I could choose my method and carry it out on my own; pills, a rope, or a hose into the car. However, if I had, as an example, a severe neurological disease, which meant I could not take pills on my own, or make the noose, or start the car, I am currently disallowed by law to be given any assistance by a loved-one or any organisation, to do exactly the same thing. It is not just that I may not be able to perform the act myself; perhaps I could, but

I would understandably fear the resultant suffering of a botched attempt.

How can that be right?

Embedded in European Law that we hear about all the time, is a Bill of Human Rights. I have not read it and do not know its details, but I know it talks of a Right to Live and a Right to Die.

Human Rights lawyers use different elements of this Bill to suit whatever agenda they currently happen to be engaged in banging-on about.

How any court can deny someone help with something they cannot do, or don't want to do on their own; help which at the same time would ensure that the act is achieved in a sensitive and humane way, is beyond me. It is like refusing to open the door for someone in a wheelchair, or in fact, more like slamming the door in their face.

I might along the way have created the impression that I do not like solicitors or barristers very much; this is so. Like all such generalisations though there are exceptions of course and so I will concede that there will be quite a few good guys around, somewhere within the legal profession.

Our next door neighbour, Eric Bray, is a solicitor, a lovely guy and from what I see, clearly not motivated by money.

As I see it, a lot of the rest of them, simply prey on others' insecurities, in order to line their pockets. I cannot take seriously any profession that resorts to running TV adverts to attract its clients. We are often forced to use solicitors because the law insists that we do, which only serves to increase their income. The financial agreement in at least two of my divorces, probably all of them, could have been resolved by a simple signed document agreed between the parties. However, the law insists that each party uses a solicitor. The pair of them, then do their utmost to generate arguments that are not needed, and by so-doing increase the exchange of letters full of unnecessary, incomprehensible legal jargon. The letters then need explaining, so generating more meetings with the client, further letters and more cash!

The law is an ass!

The reason for my dislike, I think, stems from an incident I foolishly became involved in in Hong Kong. I was the on-call doctor one night, when the Military Police telephoned me to say that a female soldier had reported that after a party in the sergeants' mess she had been raped by a male counterpart, and please would I come and examine the woman and take the necessary swabs.

I should have told them that I was not familiar with the required procedures and to contact someone else, such as a consultant gynaecologist at the hospital, for example. However, I failed to do this, and duly turned up to carry out the required examination and other necessary stuff they told me to do.

Sometime later there was held a Military Court Martial of the male soldier, on the charge of rape, at which I was required to give evidence. As is often the case in the military, and indeed the likes of the NHS, the prosecution law team was a cheap one, whereas the accused was being defended by a top London barrister; the best that money could buy.

This barrister belittled me and my evidence on the not unreasonable basis that I was not an expert in this field - which was true - but it was the hectoring and quite simply rude manner of his questioning that got up my nose, which made me feel as though it was *I* who was a guilty party on trial.

I am quite sure that mine will be a common experience for all sorts of decent witnesses, who find themselves put in similar positions. It is hardly surprising therefore, that many women do not pursue charges of rape in the court.

I did score one point against the obnoxious barrister when he asked me a leading question, to which I replied: "Are you telling me, or asking me," and was supported in this remark by the judge. However, the whole experience was an extremely unpleasant one.

After giving evidence, I later found myself alone in the lift with the pompous bastard, when during our short descent I seriously considered whether it would be worth me facing a consequent GBH charge!

Let us now return to death!

Or not, in fact!

My wife was watching a programme recently, called *Why the Rich Live Longer,* all about the various ridiculous treatments available that are supposed to bring about prolongation of life.

The narrator reported from a cryonic preservation establishment where they froze and stored bodies for them to be resuscitated years down the line when technology allowed, which of course will be never. I find it hard to believe that anyone's 'ego' can be so over-inflated as to want to do that. The arrogance of people to think that there is any reason why their grizzly old body should breathe again! Or that anyone else would want to see it again!

The narrator spoke to someone who had already paid his up-front preservation fee, and he was fat, said he did no exercise, and clearly did nothing positive for himself to prolong his life on earth *this* time round, but was happy for someone else to sort it out in order to give him a second innings sometime in the future.

This is a concept familiar to me with a significant number of overweight, smoking, and sedentary patients who want *you,* as their doctor, to sort their problems, but make no effort to do so themselves. In 2015 everything seems to be someone else's problem to solve and someone else's fault too. It appears that rarely does the culprit admit to or take responsibility for creating the state of affairs in which they find themselves.

The programme's narrator did speak to four people aged over 100 who were in good health both physically and mentally, and they said that the key to longevity and happiness was moderation and contentment. I am in trouble there!

In reality, our lifespan is probably imprinted in our genes at the outset, which we can then either lengthen by leading a healthy lifestyle, or foreshorten by a prolonged and persistent indulgence in unhealthy activities.

Every one of us would get cancer, if we lived long enough. This is why the oft-quoted statistic that more people are dying of cancer these days than before is nonsense; it is simply that as we live longer, an increase in the incidences of cancer is inevitable. More useful information might be how many of us die of cancer before a certain age - say 70, for example.

Many of us die of something else before we get cancer, while others die of lung cancer (for example) at the age of 40, having smoked 20 cigarettes a day, when without smoking they might have made it to 70. Another person can smoke 20 a day all their life, but die of something entirely unrelated, at 80.

It's luck, or bad luck, depending on who we are, but one can influence the odds.

Whilst I am on the subject of age *'the camera doesn't lie'* isn't true anymore. You only have to go to a newsagent and look at the magazine rack to realise this. On the cover of many (all) the women's magazines you will see pictures of 'celebrities'; I use the word loosely. You will notice they are 'made-up' and 'airbrushed', to look as if they are in their early twenties, when in fact they are in, and normally have the looks of, the 50 to 70 age group and beyond! Some are barely recognisable. Worse, some are *Dames*, who one would have thought would have more grace.

No doubt this then encourages gullible women to spend huge sums on 'age-defying' cosmetics, botox injections and plastic surgery. More money in the back pockets of unscrupulous companies, who are very likely in cahoots with the magazines in the first place!

Well that's 'off my chest', and that will be my last comment on the world around me in this book!

I consider my life to have been a good one.

I am a fortunate person to have had the opportunities that have come to me. Generally, I have been in good health, never been short of money, never been unemployed, and so as not to make too long a list, I've been lucky not to have suffered from a lot of the problems that many others experience.

I have a happy, healthy family. We never know what lies round the corner, but as I have said there is no point in worrying about that, because whatever it is may never happen.

I hope my readers have found this controversial journey through my life to be an enjoyable and interesting one, and have been entertained by some of my opinions - whilst undoubtedly being irritated by others, I would imagine.

We are all of us different and see things from varied positions. Remember that I am no more right or wrong than anyone else, and do not pretend to be. It has taken me a significant portion of my life to realise this obvious fact, and it is the one lesson that perhaps I wish had come to me sooner, not only for my sake, but for the sake of those around me.

Regrets?

Don't believe in 'em.

I simply know that I have made some significant decisions that will have profoundly changed the course of my life. Where would I be and what would I be like if I had done things differently is a fascinating thought, but not one I dwell upon. It is the same for all of us, and indeed if our parents had made different choices we might well not be here at all. As I have implied before, that would not matter, because we wouldn't know about it.

Whatever stage in life you the reader are, I wish you well and hope that there might be something in this book that will be of use. If I could write a letter now to myself when aged 16, would it make any difference? Hell no; I would still be insecure, impetuous, cynical, shy, angry, intolerant, and obsessive, but pleased that in many ways I have lived life to the full and 'done it my way'.

I will finish on a similar note to the way I began, with this time my favourite quote. I think I have come closer to being the 'doer' in this, than in achieving the sentiments in Kipling's *If* quoted at the start –

"It is not the critic who counts; not the man who points out how the strong man stumbles, or where the doer of deeds could have done them better. The credit belongs to the man who is actually in the arena, whose face is marred by dust and sweat and blood; who strives valiantly; who errs, who comes short again and again, because there is no effort without error and shortcoming; but who does actually strive to do the deeds; who knows great enthusiasms, the great devotions; who spends himself in a worthy cause; who at the best knows in the end the triumph of high achievement, and who at the worst, if he fails, at least fails while daring greatly, so that his place shall never be with those cold and timid souls who neither know victory nor defeat."

Theodore Roosevelt

Acknowledgements.

First and foremost many, *many* thanks and love to my wife, Julie, who has supported me in this project as she has in all my ventures over the last 11 years. She is supportive and at the same time tolerant of the ups and downs my driven nature generates.

Sincere gratitude to my eldest daughter, Fiona, and step-daughter Bethany for copyediting the book and not being too shocked by any of its content! Also, thank you to Sharon Robinson, who did a final proofread of the book.

Thanks to a number of friends who have encouraged me to write and have read the book, during its creation. They have made constructive and encouraging comments along the way. They are Pete Claydon, Jim Finnerty, Jon Maskill, Tim Moll, Chris Nunn, Guy Sheridan, Rachael Snyder and Tim Wenham. Neil Butterfield's comments were less encouraging, but he gave me some useful suggestions. To Jim special thanks for designing and creating the fantastic cover.

Thank you to my mum, Anne Swinhoe, for her help with the project. She has been there when needed over the years, whilst at the same time having to spend much time supporting the many demands of my dad, Peter.

Thank you to everyone mentioned in the book, particularly Julie, Fiona, Alec, Bethany, Heidi and Harry, and of course Charlie; as well as other family members and friends who have been part of the experiences that have given me the material for the book. Without them there would be a lesser story and a much diminished life would have been had by me.

Rightly, I should also mention Christine, Jo and Alex, who I spent many years with between them, and each of whom has added to the colour of my life.

Thank you very much to Russell Gibson at Gibson Publishing for all his help and support and Mike George for his brilliant copyediting. A much more literate man than me!

Finally, I would like to acknowledge the contribution of the crazy world we live in, for having given me so much material to comment upon and much more to ponder in the future, too, no doubt!